Local Economic
Development
in the 21st Century

Local Economic Development in the 21st Century

&

Quality of Life and Sustainability

Daphne T. Greenwood
and
Richard P.F. Holt

Foreword by Thomas M. Power

M.E.Sharpe
Armonk, New York
London, England

Library of Congress Cataloging-in-Publication Data

Greenwood, Daphne T.
  Local economic development in the 21st century : quality of life and sustainability /
Daphne T. Greenwood and Richard P.F. Holt; foreword by Thomas M. Power.
      p. cm.
  Includes bibliographical references and index.
  ISBN 978-0-7656-2093-4 (cloth : alk. paper)—ISBN 978-0-7656-2094-1 (pbk. : alk. paper)
  1. Economic development—Social aspects. 2. Quality of life. 3. Sustainable
development—Social aspects. I. Holt, Richard P.F., 1953– II. Title.

  HD75.G73 2010
  338.9′27—dc22   2009037140

Printed in the United States of America

The paper used in this publication meets the minimum requirements of
American National Standard for Information Sciences
Permanence of Paper for Printed Library Materials,
ANSI Z 39.48-1984.

∞

IBT (c)   10   9   8   7   6   5   4   3   2   1
IBT (p)   10   9   8   7   6   5   4   3   2   1

To my father, Robert Greenwood, the people of the Pikes Peak Region, and Ayla, for sharing their love of the outdoors with me.

—DG

To the people of Ashland and Medford, Oregon, who make the Rogue Valley such a very special, magical, and wonderful place to live. Also for Gay.

—RH

Contents

Tables, Figures, and Appendixes

Tables

Figures

Appendixes

Foreword by Thomas M. Power

Local "economic development" is a ubiquitous concern of almost every community over a few thousand residents. Economic development organizations, often funded with public money, tend to be layered one on top of another as the focus shifts from a small city to a county to a multicounty region to the state level.

For a variety of historical reasons as well as different interests and commitments, there often are two quite different approaches to local economic development: that taken by the business community often with local economic development organizations and that developed by research-based analysts in academia and nonprofit organizations who study what appears to work or not work.

The result is often two very different public dialogues based on two different versions of regional economics. In many local economic development organizations, the strategies proposed have not changed in the half-century or more since we have been focused on local economic development as a matter of public policy: recruit new businesses with subsidies, tax reductions, and other "improvements" in the local "business climate." Within that approach, the local economy is still modeled, as it has been for a half-century or more along "economic base" lines even if that modeling is now presented in much more detail using computer-based input-output models.

Despite this continuity in the approach to local economic development within the business community, the political realm in which public economic policy has to be developed and implemented has gotten much more complicated. When the public is invited into helping define the objectives of local economic development, the array of concerns expressed is much, much broader than "more jobs and income." Different citizens and local advocacy groups raise very complex economic issues with which they want any local economic development plan to deal. These are likely to include:

- Local quality of life, including concerns about the natural, social, and cultural environment;
- The "sustainability" of the local and regional economy, usually conveying a concern about whether natural and social capital are being permanently depleted in a way that will undermine the well-being of future generations;
- The "equity" of the developing economy, including concerns about increasing disparities in income and wealth, lack of affordable housing, poverty, and "environmental justice";
- Residential and commercial sprawl and its implications for both local government finance and local quality of life;
- The quality of public services including education, law enforcement, and transportation; the link between taxes and the provision of crucial public services makes the popular mantra about cutting taxes to stimulate the local economy quite debatable.

Local governments cannot discuss local economic development without being drawn into a much broader range of issues than the familiar bumper-sticker version of "jobs and income," "cut taxes," "improve the business climate," and so on.

Daphne Greenwood and Richard Holt directly confront this much broader set of issues as they seek to lay out a research-supported approach to *Local Economic Development in the 21st Century*. Their approach will be productive in many different ways. First, their writing is very accessible. Readers will not be confronted with the economic equivalent of "math anxiety" as they read this book. Second, they explicitly demonstrate how a broad range of environmental and social issues are actually local economic development issues. This should help draw many young people who are concerned about these issues into a dialogue about local economic development that they might otherwise turn away from. Finally, for practitioners "in the trenches," being pulled this way and that by issues that seem to be peripheral to local economic development, this book provides a productive integration of a broad range of local issues into an overriding community development framework. This can only enrich the public dialogue while providing a framework that encourages rational discussion and a careful weighing of the diverse and sometimes conflicting goals we all have for our communities.

Preface

Isn't more income the key to a better quality of life? Doesn't economic growth provide more resources for protecting the environment, for educating at-risk children, or increasing access to health care coverage? Shouldn't growth mean that paychecks get bigger and housing is more affordable? Won't this create more tax revenues for schools and roads? Most economists believe that choices would be easier if we could just get more income, making economic growth the indicator to watch.

But we all know from experience that it just isn't that simple. In the United States today, there is over three times as much "stuff" for each resident as there was fifty years ago. Yet being able to afford health care, housing, environmental protection, and high quality education is still a problem—both for people and for state and local governments. There is also increasing concern that our current patterns of growth appear unsustainable. This is not just from depletion of nonrenewable resources, but from the sheer amount of waste we generate and the effects it has on problems such as global warming.

We wrote this book in answer to rising concerns about the relationships between economic growth, quality of life, and sustainable development. All around the world—and especially in industrialized countries such as the United States—the assumption that more growth automatically brings a higher quality of life that is sustainable is being questioned. States and communities are responding to these concerns in many different ways. For example, citizen-led movements are creating local indicators for projects that measure quality of life and sustainability to supplement income as an indicator of well-being. In addition, these indicators provide early warning systems for social and environmental damage. Throughout the book, we show that the use of local indicators can be a helpful economic development tool.

We also make a clear distinction between economic development and economic growth. This is an important theme of the book. Economic development, in our view, describes a broadly based and sustainable increase in the standard of living (which includes quality of life as well as income). It is not the same as growth in market output and incomes. Many have equated economic growth with economic development, with the implicit assumption that growth brings improvement in quality of life and the standard of living. We question the assumption that income always brings improvements in other aspects of well-being. This has led us to focus on positive *and* negative impacts of population and economic growth on quality of life and sustainability. These include sustainability at the economic and environmental levels as well as fiscal sustainability—the ability of tax systems to pay for additional infrastructure and services when there is population or economic growth.

We also differ from many writers on local economic development in viewing opportunity for people as a central part of economic development. Many of our strategies are "percolate up" rather than "trickle down." An underlying theme related to these strategies is that issues of growth, quality of life, and sustainability must be tackled jointly. Too often, they are addressed one at a time in legislation, budget matters, or tax policy. We believe this approach is misguided and counterproductive. As a result, our discussion of economic development goes beyond tax incentives or urban planning, although it includes them.

This leads us to a second theme of the book: issues of growth, quality of life, and sustainability require thinking and acting *locally* as well as globally. We recognize that national and international policies and economic performance have important consequences for communities and individuals. However, economic, geographic, and social realities create substantial variation in growth and development. Booms and recessions at the national level are experienced much more strongly in some places than in others. The history of cities and regions, combined with decentralized political decisions in the United States, contributes to large differences in growth, development, and quality of life between localities. Therefore, these issues are very much local and regional as well as national. Local and state governments can make a difference in the type of economic growth and economic development that occurs in their regions despite the influence of national trends.

We believe people can influence the type of growth, quality of life, and sustainability in their communities. However, with that freedom come responsibilities. As the world becomes more and more a "global village," what we do locally—positive and negative—affects not only our lives but also the well-being of many others—now and in the future. For this reason, we hope that this book will be a useful guide not only to students of economic development, urban planning, sociology, and geography but also to opinion leaders and concerned citizens in states and localities grappling with these issues.

Acknowledgments

Special thanks are due to all who ploughed through our early drafts. Paul Kozlowski gave excellent input and thoughtful comments on Chapter 2 and Steve Pressman did the same for Chapter 5. In Colorado Springs, Thomas (T.A.) Arnold, Dottie Harman, and Lynn Peterson contributed valuable commentary, based on their experiences with state or local economic development, local government planning, schools, utilities, and land development. They are representative of the many people in Colorado who care deeply about quality of life.

Ric's class on Local Economic Development and the Environment at Southern Oregon University used a draft of this book as the primary text in spring 2009. He wishes to thank all the students in that class for their patience, insights, and valuable comments. He also inflicted rough draft chapters on some faculty members, who all responded with thoughtful comments. He also wishes to thank the many people in Ashland, Oregon, who shared their ideas and insights about what makes a good community.

We especially thank the Elizabeth Cushman Public Policy Research Fund at the University of Colorado for its support of our work on this project. With its funding Cynthia Jones, Benjamin Massey, Melissa Skillington, and Ping Tan provided invaluable research assistance at various times throughout the project. Kathryn Andrus and Andrew Castle of the University of Colorado at Colorado Springs Teaching and Learning Center provided assistance with graphs. Toni Knapp was an able editor of our final manuscript. In addition, the Kraemer Family Library staff were inordinately cheerful about requests—and Judith Rice-Jones went out of her way to be particularly helpful in coming up with sources.

Last but not least, we thank the many other writers and researchers in this field whose work we cite here. We have been inspired by many of them and hope we have done their ideas justice, along with adding some new twists of our own. We note in particular Thomas Power for his work on quality in economic development and Robert Frank's writings that inspired our views about the "negative trickle-down" effect. In the last stages of our work, we also became aware of the important insights of Steve Deller and his colleagues Gary Green, Dave Marcouiller, and others around amenities and the process of economic development.

Part 1

Defining Economic Development, Quality of Life, and Sustainability

1

Economic Growth vs. Economic Development

We wrote this book to answer rising concerns about the relationships among economic growth, quality of life and sustainability in state and local economic development.[1] One of our underlying themes is that these issues must be tackled jointly. Too often, they are addressed one at a time in community planning, state and local budgeting, and tax policies. If local governments do focus on sustainable development or quality of life, it is usually through separate policies and initiatives. Taking a more comprehensive approach will make clear the linkages among economic growth, quality of life, and sustainability.[2] Differentiating economic growth from economic development is a good place to start. Economists and policymakers often speak of growth and economic development as if they are the same. We make a very clear distinction between them.[3]

Economic Growth vs. Economic Development

Economic growth is traditionally defined as increased total output or income. People also refer to growth when there is an increase in population or in land area as a city "grows" beyond its traditional boundaries.[4] Economic development, on the other hand, is much more. We define it as a broadly based and sustainable increase in the overall *standard of living* for individuals within a community. Conventional economics has equated economic growth with economic development, implicitly assuming that growth will bring improvement in quality of life and the standard of living. However, many now question this assumption. This shows up in the questions asked by community quality-of-life and sustainability groups and the indicators they choose (Chapter 8). Some scholarly work in economics (Daly 1996, Greenwood and Holt 2010; Norgaard 1994) also raises these questions. Standard of living refers to *overall* well-being that goes beyond income. For example, if per capita income (income adjusted for population) increases but there is more crime and congestion, then the standard of living may have fallen.

This does not mean we are "antigrowth" or that economic growth is unimportant for well-being. People are generally better off with higher incomes than lower, because they can more easily afford higher quality goods and services. Higher pay can also allow more leisure or earlier retirement. Economic growth often brings a vitality that accommodates change and innovation. More income and consumer spending create local retail opportunities and can bring higher tax revenues to support schools, parks, and roads. However, growth can also subtract from quality of life and lead to unsustainable development. Growth can lead to urban sprawl and increase the cost of public utilities such as water or power. It can affect the social life of communities if neighborliness or civic engagement is harder to maintain. It can mean changes in the pace and lifestyle that people experience at home and at work that are not always positive. Growth can produce higher levels of carbon in the air and pollute water with agricultural pesticides. As we explore later in this book, rapidly rising incomes can also create a "negative trickle-down" effect through a competitive race to consume that leads to less leisure and satisfaction rather than more.

The net result is that growth can either contribute to or subtract from economic development, depending on the way it occurs. Just as important is that economic growth may not always be the most important factor in improving perceptions of well-being. Surveys indicate that while average income has risen over the past forty years in the United States and the countries of Western Europe, measures of happiness are about the same as they were at lower levels of income.[5] Studies from an even broader group of countries confirm this weak relationship between growth in income and improvement in other measures of the standard of living (Slottje 1991). After basic levels of needs are met, nonmarket elements of quality of life become more important than additional income.

Understanding the fundamental difference between growth and development is the first step in looking at the future of economic development in a new way. Economic development is multidimensional, while economic growth is one-dimensional.[6] Defining economic development more broadly than economic growth should encourage community leaders and elected officials to consider both the positive and negative impacts of all types of growth and to look beyond the immediate economic effects of their decision or policy.

The Importance of State and Local Actions to Sustainable Development

Another feature of this book is its focus on *local* development.[7] We believe that thinking and acting locally, as well as globally, are necessary when addressing quality of life and sustainability. Much of the public discussion of environmental and sustainability issues has focused on national or global issues, but sustainable practices may gain wider acceptance when tied to local (rather than global or national) outcomes. Moreover, while many economic and environmental forces transcend local boundaries to affect the globe, the source is often found in local actions. This means that some very important aspects of dealing with national and global issues must start at the local and state levels. This is where people have direct experience and can have a direct impact.

Beyond environmental and quality of life issues, there are other reasons to focus on state or local economic development. Although the role of the federal government is important for national economic growth and stability, its influence and impact on local areas can be quite limited. Just as a rising tide does not always lift all individual boats equally, growth rates in the macro economy do not have the same effect everywhere. Economic, geographic, and historical realities cause substantial regional variation in growth and development, giving local and state governments more power than they might imagine to shape economic development and quality of life.[8] For example, most decisions about land use policies are made at a local level and they have a tremendous impact on growth, quality of life, and sustainability. States and local units of government also provide many public goods that improve the standard of living, such as parks and schools. Finally, with the devolution of many policy choices from the federal government to states, counties, and cities, state and local governments are now dealing with problems of sustainability and quality of life that the federal government had greater responsibility for in the past.

Investments in Capital Stocks for Sustainable Development

How can local and state governments develop policies that support and improve the overall local standard of living? We believe this begins with (1) valuing all the capital stocks used in producing income, quality of life, and sustainability, and (2) establishing locally based indicators to track changes in these capital stocks and quality of life factors. We first turn to the idea of maintaining capital stocks.

The word *capital* is usually associated with manufactured equipment owned by private businesses that can produce future output. We use the word *capital* to describe *any* stock used to produce goods or services (public or private) that can increase the standard of living.[9]All of these capital stocks are important, as well as interdependent, in creating and sustaining economic development. Some types of capital yield a profit when goods are sold in the marketplace, and that is where private businesses invest their dollars. However, other kinds of capital are provided outside the market by nature, government, or informally by family and community. Along with manufactured equipment, stocks of human skills and talents are necessary for economic output and income. Public infrastructure represents equipment that produces services that do not yield a profit, but are equally needed for economic production and growth. Natural resources are another stock of capital, although unique in that some elements are nonrenewable. All of these are necessary for economic development. There is also the nonmarket value of civic participation and neighborliness that is sometimes called social capital. In addition, technology and innovation are important catalysts of economic growth.

In the "capital stocks" framework, new technologies are embodied in new skills (human capital), new equipment (private business capital or public infrastructure), and new uses of natural resources (natural capital). In addition to maintaining economic production, each of these capital stocks also supports future quality of life and sustainability. Education increases civic participation and influences choices toward lifestyles that are more healthful. Parks provide beauty and wildlife habitat as well as recreation and carbon (CO_2) conversion for clean air. Supporting and sustaining all of these are necessary for states and communities to grow and to have true development.

It is important to understand the interrelationship and interdependence of the different capital stocks—natural, manufactured, public, social, and human. Some of these stocks are held privately and some are held in common. For example, some natural resources are private property while others, such as the oceans or the atmosphere, are common property. Businesses own manufactured equipment privately, but infrastructure is shared equipment held in common. What we generally call "human

Figure 1.1   **The Traditional View: Economy, Environment, and Society**

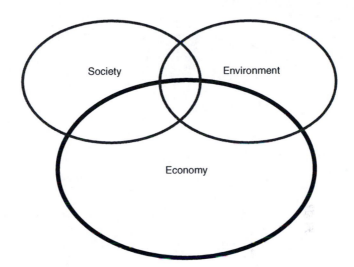

capital" is privately held, but the social capital we discuss in Chapter 3 is a common resource developed and shared by people.[10]

Investment in these capital stocks must be made to serve people and not to serve "the economy." The purpose of an economy is to serve the needs of people, not the other way around. Economic growth that supports economic development is based *on and around people* and reflects values and goals throughout the community.

The Economy as Part of the Environment and Society

In putting people at the center of economic development, however, it is important not to lose sight of how the environment supports and encompasses both the economy and society. In the traditional view illustrated above in Figure 1.1, economy, environment, and society are separate, although they have some areas that overlap.

Investments of private capital into the economy are the primary catalyst for wealth creation in the traditional model. Other forms of capital are seen as secondary except when they are used in ways that meet private sector needs. Two examples of this are the value placed on inputs into production such as oil, minerals, or agricultural land and the value placed on attractive environments such as beaches and ski slopes. Similarly, spending on education is often justified in terms of

Figure 1.2 **Sustainable Development: Economy, Environment, and Society**

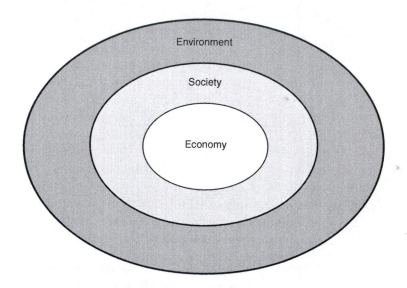

the needs of business for a trained workforce. In contrast, investments that contribute to quality of life or sustainability rather than to increased economic growth are traditionally considered outside the economy and therefore less valuable.

We think a more accurate representation shows any economy as a subset of society, as in Figure 1.2. Human beings do their first learning in informal units (families), and markets and laws are social relationships established to further their well-being. Human society, in turn, exists with the envelope of atmosphere that is "the environment." Viewed this way, the synergies between investment in the economy, environment, and society are easier to see and the inevitable trade-offs will be approached differently. We discuss this in greater depth later in the book when we focus on natural capital and the environment, and on human and social capital.

When economic development is equated with simple economic growth, the emphasis is on accommodating the needs of private capital (business) so that it can create growth and jobs. Benefits from economic growth are expected to trickle down to create investments in the other types of capital (human, natural, and infrastructure) that are also needed for production. Our approach to the future of economic development differs in three important ways from the traditional model.

First, we do not accept the trickle-down model as accurate. As we show throughout this book, extraordinary economic growth over the past half century has still left enormous gaps in education, infrastructure, health care, and environmental protection. More economic growth alone will not solve these economic development issues in the future. Second, our approach values all capital stocks for their contributions to quality of life and sustainability of development as well as their contributions to measured economic output and incomes. Third, we take a pragmatic approach to how to best sustain each of these capital stocks. While we believe in relying on market forces where they can achieve a socially desired outcome and in avoiding unnecessary bureaucracy and concentration of power, some forms of capital require more public investment than others. An ideology that values small government or low taxes above all else may mean foregoing these investments. In addition, the recent work of Nobel Prize winners Williamson and Ostrom highlights the important role of social cooperation outside of formal governments, as does the work of Bowles and Gintis on social capital that we discuss in our third chapter. Our bottom line is that results are more important than ideology when it comes to sustainable development and quality of life.

The Use of Local Indicators

We mentioned earlier that another important tool for local communities seeking to improve their overall quality of life is locally developed indicators. Currently, economic indicators such as per capita income, housing starts, or the unemployment rate, are used to measure how well a city or region is doing. People like to hear about the ups and downs of these statistics, and public officials like to quote them, so they receive attention as breaking news. These traditional economic indicators are important to watch, but a comprehensive approach to economic development, quality of life, and sustainability requires the addition of broader indicators. Without establishing new measures of success, the old measures are likely to continue to be dominate. Throughout this book, we go beyond using familiar statistics to suggest examples for new ones.

Moving away from the old ideas of economic development to a twenty-first century plan needs to be based on indicators that reflect the shared visions and priorities of citizens. That vision will differ from one community to the next. For some, cultural and educational resources are more important, while others place more value on natural or recreational resources. For some, recreation means having more parks and bike paths while for others it means better access to hunting and fishing. Measures developed with the active participation of involved citizens in the area can best reflect local history, culture, and geography, as well as the goals and priorities of residents. In Chapter 8, we develop the role of comprehensive indicators in planning for true economic development.

The Structure of the Book

In this first chapter, we made a distinction between economic growth and economic development that is the foundation for all that follows. Understanding the fundamental difference and interaction between growth and development is the first step in looking at economic development in a new way. It opens up a new path to economic development in the future that is multifaceted—a path that *includes* quality of life and sustainable development rather than *opposing* them. It leads to a focus on all capital stocks as important and to considering the ways in which the economy, environment, and society are related.[11]

Chapter 2 examines the conventional wisdom about achieving economic development through tax incentives and subsidies to private business. Some examples of this are the economic base model, the emphasis on "export" industries, the use of business incentives, and the focus on improving the local business climate. All of these traditional economic development strategies assume that other benefits will follow from supporting investments by private business. They often emphasize low taxes at the expense of public goods. We differ by advocating a very limited role for government in influencing private investment decisions. We also present alternative strategies for local economic development.

In Chapter 3, we look at ways to define and measure quality of life and the importance of social capital in quality of life and the standard of living. Higher income is not always accompanied by better quality of life. Instead, some kinds of growth enhance economic development, while others do not because they come with too many social or environmental costs. Pursuing undifferentiated economic growth and expecting quality of life to automatically follow are failed recipes.

Chapter 4 explores, first, how to create environmentally sustainable development and, second, the role that state and local policies play in this process. Sustainable economic development starts with recognizing the unique qualities of nonrenewable natural capital that has no substitute.

It may be irreplaceable, either for technical reasons or based on spiritual or aesthetic values. States and localities have important roles in making development sustainable, which we highlight.

In Chapter 5, we look at the relationships among human skills and talents, opportunity, and local economic development. Growing gaps between the incomes of the rich, middle class, and poor have effects on individual opportunity as well as direct costs to state and local governments. We consider the relationships between inequality and health, inequality and crime, inequality and a good education, and the more general effects of inequality on social capital, affordability, and long-term opportunity. We also explore what we call a "negative trickle-down" effect that widens the gaps in well-being even more.[12] We devote a large portion of Chapter 5 to local or state actions that can moderate inequality or increase affordability and opportunity.

Chapter 6 is about land use and infrastructure, such as transportation, parks, and schools, where local and state governments have a substantial impact on economic development. Governments must invest sufficiently in infrastructure for sustainable growth, but it is also important that it be the *right type* of infrastructure for a twenty-first-century economy. The shape of a community—its neighborhoods, commercial districts, transportation networks, schools, public buildings, and parks—is what determines its character and its attractiveness as well as the costs of living and doing business there. We believe that when communities use outdated planning and land use models, they will face problems in the future as quality of life and sustainability become more important to people.

In Chapter 7, we consider how growth in population, land area, or the economy affects the "bottom line" of state and local governments. The effects of growth depend on tax structure as well as patterns of land use. These both affect the ability to maintain infrastructure and public services per resident when growth occurs. We explore how traditional assumptions about growth and budgets can ignore the conditions required for fiscal sustainability and lead to budget crises even in the midst of economic growth.[13] Communities that move in new directions for sustainable development and better quality of life must shift their budget priorities.

Finally, Chapter 8 explores policy recommendations for local, county, and state governments that want to integrate their strategies for economic growth, quality of life, and sustainability. One of these recommendations is to construct a set of comprehensive local indicators. This should include several kinds of measures that we do not see in traditional economic indicators. The first is a new set of measurements of success that can be integrated into strategic plans. The second is a set of measures that clearly show the effects of economic growth, population increase, and changes in land use. The third is a set of measures that can increase the accountability of the public sector. In a brief concluding section, we summarize the issues raised in this book through ten myths and four rules for economic development.

Concluding Remarks

As a way to help readers understand our vision for local economic development, the book also addresses many common myths about economic growth and economic development and why they should not be accepted at face value. Some myths reflect a lack of understanding of both economic thinking and the economic history of the United States. Others linger on as part of what we call the conventional wisdom or folk economics of economic development.[14] Throughout the book, we compare those myths to the evidence. Good decisions that will stand the test of time rather than satisfy the political winds of the moment or the pleas of special interests must be based on solid evidence.

We believe that many non-economists who are confronted with policy problems know there are important economic dimensions to them but have given up on "economics" in frustration. Too often, they are presented with a narrow view of economics and how it applies to problems they care about. However, this book incorporates a wider range of economic thinking than most we have seen. We recognize the power of market theory in analyzing many problems and solutions and use it where we think appropriate, but we also explain why and where we see limits to the application of traditional economics. To us, this does not mean abandoning the use of standard economic tools, but a need to expand the "toolbox" available for thinking through problems. This becomes particularly necessary when social values or environmental concerns are being considered, as they are when dealing with quality of life or sustainability.

Since this book is oriented toward students in the field and policymakers who are not economists, we have attempted to minimize jargon and technical material—or at least consign it to our numerous endnotes or to appendixes. We hope the book will be useful to those directly involved in public policy analysis at the state and local level, particularly in the United States. We also hope that it will serve as a supplementary reading text for students of public policy—whether they are approaching the subject from the areas of public finance, political science, urban planning, regional economics, sociology, or geography. We have provided detailed references and more extensive discussion (primarily in endnotes) for those who wish to delve deeper. Finally, to help guide readers as they go through the book, we end this chapter with four rules that summarize our main points:

Rule #1: Economic Development Is Much More Than Economic Growth

True economic development is represented by increases in the standard of living that are broadly based and sustainable. Economic growth may or may not support that goal, depending on the composition and distribution of growth.

Rule #2: Improvements in the Standard of Living Require Consideration of Both Quality of Life and Income

The standard of living, or well-being, includes many aspects of quality of life, such as health and safety, as well as access to educational, recreational, natural, and cultural resources. Overcrowded parks or schools or rising crime rates can offset the positive effects of an income increase.

Rule #3: Improvements in the Standard of Living Must Be Sustainable

In addition to contributing to a better quality of life, true economic development (in contrast to growth alone) is sustainable over time. Sustainable development allows future generations the opportunity to have *at least* the standard of living we do today. This means monitoring all capital stocks that contribute to quality of life and economic growth.

Rule # 4: Improvements in the Standard of Living Must Be Broadly Based and Affect the Majority of People

The purpose of any economy is to raise living standards for most of the population. When the benefits of growth are skewed toward some groups or the costs of growth are borne by some more than others, true economic development is not achieved.

2

Traditional Economic Development: Incentives for Business

In this chapter, we question how well traditional economic development strategies achieve economic growth.[1] We begin with a review of the traditional local "economic development" model, which is focused on the general business climate and providing tax incentives to attract new firms. The conventional wisdom sees encouraging private business as the way to increase average income and bring better quality of life. Even if the benefits of growth go first to those at the top, they eventually trickle down to the rest of the population and everyone becomes somewhat better off. To the degree that sustainability is viewed as important, market forces are assumed to provide it. We find that the conventional wisdom embodies a kind of "folk economics" that is based on several myths. These myths are not supported by research on what causes economic growth. Instead, the popular definition of economic development supports the profitability of *some* businesses and landowners, but not all.[2] Small local entrepreneurs would benefit more from an economic development model focused on local needs, but are largely left out of the process. This dominant strategy of economic development is actually a less cost-effective way to increase average incomes and the state or local tax base than others we will discuss throughout the book.

Later in the chapter, we review alternative economic development strategies that recognize, as did early economists like Adam Smith, that the source of wealth and of a higher standard of living lies in people and their productivity. Some of these strategies focus on increased local economic activity instead of export-based models. Others emphasize entrepreneurship, flexibility, and creativity. The alternative strategies have as their goal economic growth that is compatible with improved quality of life and sustainability. We begin first with the traditional local economic development model.

The Traditional Approach: Primary Jobs and the Multiplier

Most local economic development models, formal or informal, revolve around the creation and retention of jobs. Certain jobs are defined as "primary" because they produce goods and services for export *outside* the local economy. Their value derives from bringing "new" or outside income to enlarge the economic base. As this new income is spent, there is a multiplier effect, creating secondary and tertiary jobs such as home building, grocery and retail, and many other service jobs. These service sector jobs range from high end (doctor, lawyer) to low end (gardener, dishwasher, and busboy). The export-base/primary-jobs model is very popular with economic development practitioners.[3] As a result, they have pressured state and local governments to provide special incentives to bring new firms or industry to the area. Their rationale is that the incentives create new jobs, which generate income that trickles down to create more service and retail jobs within the community.

In spite of its widespread use and popularity, however, this vision of economic development is a partial and confusing view of reality. While bringing in new industries to create "primary" jobs may sound as if it should be the highest priority, the same economic impact can be achieved in other ways that may be better suited to particular communities. When export jobs dominate a local economy, relatively few workers produce goods and services for their neighbors. Instead, local dollars are spent elsewhere, by traveling to where the goods or services are to shop or by having them shipped in. On the other hand, when more of the local economy produces and sells for their neighbors the size of the local multiplier increases. In addition, less dependence on faraway export markets means that the local economy has less volatility from national and global business cycles.[4] Finally, when local jobs depend on branches of national or international companies, profits from production go to stockholders who live far away and spend their profits elsewhere.

The economic base model, while having some truth, is not a sufficient answer to how a local economy should develop. If growth in total employment is the primary goal, following the economic base model is likely to deliver (see Polzin 2001). However, if growth in per capita income is the goal, the model is less likely to deliver better economic opportunities and a higher standard of living. In other words, economic development means more than ensuring that people have a job; it also means having

Table 2.1

Per Capita Income Growth: High and Low Population Growth States, 1989–1999

Top ten	Population growth	Income growth	Bottom ten	Population growth	Income growth
Nevada	66.3	23.7	Massachusetts	5.5	21.0
Arizona	40.0	21.0	New York	5.5	19.4
Colorado	30.6	37.0	Iowa	5.4	24.9
Utah	29.6	31.0	Ohio	4.7	26.8
Idaho	28.5	3.0	Rhode Island	4.5	21.4
Georgia	26.4	17.0	Maine	3.8	22.5
Florida	23.5	23.0	Connecticut	3.6	26.0
Texas	22.8	26.0	Pennsylvania	3.4	25.6
North Carolina	21.4	19.0	West Virginia	0.8	28.8
Washington	21.1	22.0	North Dakota	0.5	26.4
Avg. growth over decade		22.3			24.3

Note: Both population and income growth are cumulative over the entire period.

jobs that pay enough for a good standard of living. To show the difference, we compare states with high population and job growth in the 1990s to those with low or little population and job growth. The top ten states for population growth had *lower* average real income growth than the ten *slowest* population growth states (see Table 2.1). The fastest population growth also had low unemployment rates, so job creation did keep up with population. But creating more jobs clearly does not automatically raise average incomes, the stated goal of most economic development. Even new high-paying jobs may lower average incomes if each highly paid worker requires several low-paying service jobs.

Many local governments and economic development consultants, however, continue to use the economic base model for its ease and familiarity, although there are more sophisticated models available.[5] This leads to two folk myths that put local economic development on a path that often conflicts with quality of life and sustainability. The first myth is that a larger economic base of export-oriented industries will automatically increase total employment and, with that, raise the standard of living. But, as we discussed above, new jobs can be created (indicated by more population and low unemployment) without per capita income increasing. And even with increasing per capita income, the overall standard of living will not increase if income flows primarily to a small group or comes with high environmental or social costs.

In addition, there is no guarantee that new jobs created will actually go to local workers.

The second myth, which rests on the first, is that individual business incentives are necessary for a local economy's growth. This seems to be common sense based on the conventional wisdom that private, profit-making investment is the best and only way to create economic prosperity. However, nonprofit or public-sector investment also brings new income into the economy. Hospitals that draw patients from a large area pull in "new" dollars (Bartik and Erickcek, 2008). A university that draws students (and dollars) from other regions is likely to bring more "outside" money into an area than a manufacturing plant importing raw materials, adding an additional layer of value to them, and shipping them elsewhere.[6] This is not to say that public or nonprofit expenditures are any better than private spending, but that they both can have the *same* economic impact on a local community.[7]

New jobs and income flows can come from a variety of sources. Retail stores are often described as generating secondary jobs since they receive dollars from income already earned in other jobs. However, a specialty store that brings shoppers from other towns also brings in "outside" dollars. By different criteria, it could be called a primary source of jobs and income just as much as a new manufacturing company. A large retirement community brings in "outside" income from social security and pensions, which supports retail spending and local jobs in health care, the arts, and recreation. The belief that only manufacturing employment can lead to sustainable economic growth does not hold water. For example, the growth in financial services in the 1990s does not fit the traditional manufacturing export model. The classifications into primary vs. secondary employers often appear to derive more from the size of the business or its influence with the local chamber of commerce or economic development directors than from consistent evidence about effects on the local economy.

Examined carefully, the core ideas of the economic base model—manufacturing more exports and creating primary jobs—turn out to be fuzzy and amorphous rather than simple and concrete. A major weakness of the model is that it rarely considers the contribution of universities, local nonprofits, or tourist and retail establishments or small businesses in general. These groups are believed to create only secondary jobs. The definition of what is primary and secondary in a local economy and what brings in outside money are somewhat arbitrary. And when it comes to the multiplier effect, all dollars are equal! They do not need to come from a "primary" or manufacturing job. Let us now look more closely at the conventional wisdom about the use of specific business incentives in economic development.

Location Incentives: Economic Development or Business Development?

In contrast to providing a low tax, pro-business climate (which we discuss later in this chapter), location incentives are targeted toward specific firms to encourage them to move to a community, to remain in a community, or occasionally to expand their operations. Commonly given incentives include tax credits, abatements, or rebates as well as free or reduced-cost land. An alternative form is public infrastructure that is built (or tailored) to the needs of a new business. All these actions do help particular businesses or sectors develop, but they do not create broadly based and sustainable economic development. Location incentives were first used during the Great Depression of the 1930s by the state of Mississippi. Since then billions of dollars of targeted incentives have been granted, with very little solid evaluation of result in jobs or tax base increments relative to dollars spent (Buss 2001).

However, most incentives are too small to make any difference in a firm's decision. The highest level of incentives was a deciding factor in only three out of ten location choices (Fisher and Peters 2002). Often the specifics of the incentive deals are secret or buried in budgets, making them difficult to track. This lack of transparency and accountability makes it less likely that the financial soundness of the decision will ever be seriously evaluated. North Carolina offered $260 million in incentives for Google to create 210 jobs, on the heels of a study of North Carolina incentive programs just two years earlier that showed a cost of nearly $40,000 per job relative to the benefits received (Luger and Bae 2005). Evidence about the effectiveness of incentives is regularly ignored, as several chapters in *Reining in the Competition for Capital* (Markusen 2007) make clear. A broader geographic picture of the spread of incentive competition across the United States and even into other countries over the last twenty years is painted in Markusen and Nesse (2007).

How common is a zero or negative return on public investment spent on location incentives? Timothy Bartik (2005a) of the W.E. Upjohn

Institute, the guru of economic development incentives, concludes that a *fiscal* loss to government is almost certain.[8] However, if there is high unemployment or underemployment (people working at jobs below their skill level) among current residents and if the new jobs *actually go* to these people, there can be a net social benefit to the community. Only two of ten new jobs brought into a metropolitan area are likely to go to existing residents according to Bartik's (1991, 1993) own studies.[9] Attracting new jobs may not lower the local unemployment rate. It may even increase, since job seekers are attracted to areas with growing employment and this increases the number of people looking for work.

How can a community ensure that tax dollars are used for incentives only in the limited situations that are appropriate? Local decision-making processes must be more democratic, with full information, better benefit–cost analysis, and performance requirements. Businesses receiving tax or infrastructure incentives should have contractual obligations to satisfy and "claw back" and recapture provisions when they cannot meet performance benchmarks (Bartik 2007). Greg Leroy of Good Jobs First believes that the most important part of incentive reform is plain old sunshine. Leroy's (2007) list of top ten reforms for incentive processes includes: (1) having site consultants register as lobbyists, (2) adopting unified economic development budgets, and (3) capping the total amount of incentives granted annually. The lobbyist registration requirement keeps site consultants from working "both sides of the fence" without disclosing this to local governments. Unified economic development budgets make clear the direct spending as well as the indirect loss of revenue from tax breaks. To ensure that incentives are used only when benefits clearly outweigh costs, much stricter standards around their use are needed.

In addition to these criteria provided by Bartik and Leroy, we believe that the costs and benefits weighed should relate to true economic development—not to simple growth in employment or income. This means (1) accounting for the impacts of growth in employment or population on quality of life and sustainability, (2) looking at the breadth of gains across the income distribution as well as per capita income growth, and (3) assessing the effects on the fiscal health of local governments (see Chapter 7). If granting tax incentives takes money away from other community needs, such as the ability to fund schools, it will not have contributed to the net benefit of the community. If it brings in new residents, crowds roads, or overloads wastewater systems in the absence of enough new revenue to offset these new costs, it will not have contributed to true economic development. Instead, the incentives will have adverse effects on the quality of life that outweigh the income gains.

In many cases, local policymakers overestimate the net benefits from a proposed new incentive plan. We think there are two major reasons for overstatement. First, the limited debate about any particular incentive tends to be dominated by local business interests and has little public oversight. Both benefits and costs are often hastily calculated using ad hoc assumptions and dubious data. Second, when formal impact models are used to assess a deal, they rarely consider all the costs associated with a new business or the new workers it will bring. Benefits are attributed to the new jobs that may reasonably be expected to occur from other kinds of local activity. Rigorous and complete cost analysis could increase the breadth of debate on incentive packages if that analysis is transparent and conducted in a timely manner.

In the end, the usefulness of any analysis of location incentives depends on three factors. The first is the tools and information evaluators have to work with. The second is the assumptions made in that analysis. The third factor is the background and experience evaluators have to correctly make a full analysis. When decisions are made in the rush of excitement of a new "prospect" and a perceived bidding war with other cities or counties, they tend to be less useful for the reasons outlined above.[10] Establishing a regular process to assess the overall economic impact and the impacts on various groups (including local governments) is important. Sticking firmly to that process is the only way to have a reasonably objective evaluation of the cost effectiveness of incentives up front. We turn now to another topic closely related to incentives: economic development through improving the general business climate.

Improving the Business Climate: The Conventional Wisdom vs. the Evidence

The conventional wisdom holds that a good business climate is important for attracting and retaining businesses that create jobs and wealth. Some indexes have been created to measure business climate. There are also ratings that assess the "business friendliness" of an area. Some measures, such as the Economic Freedom Index, have a libertarian political bent rather than being focused on business, including issues like school voucher policies.[11] The Beacon Hill Institute's (BHI) multidimensional State Competitiveness Index is another well-known measure. It assesses each state in terms of "the policies and conditions that ensure and sustain a high level of per capita income and its continued growth" (Beacon Hill Institute 2001, 5). Though the stated purpose of these indexes is to provide objective and predictable data, the overall quality is low.[12] For example, the business climate factors chosen by BHI to predict personal income growth did not predict that growth. As we show in Table 2.2, BHI's *top ten* rated states in 2001 had *lower* average per capita income growth over the next several years than their *bottom ten* rated states. How did the states with a "poor business climate" fare? Only one of them (Arizona) had a growth rate in per capita income that was below the average growth rate of the top ten! Yet Table 2.3 (see page 23) shows that over half of the predicted top ten performers in 2001 remained on that list in 2007 despite the results. Rather than being humbled by this poor performance, BHI has established a city competitiveness index, indicating that the demand for indexes is thriving even if their predictive performance is not.

It is hard to know what *is* driving the BHI index, but even for the limited use of evaluating how well business needs are served, the rankings must be taken with *very* large grains of salt. A close examination of competing indexes is likely to reveal the same problems. They purport to measure ability to generate income growth—the goal of many states and communities—but do not. An earlier analysis found that many give equal weight to very different kinds of measures, which may be of varying importance. However, most states "can brag that they are in the top ten in terms of business climate or competitiveness: they just have to pick which of the five indexes they want to point to" (Fisher 2005, 71). On the other hand, in all but eight states, businesses pushing for tax cuts or less regulation can also point out to state policymakers that their state is in the bottom half of competitiveness on at least one index. Having said this, let us look more carefully at the evidence of the impact that these business climate ratings have on local communities.

As we outline in the next few chapters, economic output, quality of life, and sustainable development depend on more than business capital. Human, natural, and social capital are also necessary, along with public infrastructure. However, business climate indexes do not give them much weight. Not surprisingly, the business indexes focus on how well the needs of business are satisfied rather than social, environmental, and human needs. The BHI Competitiveness Report is typical of many others in citing low tax rates and little regulation as attractive to business. But numerous studies by economists over the past thirty to forty years

Table 2.2

Annual Per Capita Income Change (%)

BHI ranking 2001	State	2001–2	2002–3	2003–4	2004–5	2005–6	2006–7	Average
1	Delaware	2.63	1.88	5.53	4.64	5.52	3.77	4.00
2	Massachusetts	-0.03	1.51	5.06	5.23	6.16	6.01	3.99
3	Wyoming	2.42	5.73	7.30	5.76	8.95	6.32	6.08
4	Washington	0.84	1.82	6.40	1.56	6.62	5.76	3.83
5	Vermont	1.24	3.35	5.40	2.73	6.21	5.16	4.02
6	Colorado	-1.40	0.10	4.51	5.85	5.03	3.93	3.00
7	New Hampshire	0.62	1.30	5.52	3.01	5.85	4.42	3.45
8	Connecticut	-0.88	0.60	6.82	4.77	5.88	6.61	3.97
9	Minnesota	1.95	3.26	5.26	3.07	4.30	5.60	3.91
10	California	-0.17	2.22	5.62	5.71	5.78	4.91	4.01
								4.03
41	Arizona	1.07	1.95	6.38	5.84	5.10	3.42	3.96
42	New Mexico	0.74	2.61	5.54	7.02	6.23	5.16	4.55
43	Hawaii	2.68	3.06	7.23	6.79	5.98	5.99	5.29
44	Oklahoma	-0.58	2.26	7.51	5.85	7.59	5.44	4.68
45	Alabama	2.91	3.57	6.20	4.64	5.42	4.89	4.61
46	Nevada	0.07	3.46	8.30	8.73	4.12	3.81	4.75
47	Arkansas	1.55	4.48	5.47	4.71	5.50	5.57	4.55
48	Louisiana	2.14	2.43	5.41	-8.66	27.79	9.22	6.39
49	West Virginia	3.29	1.05	4.13	4.77	6.35	4.72	4.05
50	Mississippi	1.78	3.30	4.45	5.57	6.03	6.72	4.64
								4.75

Sources: Bureau of Economic Analysis, *State Annual Personal Income;* Beacon Hill Institute, *State Competitiveness Report* (2001).
Note: Real growth rates, adjusted for inflation.

Table 2.3

BHI Rankings of Best States for Business, 2001 and 2007

	BHI ranking 2001	BHI ranking 2007
1	Delaware	Utah
2	**Massachusetts**	**Massachusetts**
3	**Wyoming**	**Colorado**
4	**Washington**	North Dakota
5	Vermont	Idaho
6	**Colorado**	**Minnesota**
7	**New Hampshire**	**Washington**
8	Connecticut	South Dakota
9	**Minnesota**	**New Hampshire**
10	California	**Wyoming**

Note: The six states in bold font are in the top ten in both years.

do not support this piece of conventional wisdom. Lower taxes are (of course) preferred to higher taxes, but when spending cuts are factored in, the positive effects disappear.[13] Tax levels alone are a neutral factor in business location, it is more important what the taxes are spent on and how effective the spending is. Some studies have found clear *negative* effects of combined tax cuts and spending cuts, when the cuts were in either higher education or basic infrastructure spending (Lynch 2004).

Areas with *higher* incomes generally have *higher* rates of labor and environmental regulation, rather than less union membership, lower minimum wages, and lower unemployment and workers compensation coverage. Perhaps this relationship shows that higher incomes result in more willingness to give protection to workers, rather than the other way around. However, it is difficult to argue that pro-worker policies or environmental regulations *prevent* achieving higher incomes. An objective look at what supports economic development must balance the trade-offs of one form of capital needs against those of another.

Business climate studies are popular not because they tell anyone much about what it is like to do business in a city or state but because they are fun to look at and easy to use. Their use of numbers gives them the aura of an objective scorecard. Ranking invites people everywhere to see how they measure up relative to other states and to their own past rankings. Is there anyone who does not look first at the ranking for where they live (and next at where they grew up) to compare that with others? However,

Figure 2.1 **The Relative Importance of Various Measures in National Ratings of Cities for Individuals and Businesses**

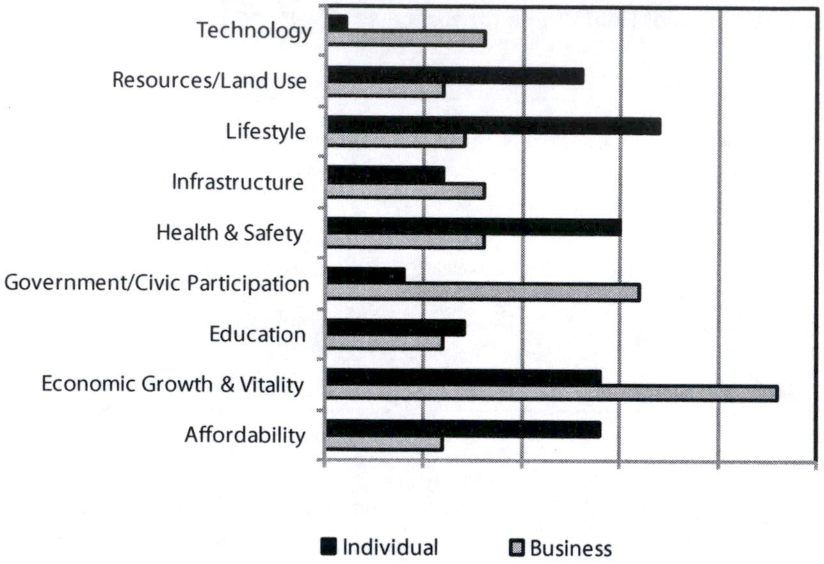

■ Individual   ▨ Business

Source: Greenwood and Skillington, 2008.

competitiveness and business climate rankings are more than a harmless exercise. They often carry weight with state and local governments. Based on a low position in the business climate rankings, pleas are made by business groups for weakened environmental regulations, for fewer legal protections for workers, and for lower taxes. Requests for more public spending on education or healthy environment are less likely to be heeded.

As Figure 2.1 shows, indexes oriented to business needs have a different emphasis than indexes rating a good place to live (from Greenwood and Skillington 2008). Aspects of quality of life such as lifestyle, health, safety, and affordability predominate in the best places to live indexes. On the other hand, business climate indexes emphasize economic growth, technology, and infrastructure. Not surprisingly, many cities rated in the top half of "good places to do business" are in the lowest quarter of rankings for "good places to live" (Gabriel and Rosenthal 2004).

The different priorities of businesses and of individuals are just one example of the complexity of the road to true economic development. We recognize that the future of economic development must accommodate a variety of different interests and concerns. The best way to achieve this, we believe, is through strategies that support a combination of economic growth, improved quality of life and sustainability. Replacing the pressure on elected officials to follow the conventional wisdom on economic development must come from more than criticism—there must be alternative strategies. Before describing several more integrative approaches to economic development that are alternatives, we look first at the true sources of economic growth.

Economic Development: Wealth Comes from People and Productivity

An evidence-based approach to economic development must start with the fact that the underlying source of sustainable income growth lies in increased productivity. This requires more efficient use of labor, resources, and capital so that more value can be created from the same level of resources. Bringing new firms to town, increasing total output, or raising the price of land are often labeled "economic development," but they do not guarantee higher productivity. Focusing on *people and productivity* is the most effective strategy for increasing economic growth and quality of life simultaneously. It goes back to the father of economics, Adam Smith.

In the *Wealth of Nations* (1776), Smith questioned the conventional wisdom of his day. The influential merchant class claimed that a nation's wealth depended on the amount of gold and silver it acquired by selling exports to other nations. Smith, on the other hand, identified the true source of national wealth in how productively people use resources to create a better standard of living. It seems ironic that so many business people today use the same mercantilist arguments of export-driven growth that Adam Smith worked hard to disprove.[14] We should remember from Smith that it is innovations in how resources are used that create wealth.

With increased productivity, more value can be created in fewer work hours. If the benefits of higher worker productivity are shared with local workers in wage or salary increases, then local incomes will rise. Developing new technologies to make this increased productivity possible does not require location incentives or new infrastructure. Instead, it requires an increase in knowledge and its practical application. The increased knowledge that comes from new technology development is permanent and will not disappear when a tax break has expired (as often happens with a plant location), or when a natural resource is exhausted. If some of the benefits from increased productivity are reinvested in the community, this helps economic sustainability. A community that invests in its education, social fabric, and quality of life is a place where entrepreneurs and workers want to stay. It is also supportive of higher productivity, which depends on the ingenuity of people operating within a social framework that supports creativity. Even after a natural resource is depleted, technology changes, or demand for a particular product shifts, these elements remain as the basis for further economic development. But what policies can be used to encourage increased local productivity?

"High road" regional development strategies include competition based on high quality of labor and other resource inputs rather than competition based on low cost. This means avoiding a "race to the bottom" with less-developed countries. Luria and Rogers (2008) advocate investing in energy efficiency and coordinated rebuilding of infrastructure to reduce costs for manufacturing firms in the troubled areas of the industrial heartland, along with making investments in education. However, it is equally important to close the low road as well as to choose the high one, according to a recent report by the Corporation for Enterprise Development (Schweke 2006). This means taking a hard look at what can result from pursuing a "good business climate." The conventional wisdom supports flexible labor markets, low regulation, low taxes, weak unions, low workers' compensation, and low unemployment insurance rates as good for business. These elements appeal to many business managers, but low bargaining power of workers often means low wages, benefits, and job security in the community. Since the multiplier effect on dollars spent locally operates both ways, the negative effects on individual workers ripple throughout the local economy. Low pay means fewer dollars spent at local businesses. It means less tax revenue per worker to pay for their public services. Low benefits mean more uninsured patients at community hospitals and clinics. Job insecurity combined with restrictive unemployment insurance policies means more periods of economic distress for the entire community.

The future of local economic development requires new tools and a new debate that is focused on the high road and on closing the low road. Along with questioning the effects on people of a "good business climate," we must question whether tax incentives to firms are the most effective strategy. Considerable research has confirmed the minor role tax rates, tax cuts, or special incentives play in most location and investment decisions. Since the use of business incentives by cities, counties, and states continues to increase despite this evidence, closing the low road requires regularly evaluating these indirect expenditures for benefits relative to costs of lost revenue.

The most distinctive aspect of "closing the low road" is the assertion that many policies good for workers are *also* good for the economy, something we explore later in the book. The high road strategy represents a "U-turn" from asking workers to sacrifice for the economy in hopes that the benefits will trickle down to them. It recognizes that people are at the heart of true economic development. Let us now explore in detail other alternatives to the traditional model.

Another Strategy: Increasing Incomes through Local Production of Local Needs

Besides focusing on efforts to increase productivity of individuals within a community, communities can also pursue alternatives to the export-base model of the economy. It does not take a business from out of town to produce exported goods and "prime the pump" for income growth. Instead of a person's having to drive to the big city for shopping or leaving it for recreation, if these amenities are available close to home more dollars circulate locally. If clothing or furniture were purchased previously by mail or on-line, they can now be bought from a local retailer. The effect will be the same—more dollars in the local economy. If grocery stores find local sources for eggs, meats, or vegetables that used to be brought in from elsewhere, the local multiplier rises. A higher percentage of *any* dollar in the economy circulates locally rather than leaving.[15] Community-based financial institutions also have advantages. They have less overhead and are more likely to be willing to lend to small local businesses. This is partly because closer oversight results in fewer bad loans. While the trend in banking has been to more consolidation and fewer locally-owned banks, there could be a reversal in the post-financial meltdown climate of 2009 and beyond.[16]

Local banks and businesses both play valuable roles in increasing what economists call "import substitution" (buying goods made locally and substituting them for goods made elsewhere). This increases the size of the local economy just as much as any "export." An added benefit is that this flow of dollars is likely to be more sustainable than one coming from manufacturing for export. The evidence shows that branch plants of companies operating globally, or even nationally, have weak attachments to any one location (Power 1996a). In contrast, businesses started by local residents—whether to export products or provide for local customers—generally have ownership or management ties to the area and preferences for staying there.[17] They are much less likely to look at a new location based on a few years of lagging sales or a tax incentive offered elsewhere than branches of national and global companies will be.

When a community shifts away from reliance on an export-based economic development model to an import-substitution model, this changes the view of how jobs are created and how economic growth occurs. The import-substitution model supports government policies that focus on economic development for local entrepreneurs and increased productivity of local workers, instead of policies that are hunting for outside industry to lure in. We believe this model is likely to be much more compatible with quality of life and sustainability. The following section presents an example.

Economic Gardening and Entrepreneurship vs. Hunting for Jobs

Growth that supports true economic development is sustainable, compatible with high quality of life, and based on and around people. Focusing on these goals simultaneously led the Littleton, Colorado (just southwest of Denver), city council to a different strategy. In the economic downturn of the mid-1980s there were major layoffs by its largest employer, Martin Marietta. The new economic development director, Chris Gibbons, was asked to work with local businesses to develop good jobs. Rather than using incentive payments to attract more corporations with out-of-state headquarters, community leaders wanted Littleton's future in the hands of local people. They chose to use their resources to build from the inside out, fostering creativity and resilience. Their strategy is called "economic gardening," and we summarize it below.[18]

Like many others, they had seen the work of David Birch (1981) at MIT revealing that the great majority of jobs created each year is in small business. However, the problem with encouraging small businesses is their very high failure rate, especially for startups. Many small businesses that do survive may limp along with low wages and benefits. When jobs do not include good health insurance packages or pay enough so that workers can afford to live nearby, they put other burdens on a community. Birch's study identified certain businesses that could support good jobs that would last. The success of these "gazelles"—innovators with high growth rates—was not based on tax breaks or subsidies. The success of new and rapidly growing companies was influenced considerably by the willingness of their leaders to shift how they look at the world.[19]

The critical factor turned out to be the temperament of the CEO or the entrepreneur. Of course, temperament is not and cannot be taught in small business training programs. Any influences that the community has on individual temperament are through a culture of innovation that supports (or attracts) the right entrepreneurs. If this approach to economic development sounds a lot like what best-selling author Richard Florida (2002, 2003) called "creative centers"—it is. If the local culture concentrates on attracting "good paying jobs" rather than on wealth creation from their own ideas, this focus is almost sure to affect local education and socialization of the next generation (see Power [1996a] for more discussion of this). In the long term, "hunting" for jobs in the worldwide market can actually *hurt* the entrepreneurial culture even if it is successful in bringing in business in the short term. An economic base of large companies or military bases may actually quash the spirit of entrepreneurship.

Economic development director Gibbons says the conventional economic language of "revving up the economy," "steering the organization," and "priming the pump" reflects a mechanical view of organizations and the world. He believes that biological analogies make more sense when it comes to economic development. The biological view describes a world in which growth can have limits. It is a world where change can occur without growth in size. Innovation and long-term survival take place at the "fine line between stability and chaos" in a world of feedback loops and unpredictability. Gibbons goes on to say:

> In nature, it is massive disruptions that allow newer species to change their position relative to others. It took the dinosaurs dying off before the mammals (who had been scurrying at their feet) got a chance to thrive. Nature finds the next fitness peak by placing a lot of small bets and doubling up on the winners.
>
> In Complexity Science, these changes are called "punctuated equilibrium" meaning that things go along fine for a while and then the bottom drops out. . . . A business will have a really hard time breaking the status quo in any industry without these massive disruptions. For that matter,

the same is true of communities. Detroit was a small fur-trading/farm town, not growing because it was locked in the hierarchy of town sizes. It took the massive technology disruption of the auto to decimate the horse and buggy towns and turn Detroit loose to find a new position in the food chain.[20]

Gibbons sees companies searching for local "fitness peaks" on the landscape. In volatile environments, those peaks disappear quickly. "Open source" distributed innovation is a way of doing this faster. In *The Origins of Wealth,* Eric Beinhocker (2006) expands on the point that competitive advantage is rare and short-lived in economies as well as in biology.[21] Successful communities as well as successful organizations must arrive at their own special balance of stability and flexibility. It is vitality and openness to change that are important for long-term community survival, not growth in terms of getting larger.

Communities that are most resilient to the ups and downs of large companies and international shifts in demand are those where a culture of entrepreneurship and self-employment exists. This encompasses both traditional small businesses that stay small but provide stability of employment[22] and continuity for the community[23] and the high-impact "gazelles" that have the potential to become high-growth companies with a broader economic effect on the region. The critical regulatory and infrastructure support for these is not always the same. For example, most "small business" programs from the Small Business Administration of the Department of Commerce are oriented to businesses with annual revenues of $500,000 to $1 million. This is small compared to the Fortune 100 or even 500, but still out of range of what is meant by a local small business with only a few employees. The Kauffman Foundation and the Edward Lowe Foundation have been particularly interested in the geographic variation in entrepreneurship (defined as new business start-ups) for truly small businesses and have each devised several measures to track this. They represent some new resources in this important area.

Firms with high revenue growth as well as employment growth are the high-impact firms of today. Their number grew significantly between 1998 and 2002. Ranging across many industries (not just high tech) and throughout the country, they account for almost all of the private sector employment and revenue growth in the United States' economy today. On average, these firms are twenty-five years old, which is considerably less than the average age of low-impact firms. They have fewer than twenty employees, and their leadership is relatively young. They have seen little job loss even in most recession spells.[24]

Between 1989 and 2004, the city of Littleton pursued an economic gardening strategy and spent no money on incentives or tax breaks to recruit businesses. It doubled the number of jobs largely by being a "quality of life" destination and kept its small town center even as the metropolitan area around it grew.[25] Pursuing similar strategies of economic gardening rather than hunting has attracted the interests of many small to medium-sized cities in the United States[26] and around the world. It replaces chasing "commodity businesses," those that shop around for the cheapest location and will therefore always be footloose. Since they are based on lowest cost, their locations are constantly changing in search of cheaper labor or more lax regulations.

How does a city or state support economic gardening ideas with concrete actions? Providing the kinds of information available through geographic information systems (GIS), detailed census data, and searches of other databases that are out of the reach of small and start-up businesses, gives them a leg up.[27] This avoids picking winners and losers, something governments are notoriously bad at doing successfully. Some communities adopt a similar strategy by accident rather than design. Since community attitudes about innovation and creativity are important for fostering start-ups, it is no surprise that university towns are now among some of the most successful local economies. Cambridge (Massachusetts), Madison (Wisconsin), Ann Arbor (Michigan), and Boulder (Colorado)—to name a few—are doing well not only because they have a high quality of life but also because their environment attracts and nurtures people of ideas.

Not every community can have a large research university; however, it can adopt strategies to foster the innovation and development that lead to job creation. For a more extensive discussion of the relationship between various amenities and local economic performance in rural areas and small towns, see Deller, Tsai, Marcoullier, and English (2001) and Lledo and Marcoullier (2008).

However, for businesses to move from what is often called "stage one" to the "stage two" level of expansion (Schweke 1990), an infusion of financial capital is required. The availability of venture capital is critical to this expansion and is often lacking. Venture capitalists tend to live in larger cities and often want businesses they invest in to move closer to these business centers. This is a difficult barrier to overcome in the short run, but a long-run strategy is to attract residents who can finance these start-ups. Focusing on community quality of life and developing an economic development plan that supports entrepreneurship and creative thinking are part of that strategy.

Conclusion

An effective economic development strategy must include two things. The first is a systematic evaluation of the cost effectiveness of incentives (direct or indirect) given to companies today. The second is a recognition of the effects of business and economic development activities on quality of life and sustainability. The future of economic development is in moving beyond the assumption that it is always more effective to spend money on private business capital than other kinds of capital. All kinds of capital are important components of economic growth and development, along with an environment that encourages entrepreneurship and innovation in all areas. This means fostering creativity and the pursuit of knowledge—something that often comes from valuing cultural diversity in music and the arts as much as in technological development.

Throughout the remaining chapters, we continue to explore other economic development strategies that are based on factors local and state governments can influence. These include urban design, environmental quality, public education, and value per dollar of public goods and services. Rapid change experienced within amenity-rich communities continues to point to the importance of these less tangible resources as key drivers of community development. The amenities that contribute to economic development may be natural, cultural/historical, or lifestyle related. We explore some of these further in Chapter 3, where quality of life is our focus.

3

Quality of Life and the Standard of Living

Following our Rule #2, quality of life and income are *both* important parts of the standard of living. We use the term "quality of life" to encompass many non-market goods, such as health, education and culture, open spaces and parks, air and scenery, and safe neighborhoods and streets, that are important to the standard of living. When economic growth has negative impacts on quality of life, this offsets the benefits of income growth.

To minimize potential negative effects of growth, public policies should support growth that is compatible with quality of life. Pursuing undifferentiated economic growth and expecting quality of life to follow automatically are a recipe for continual problems. Growth that leads to more cars on the road can mean traffic jams and pollution that subtract from quality of life. Certain types of growth can create urban sprawl, causing economic and social segregation that diminishes a community's social capital. On the other hand, other kinds of growth can revitalize neighborhoods or reduce pollution, through better transit options or cleaner fuels.

Some have called quality of life a "luxury good." Instead, we suggest that the non-income factors that make up quality of life are a significant part of our standard of living. They are actually becoming *more* important for "win–win" economic development planning that wants to attract and retain talented individuals and private capital to a community, and improve the overall standard of living for current residents.[1]

In Chapter 1, we maintained that economic development is sustainable only when investments are made in *all* capital stocks. In this chapter, we look more carefully at what "social capital" means and why it is particularly important to local quality of life. We also introduce the use of local indicators of well-being as part of an economic development strategy concerned with improving quality of life. But first, we look more at what is meant by the term "quality of life." Quality implies subjectivity and personal preferences that are more difficult to measure than quantities.

Traditional economics views "quality" as too subjective and normative for value-free economists to deal with. Quality of life is often viewed as "outside" the economy. We disagree and cite the work of economist Thomas

Power. He argues that most of what our private market economy produces and sells has always has been centered on the pursuit of qualities:

> [W]hat we seek in food is not primarily health or survival. . . . If it were . . . we would all be eating a diet of soybeans and leafy greens. . . . We primarily pursue taste, texture, visual attractiveness, variety and a set of cultural values associated with food. . . . The pursuit of quality, as guided by our individual aesthetic judgments and the larger society's cultural values, clearly dominates the commercial economy (Power 1996a, 11–12).

This is clearly not the view of a vegetarian! But Power's point about the willingness to pay for aesthetic "quality" in food and other basic items is right on target. He contrasts the costs of a diet meeting United States Department of Agriculture nutritional needs with average spending on food in the United States. He estimates the cost of basic clothing from military budgets and shows how much more is spent in the private sector, presumably to get quality of design, fashion, and the like. While the conventional wisdom usually contrasts hard-headed and practical economic concerns with subjective "social" or "aesthetic" concerns about quality of life, Power disagrees. He writes that the language of everyday folk economics, which implies that *quality* is something separate from *economic needs,* is just plain wrong:

> Basic economic issues are "bread-and-butter" issues and qualitative concerns are dismissed by noting that "you can't eat the scenery," but it is . . . actually discretionary qualities—subjective, disputable, aesthetic qualities—*that both motivate economic activity and provide its primary outputs* (Power 1996a, xiii; emphasis added).

Power argues that economic activity has always been centered on pursuing qualities we find to be attractive and, therefore, important. Quality (or aesthetic consideration) has economic value whether in the private or public realm and plays a much larger role in economic analysis than many economists seem to admit. Economic development should be just as concerned with increasing quality of life as with increasing income.

Quality of Life and Income

When confronted with measuring quality of life, many economists and policymakers use income as a proxy.[2] Even though they know it is an imperfect substitute, income is an accessible and familiar measure.[3] The founder of *Forbes Magazine,* Bertie Charles Forbes, is quoted as saying, "Business was originated to produce happiness" (Carr 2009). This reflects well the conventional wisdom of the modern world that more income produces more happiness. But there is substantial evidence that makes us question this assumption. Higher income is positively related to improvements in happiness and the standard of living, but the relationship is quite weak (Slottje 1991). At very low levels of income close to minimum subsistence, sustained income growth makes people permanently happier. However, at moderate and high levels of income, increases in satisfaction from higher income or consumption are *temporary,* fading as people become used to higher income or consumption (Deaton 2008). Robert Frank (1989, 1999) explains that when income increases, individuals develop a new frame of reference for their income. Higher income or consumption when everyone else has it is less valuable in both a psychological and a real economic sense than when it represents being at the top of the heap.[4]

People in poor societies who have enough to eat and are not subject to war or major natural disasters are often as happy as people in wealthy societies (Slottje 1991). Economists generally argue that because increased income makes more choices possible, it makes people better off. But recent work in behavioral economics indicates that having too many choices can actually take away from your happiness (O'Donoghue and Rabin 2001). Despite a tripling of real per capita income and output, self-reported measures of happiness in the United States have remained about the same since the 1950s. This has been true even in years of robust income growth, and for Western Europe in recent decades (Easterlin 1974, 2001).

In addition, studies on *individual* well-being and quality of life find that attitudes and relationships are more important than income (Diener and Suh 1999).[5] Personality and coping skills are often even more important than one's life situation (Diener and Lucas 1999). These studies provide evidence that increased income *alone* is not a good predictor of happiness or better quality of life.[6] There is also evidence that affluence itself can lower quality of life. Health is one of the most important aspects of the standard of living, which has a high correlate with quality of life indexes around the world (Rahman 2007). With lower incidences of some diseases and conditions, people in affluent countries have higher standards for "good health" than in the past. On the other hand, new health problems related to obesity are growing because of the availability of tasty, inexpensive, and unhealthful food, lack of physical exercise, and passive leisure activities. Rapidly increasing obesity among children in the United States is likely to result in billions of additional dollars spent on health care, shorter life expectancy, and lower worker productivity.[7] Lack of access to healthful foods is becoming a recognized problem in the United States and is an issue that we address in Chapter 6 as part of urban development patterns.

Economic growth and the resulting affluence allow the United States to spend far more per person on health care than any other country in the world, yet this has not translated into better results in health.[8] This is a prime example of how spending more does not necessarily lead to more satisfying results. Good health is a product of environment, lifestyle, diet, and many other factors as well as a product of medical care. Having access to all of those other factors often depends upon non-market "quality of life" factors as well as income. In addition, the distribution of health care spending throughout the population and the procedures for which it is used are as important as total spending, according to many health experts.[9]

State and local governments in the United States have limited influence on medical care access today. However, they have a substantial impact on community and lifestyle factors that influence health and health care use. They have an even larger impact on some other aspects of quality of life, such as public safety, access to recreation, and clean water. A broader view of economic development that includes quality of life as well as income growth will address many of these concerns. However, when communities focus on quality of life they want to be able to measure their progress. Before we examine locally developed indicators, we turn to how economists estimate the somewhat elusive idea of quality of life.

Estimating Quality of Life

Economists sometimes estimate quality of life or amenities through "compensating differentials" that explain why people choose to move to an area with a higher ratio of housing cost to salary or with higher tax rates (Berger et al. 1987; Blomquist et al. 1988; Roback 1982). This method implies that, over time, the overall "package" of wages, housing prices, and amenities or disamenities, will become equal everywhere. Some places will have higher wages and fewer amenities, while in other places low wages will be compensated by higher quality of life. Population movements will continue in search of a better package until the negatives and positives balance out everywhere. In the end, no place will have an advantage over any other.[10]

This model suggests that a locality attracts people until it has accumulated enough "unattractive" factors, such as congestion, pollution, higher taxes, or unaffordable housing, to cease attracting people away from other places (Alfeld 1995).[11] It is this negative effect of growth on communities that we focus on here. Most economic research on quality of life is focused on how to *explain* the causes of population movements and wage or housing price differentials, rather than on how to *improve* quality of life. But the people who live in an attractive community don't want it to become so unattractive that no one wants to move there! They are interested in maintaining or improving the quality of life that is right where they live.

Jacksonville, Florida, was among the first places to try to define local quality of life rather than just measuring it indirectly. They called it "a feeling of well-being, fulfillment, or satisfaction resulting from factors in the external environment" (Jacksonville Community Council 2007). This definition is subjective in representing the values and goals of a particular community, but its translation into measurable indicators is objective. Measurements of quality of life that are tied to place have played a role in local and regional economic development for some time. We have all read the popular rankings generated by national magazines and heard them quoted. Local measurements of quality of life can be important in economic development strategies, but as we will see, some do a better job than others at representing the goals and values of a community.

Measuring Quality of Life: Local Quality-of-Life Rankings

The first local measures of quality of life were published in Garoogian's *Best Places to Live, Money* magazine, *Ladies Home Journal,* and others soon followed. Each of these had their own criteria to rank quality of life. The many more specialized indexes produced by *Runner's World* and *Senior Living* have even more specifically targeted criteria. Obviously, some communities will rank high on one index and not on another. While many community leaders pay attention to these popular indexes, the results of "quality-of-life" rankings need to be taken with large grains of salt (see, for example, the analysis of Cortright and Mayer 2004).

The ratings developed by various publishers differ wildly from one publication to another (and sometimes from one year to another). There are also many problems and inconsistencies in the ways they measure quality of life. For example, some ratings use statewide averages for property taxes that may vary considerably by city or county. Others omit apartment rentals from housing costs. In addition, the rank of any one city is very sensitive to changes in the way climate, geography, economic opportunity, housing costs, taxes, educational quality, and other cultural and recreational aspects are weighted in the index. Climate is used in almost all ratings systems, but what is a "good" climate? Most indexes use average daily temperature and therefore reward moderation in the range of temperatures. However, using the average temperature misses the fact that many sunny winter days in the mountain West are perfect days for hikers, bikers, and runners, even though evening temperatures drop sharply. Equally important, this measure of climate ignores the amount of snowfall, rain, and the level of humidity. The measure of "climate" is a good example of how popular indexes use oversimplified measures in order to be able to easily apply them to cities across the country.

Cities and their economic development directors brag about top ratings wherever they get them and grumble when they do not, because ratings are a tool to attract new residents and businesses. The primary weakness we see in these commercial "quality-of-life" indexes is that they do not focus on how to *preserve* quality of life amid the growth and change that occur in local areas. Sustainable economic development is just as much about preserving and protecting as growing and changing. Seattle (Washington) and Austin (Texas) are examples of communities with high popular ratings that have also been leaders in developing locally based indicators. Their indicators are not for promoting the community to the rest of the world, but are for protecting and enhancing the amenities most valued by local residents. We look next at some alternative measures of well-being that do focus on preserving and improving local quality of life.

Alternative Measures of Well-Being

Many communities in the United States and Canada have chosen to identify their own indicators to supplement the use of income. Some are labeled "quality-of-life" indicators while others are called sustainability or community indicators. Although theoretically distinct, in practice the terms quality of life and sustainability are used almost interchangeably in local projects.[12] In Chapter 8, we describe in more detail how several cities have developed and used local indicators to improve quality of life and sustainability. Indicators focus on many non-income factors that show long-term investment in children and youth (low birth weights, child care quality, graduation rates, and alcohol or drug abuse among teens). They also look at economic equity or fairness, through affordability of housing and health insurance as well as poverty rates. The community groups choosing these measures did not assume that higher average incomes would automatically improve people's quality of life. Their members had observed through experience that separate measures were appropriate, so they developed indicators to follow various aspects of quality of life as well as to track economic growth.

Local projects also include environmental indicators that reflect land use, as well as water and air quality. Some of these reflect concerns specific to the geography and climate and cultural history of the city or region—salmon spawning in the rivers of the Northwest or farmland preserved in northern Florida. The indicators also include measures of health outcomes and public safety, of clean air and water, the quality of the "built landscape," and the growth in impermeable surfaces that affects vulnerability to flooding. Quality of life includes such a wide range of aspects—some economic, some environmental, some social—that it requires many measures missed in traditional economic indicators. Clean air or access to parks can be measured objectively, but other aspects of quality of life are based completely on individual perception or evaluation. Only surveys that allow for subjective responses can measure some of these. Alternative community indicators show that many people believe that income and production numbers alone give a very incomplete picture of the standard of living. Traditional economic indicators do not address the role of public goods and services or how much of the population participates in income gains. They do not deal with depletion of natural resources, investment in future generations, or the effects of growth on society and family. Indicators of quality of life can better equip local communities to deal with a variety of issues and to develop an economic development strategy that improves the overall standard of living.

Improving Quality of Life: Two Different Strategies

Individuals can improve their quality of life in one of two very different ways. The first is to move to a new community that offers more of what is wanted.[13] This search for improved quality of life has dominated migration in the United States for the past several decades, as economic factors have become relatively less important (Graves 1979). But this strategy has a downside. Recent research on measures of quality of life across the United States (Gabriel, Mattey, and Wascher 2003) finds that states with rapid population growth that did not adequately address congestion, air pollution, and infrastructure investment had substantial deterioration in quality of life.[14] New residents may feel better off from their change in location, but the original residents may experience declining quality of life from the in-migration. The strategy of improving quality of life by moving can benefit some, but in the end may lead to an overall decrease in quality of life. There is, however, a second strategy for improving quality of life that is sustainable. Whole communities can improve when their members choose to focus on quality of life in the place where they already live.

This second way to improve quality of life, through joining with fellow citizens, has been characteristically American for quite some time. "Americans of all ages, all stations of life, and all types of disposition are forever forming associations. . . . In democratic countries knowledge of how to combine is the mother of all other forms of knowledge; on its progress depends that of all the others" (De Tocqueville 2000 [1830] 211, 214).

One example of a new form of community governance is the development of locally chosen indicators that focus on quality of life or sustainability. Individuals who are likely to be ineffective acting alone can collaborate to exert some control over their external environment rather than having it defined by impersonal economic markets or government decisions. This provides an increasingly popular mechanism for individuals to join together in common action. As economists Bowles and Gintis (2002) observe, community governance is neither traditionally "left" nor "right," because it does not put ultimate faith in either the market or the government.

The growing popularity of community indicators is probably due in part to the prosperity and higher incomes of the last fifty years. With most people able to meet basic needs, they now express desires for amenities such as parks, bike trails, and the arts. From this perspective, indicators are evidence of the success of economic growth: it has allowed higher-order needs to surface. On the other hand, some of the areas that community indicators measure (environmental degradation, traffic congestion, and loss of sense of community) reflect the increased costs of economic growth.[15] Other measures, such as child poverty rates or extent of health insurance coverage, demonstrate public concern about the effects of unequal distribution of growth. The need to measure each of these in addition to per capita income makes clear that income levels alone are not adequate measures of how health, opportunity, and other aspects of quality of life are changing. Economic development must explicitly pay attention to changes in quality of life as well as in income. This requires attention to more than private business capital, such as infrastructure, human resources, natural resources, and the formal and informal institutions that make up community social capital.

Once local governments make a commitment to decide what aspects of quality of life they value most, and how to measure changes in them, the next step is to decide on actions. At the beginning of the chapter, we mentioned the importance of investments in social capital as a way to improve the quality of place in which people live. A vital aspect of carrying out the second strategy mentioned above is building on existing social capital in a community and improving it. We look next at what social capital is and its importance to economic development.

The Importance of Quality of Place and Social Capital

Social capital is best defined as the intangible laws, customs, and institutions that help any community function.[16] The idea of social capital originated in studies showing that the educational progress of individual students was significantly affected by family and neighborhood factors (Coleman 1988). Robert Putnam (1993) reinforced its importance when he explored the effects of civic and social relationships on economic development in the towns of northern Italy compared to southern Italy. Then, in *Bowling Alone* (2000), Putnam documented declining rates of participation in PTAs, churches, and bowling leagues in modern America and raised the question of what they meant for future levels of social capital.

There is widespread acknowledgment that human customs and institutions support the functioning of people and of commerce. These relationships and institutions—including neighborhood watches, block parties, carpools, bridge clubs, and book groups—often encourage trust and cooperation.[17] Many elements of quality of life that people value are nonmarket services, such as public safety, parks, museums, hospitals, roads, and education. These services are provided by either public sector or private not-for-profit organizations. Another part of that framework includes the network of relationships between family, friends, and neighbors within both formal and informal institutions.

Social capital has been criticized as a catchall term that is difficult to define or measure (Robison, Schmid, and Siles, 2002; Schmid, 2000). But we believe the term is valuable in spite of its shortcomings, since it incorporates aspects that are important for any local economic development plan. Quality of life is becoming more important as a way of attracting and keeping talented people in a community for economic growth. Just as important, the amenities often called quality of life are what make a community livable, safe, and enjoyable. A comprehensive look at what leads to improvement in quality of life and economic development must include both the *level* of social capital and *changes* in social capital.

Preserving and Investing in Social Capital

Economists, not surprisingly, suggest that people invest more in building social capital when the incentives are right. This means that the benefits received from an investment are expected to be greater than the costs of undertaking the investment (see Glaeser, Laibson, and Sacerdote 2002). It is easier (lower cost) to form relationships in a community when people stay in the same houses, neighborhoods, or cities. In addition, the longer that people stay in one place, the more benefit they receive from these relationships. Since more stability encourages social capital formation, relatively high mobility in the United States poses a challenge. Although it is individuals who decide how involved they will be in schools or community groups, or whether to become acquainted with their neighbors, the effects of their choices and actions spill over to the larger society. Evidence shows that weakened social capital affects community quality of life and the sustainability of community development (see Turner 1999).

For community leaders and policymakers, the question is how to encourage formation of positive social capital that benefits the entire community. Racial and cultural tolerance and opportunities for all economic groups strengthen the social fabric of a community, while ethnic or economic divisions weaken it. Social capital may also be increased by the renewed interest in community organizations and walkable neighborhoods. Neighborhood schools, food markets, corner coffee shops, and pocket parks can all make it easier to connect with neighbors. These are just a few examples of factors important in improving quality of life related to place, which in turn affects the attractiveness of locations.

Investment in public goods or the arts and other forms of social capital in a community creates or preserves valued amenities. These "nonmarket goods and services such as amenities and public services can be viewed as part of a community's set of economic assets," according to community development economists Ron Shaffer, Steve Deller, and Dave Marcoullier (2006, 64).We add that amenities are more than the physical characteristics of a place. Ties of family, friendship, and organizations hold many people to their community of origin or influence the choice of community where they relocate. Today, not only industries but people move to areas to be with other people who are like them—economically, socially, or otherwise.[18] Social capital is important for the quality of life in a community; it is also important for sustainable economic development.

Creative people want to live and associate with other creative people, and the amenities in a location draw people with particular characteristics that help spur economic development.[19] Richard Florida's *The Rise of the Creative Class* (2002) popularized the idea that jobs follow creative people, rather than the other way around. He looked at the places that have attracted these workers and found not only high concentrations of high-tech industry growth but innovation in many non-technical areas such as the arts and music.[20] Florida concluded that many growing population centers do not thrive "for such traditional economic reasons as access to natural resources or transportation routes . . . [or] because their local governments have given away the store through tax breaks and other incentives to lure business. They are succeeding largely because people want to live there" (Florida 2002, 217–19).

The increasing overlap between work, safety, and play leads to a desire to live in communities that provide stimulation in three dimensions: (1) *What's there?* in the city or town and natural environment, (2) *Who's there?* in the mix of people and (3) *What's going on?* in the vibrancy of endeavors that allow participation as well as observation in many aspects of life (Florida 2002, 232). This may be expressed in urban culture and entertainment or in opportunities to enjoy natural beauty and outdoor recreation. Florida writes that creative workers (whether involved in technology, art, marketing, or research) are not lured by: "sports stadiums, freeways, urban malls and tourism and entertainment districts that resemble theme parks but by amenities, experiences, and openness to *diversity of all kinds* and above all else the opportunity to validate their identities as creative people" (Florida 2002, 218; emphasis added).

We note that people often treat diversity as a code word for a larger minority population or for being gay-friendly, but diversity of all kinds includes openness to different political and religious views as well as cultural values and immigrant and ethnic groups. Communities might be much more open to diversity in one area (ethnic background) than in another (political tolerance) or vice versa.

Will Florida's formula for attracting jobs work across different types of communities? To begin with, future economic development may not be based on the same factors that led certain cities to boom in the 1990s, his period of focus. In addition, the classification system that Florida used to determine a "creative worker" and his vision of a new era of post labor–management conflicts have both been questioned as oversimplified.[21] But our interest here is primarily in the first and third dimensions of Florida's characterization of quality of place (*what's there? what's going on?*). We believe that he is correct in recognizing that amenities and quality of life are important for a healthy, vibrant, and productive community. The standard of living is truly higher—economically and personally—in places that make investments in amenities that support quality of life. Amenities are part of the social capital of a community.

Conclusion

In this chapter, we further developed our second rule for economic development: it must lead to a better overall standard of living, which includes both income and quality of life. As we observed above, the increased popularity of local indicators demonstrates two very different aspects of our modern-day "affluent society."[22] Higher incomes and widespread satisfaction of basic economic needs have led to increased demand for the amenities often called quality of life. At the same time, increased costs of growth are reflected in concern over many environmental and social measures. The movement for quality-of-life indicators reflects both the successes of growth and the desire to move beyond growth as the only primary goal.

These local community movements show that people have another option besides relocating to a "better place" when they seek to improve their quality of life. They can also promote public policies and private actions to deal with the effects of growth on their daily life. States and communities often focus on how to attract people or businesses to increase income. With more interest in quality of life from the public, economic development strategies are now increasingly attentive to environmental, quality, and cultural amenities. Economic development and quality of life, however, are too often pursued separately rather than in tandem. This is an inefficient strategy for communities to follow—both in terms of dollars spent and results achieved. In later chapters, we address how communities can influence economic development and quality of life in a combined strategy rather than having the two at odds with each other.[23] In Chapter 4, we look at another important factor in well-being, the sustainability of development that depends on nonrenewable resources.

APPENDIX 3.1
GDP Measures of Economic Activity

Gross domestic product (GDP), the most well-known number from the national income accounts, is the dollar value of all output of market goods and services produced in our economy each year; increases in GDP (adjusted for price changes) show growth in the size of the economy. Since market production always creates a corresponding amount of income (wages, interest, rents, profits, etc.), GDP also measures total national income. GDP adjusted for population growth shows whether income growth is outpacing population growth (or vice versa).

When the United States was coming out of the Great Depression of the 1930s and gearing up to support the Allied war effort in World War II, leaders in business and government realized they needed to know more about the national productive capacity. There was almost no information available nationally about prices, employment, or production. Simon Kuznets later won a Nobel Prize for devising our national income accounting measures. They became a model for other countries around the world also wanting to understand more about the basic workings of their economies. Kuznets and his colleagues in the early measurement efforts issued warnings—largely unheeded—that these were measures of output potential, rather than measures of national well-being. Yet GDP has come to be treated as just that—a measure of how well we are doing.

Over the years, many concerns have been expressed about interpreting even real GDP per capita (after it has been adjusted for population and price changes) as a measure of well-being.[24] One problem is that GDP does not differentiate between "goods" that have a positive effect on well-being and those that may be necessary only to deal with problems humans have created. For example, more police officers and prisons to deal with rising crime rates cause GDP to rise. So does treating polluted water to make it safe to drink. Spending on police and prisons is necessary and prudent because of crime, just as building a plant to purify polluted water is necessary. But it would be even better for an economy *not* to have to pay for these costs. That is why they are often called "defensive expenditures." In addition, GDP measures only production that involves a money transaction, so leaving work to stay home with a new baby or an elderly parent causes GDP to decline even though a valuable service is being provided.

States, counties, and cities do not have a GDP measure, but they use personal income as calculated from these same national accounts to measure changes in economic activity. Personal income differs from GDP, in that depreciation of business capital has been subtracted out, along with certain indirect business taxes and income flows from the rest of the world. Personal income is also often interpreted as a measure of well-being, but measures only market economic activity. It is valuable in its own right, but not meant to measure well-being any more than GDP is.

We believe that providing alternative indicators to supplement per capita income and GDP by measuring other aspects of the standard of living is an important step toward incorporating quality of life and sustainability into economic development. Measures of quality of life are among these indicators.

APPENDIX 3.2
Alternative Measures of National Well-Being

The genuine progress index (GPI) adjusts GDP by subtracting some of the costs of growth and adding estimated values for non-market activities such as household and volunteer work. It specifically addresses the depletion of nonrenewable resources and the costs of pollution,

Figure 3.1A   **Real Gross Domestic Product (GDP) and Genuine Progress Index (GPI) Per Capita, 1950–2000 in 2000 Dollars**

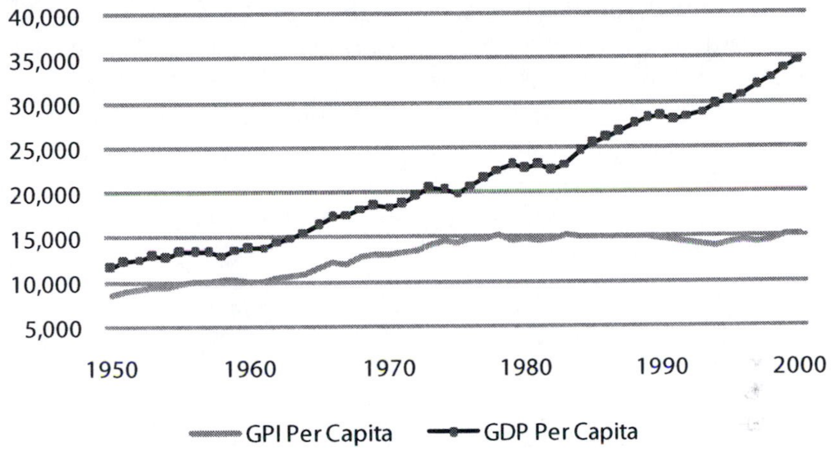

Source: Redefining Progress, www.rprogress.org/sustainability_indicators/genuine_progress_indicator.htm.

commuting, auto accidents, crime, and lifestyle-induced disease. While the U.S. GDP advanced steadily since the 1950s except for occasional brief recessions, GPI rose until the mid-1970s and since then has remained fairly constant (Figure 3.1A). Although GDP continues to show a growing U.S. economy during the past few decades, increased social and environmental costs now cancel out the benefits of growth in the GPI.

Are the factors added to and subtracted from GDP to derive GPI the "correct" ones? The devil is often in the details, and others might calculate it differently. However, the failure of GPI to grow since the mid-1970s is roughly consistent with public opinion. Numerous polls over the last few decades show many people feeling either that they work harder without becoming any better off or that they have concerns about the long-term economic future of the country as a whole.

In addition, the lack of increase in the GPI is generally consistent with findings in *America's Social Health: Putting Social Issues Back on the Agenda* (Miringoff and Opdycke 2008). The authors observe a drop of almost 20 percent in their Index of Social Health from 1970 to 2005; a period when real GDP per capita more than doubled. Steep declines in the late 1970s and early 1980s were followed by a decade of little change.

While the GPI stayed about the same throughout the 1990s, progress in various social health measures almost restored prior losses in the Index of Social Health during that period. When the index began to drift steadily downward again from 2000–2005, it was because improvements in infant mortality rates were offset by higher incidences of child abuse and higher rates of child poverty. Similarly, reduced teen drug abuse was offset by higher teen suicide rates and less frequent coverage by health insurance, and less poverty among the elderly was offset by more overall income inequality and major housing affordability problems (see Miringoff and Opdycke 2008, 71–74).

4

Environmentally Sustainable Development

In this chapter, we focus on environmental sustainability and natural capital. We begin by examining how natural resources are both similar to other capital stocks that must be maintained, but also different from them. In line with our rule #3, that the standard of living must be sustainable, we review definitions of sustainability and sustainable development. We then discuss the ways in which local-land and water-use decisions, recycling, and power generation have impacts on sustainability at home and far beyond. Next, we look at the costs of sustainable development. The word *sustainable* immediately raises the specter of costs for business, individuals, and local governments.

We call for a fuller look at costs that goes beyond the immediate price paid. Currently many costs associated with economic development are shifted to others nearby, far away, and even in future generations. Sustainable development requires a hard look at what has been considered cost-effective, so that growth reflects all costs. But we also note opportunities to reduce costs or spend less to produce and consume in a more sustainable way. Many of these opportunities have not been fully pursued to date. Since many rural communities are particularly dependent on natural resources for their livelihood, we devote a special section to how they are affected by environmental sustainability. We close with a section of examples of towns and cities that have already made formal commitments to sustainable development.

Natural Resources as Capital

Our view of economic development emphasizes sustaining *all* capital stocks that contribute to a healthy economy and society in the future as well as today. The natural resources we focus on in this chapter are more accurately called *natural capital* because air, water, forests, and soil are *stocks* that provide *flows* of resource use. This is true of oil reserves that provide gasoline, and of rivers that provide transport, fresh water, and a habitat for fish and wildlife. It is true for the atmosphere that provides the air we breathe and the sun that warms us. In this way natural resources are similar to other capital stocks, such as machines or roads or a set of human skills. They differ, however, in four important ways: first, the extremely high degree of global interrelatedness; second, the combination of initially "free gifts of nature" with the inability to renew some of them; third, the impossibility of using technology to substitute for some natural resources; and fourth, the incorrect pricing that the market mechanism places on many natural resources.

Natural Capital Interrelatedness and Uniqueness

In comparison to other forms of capital, natural capital has many more aspects that are not under the control of any one community or nation. "Think globally, but act locally" reflects both the global effects of actions by individuals in their communities and the effects on any community of actions by others around the world. For example, transportation produces 21 percent of the carbon pollution that creates greenhouse gases (Hawken, Lovins, and Lovins 1999, 40). Reducing the contribution of automobiles requires national regulations,[1] but traffic patterns and driving habits reflect local land use and transportation options. Similarly, the quality of local water sources is often affected by actions elsewhere.

Another way in which natural capital is very different from many other forms of capital is it was formerly called "free gifts of nature" (because it was here before we were). Today we are more aware of the limited supply and uniqueness of many forms of natural capital. Some forms, such as forests or fish, are renewable if well managed. Fossil fuels such as coal and oil are not renewable, but alternative energy sources can substitute for their depletion. Substitutes are unlikely, however, for environmental services, such as the water we drink or the air that we breathe, and the natural waste absorption properties of the atmosphere and of rivers, lakes, and oceans. Some kinds of natural capital are inputs for production, and it is probably possible to devise substitutes for many of them. Other kinds of natural capital providing life-giving services (such as the air and water of the atmosphere) are not replaceable and have no substitute.

Understood this way, the environment is not a competing interest to be balanced with the economy, but rather an envelope surrounding human society and the economy. Figure 4.1 (first shown in Chapter 1 as Figure 1.2) illustrates the important role of environmental services.

Figure 4.1 **Sustainable Development: Economy, Environment, and Society**

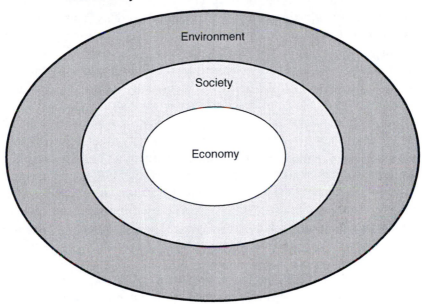

Technological Replacements for Natural Capital?

With technological progress, there will be substitutes for some forms of natural (or social or human) capital, but not for others. While machines, electronic devices, and other new processes have increased the productivity of labor and land enormously over the past century, there are two fundamental reasons why this is only partially transferable to natural capital. There are both technical limits on substitution and individual and social values that limit this possibility (Holt 2005). We look first at technical limits for environmental inputs and environmental services.

Human ingenuity can find replacements for some natural resources that are depleted, but not all. Recent history demonstrates that even while knowledge grows continually, its results are uncertain. If incentives were enough to guarantee a solution, someone would have invented a cure for the common cold and become rich! New knowledge can *decrease* rather than increase available resources. For example, asbestos and chlorofluorocarbons were widely used in the past, but we now know that they cause severe harm to human health (Daly and Farley 2004). This new knowledge has made remodeling older buildings considerably more costly if they contain asbestos materials. The most important technical limitations are on substitutes for ecosystem services (conversion of carbon dioxide into oxygen in the atmosphere and filtration of water by natural systems) that sustain life. Regardless of the level of incentives provided, technological fixes or the development of substitutes for this are unlikely (Costanza 1991). Relying on "technology" to provide absolute life necessities that are at risk is a dangerous strategy.

Substitution also has social limits. Some aspects of nature are valued for spiritual or aesthetic reasons, such as the beauty of rainbows, mountains, seashores, and the songs of birds. There either are not adequate substitutes or substitution may be contrary to social or ethical norms.[2] Values are as important as technical limitations in maintaining particular aspects of each capital stock rather than considering substitutes for it. Preserving capital stocks for their unique and non-substitutable values is part of sustainable development, but may not be encouraged by watching the bottom line of profitability today. This leads us to the final way in which natural capital differs from other forms of capital. It stems from the fact that some of the most essential environmental services are not marketable and therefore are undervalued in a market system.

Why Prices May Not Provide Correct Signals of Value for Natural Capital

Nature provides many services essential to human life (such as air and sunshine) and gives pleasure to us directly through sunsets and cool breezes without going through a market. Since these services are not marketable, there is no price tag for them. As a result, they will be undervalued. Official accounting practices in private business, the public sector, and the national income accounts (Appendix 3.1) all ignore benefits and costs that do not go through a market, as well as costs that can be shifted to others. These costs may be financial or show up in lower quality of life. Some costs are not borne by the consumers, businesses, or investors who enjoy the use of a good or service (or the profit from making and selling it). When these costs are shifted to other parties, they are called "spillover" costs. (A more extensive explanation of why market mechanisms and spillover costs and benefits is provided in Appendix 4.1, for readers who want a short introduction or review of these arguments.)

Just as pollution costs can be shifted, spilling over to others, damages to scenic beauty or sense of community are also costs that can be shifted. Without accountability by producers and consumers for the costs shifted to others, there are not proper price incentives for using scarce resources carefully and for preserving nonrenewable capital. Because of these spillover effects, conventional cost–benefit analysis is not only difficult but perhaps inappropriate, since neither spillover benefits nor costs may be able to be calculated in terms of prices.[3] It may be better simply to admit that there are important social and human values that must be taken into account, and proceed with the most cost effective way to achieve them. Because of the importance of certain natural resources for quality of life and sustainable economic development, this lack of marketable value or incorrect pricing means that public action is necessary. We now turn to defining the terms sustainability and sustainable development.

Defining Sustainability and Sustainable Development

The classic definition of sustainability is "meeting the needs of the present without compromising the ability of future generations to meet their own needs" (Bruntland 1987, 7). Sustainability requires attention to all forms of capital, but natural capital has unique qualities that give it particular importance. Private business capital and public infrastructure are assigned primary roles in the conventional wisdom and traditional economics.[5] But they are both derived from natural and human capitals, and they depend on them for renewal.

Sustainable development is development that considers the economy, environment, and society as a whole system.[4] This system meets a variety of human needs—not all of which are economic. To increase the standard of living, many aspects of quality of life (discussed in Chapter 3) are also important.

Sustainable development requires awareness of the unintended consequences to one capital stock that may come from increasing another. For example, in the process of improving infrastructure, communities sometimes destroy wetlands. Flooding due to lack of water absorption then requires building more infrastructure to solve the flooding problems. This is somewhat analogous to getting medical treatment for one problem and having it create or worsen another problem. Approaching sustainability through a systems perspective should heighten awareness of the complex interrelationships between various capital stocks.[6]

The first major local sustainability project followed this systems approach when it asked: "How do we protect our environment, meet everyone's basic needs, keep our economy dynamic, and maintain a just society? How do we make difficult trade-offs and balanced judgments that take everyone's interests into account, including those of our children and grandchildren?" (Sustainable Seattle 1998). We develop this approach by looking at five areas of environmental sustainability where states and localities have direct control. These are regulation of land use, water use, non–point-source water pollution, solid waste, and power generation. All of these affect economic development and quality of life as well as environmental sustainability of the community. They also have consequences for the larger society and environment.

Regulation of Land Use

Determining appropriate possible uses for any particular piece of land is a primary function of local and state governments. This is an area where sustainability and quality of life are very dependent on local land-use development plans. Through zoning and planning, local policies determine which land may be used for agriculture, for mining, and for industrial or commercial development. Local planning affects how residences and retail fit into the existing natural and built environment. In some parts of the country, protecting "viewscapes" along with landscapes has become an important part of public land-use policy. The "green infrastructure" of open fields, lakes, and trees in local communities probably affects health just as much as private and public expenditure on health care and safety. Parkland and open space encourage biking, walking, and athletic activities that are valued as part of quality of life. They also provide a safe haven for bird and wildlife habitat and improve local air quality, even for those who never visit a park.

As state and local governments think creatively about how to preserve and develop their green infrastructure, land-use policies will play an important role. For example, a new opportunity in already dense urban areas comes from reclaiming "brownfields"[7] caused by waste disposal prior to current environmental regulations. Some contain toxic substances that preclude construction but can still be beautiful park and recreation areas. Brownfield development was encouraged by Illinois and Minnesota before the Environmental Protection Agency began grants and incentives nationwide to encourage this kind of development (see Benedetti 2008).

We note that this type of incentive is quite different from the location incentives discussed in Chapter 2. Incentives for brownfield development spend public money to encourage action (the cleaning of the site and its productive reuse) that would not otherwise be privately profitable. This results in a social benefit and encourages long-term and sustainable changes in development practice. However, a much lower effectiveness rate of these incentives in New York (compared to neighboring Massachusetts, New Jersey, and Pennsylvania) demonstrates that they must also be carefully targeted and monitored.[8] Today's brownfields serve as potent reminders of the potential future costs of waste disposal practices we follow today. We turn now to the effects of waste on water quality.

Ensuring a Clean and Safe Water Supply

Access to good quality water at a reasonable price is necessary for sustainable development in agriculture, industry, and urban areas. While federal clean water laws apply to industry, non–point-source pollution of water from diverse actors in agriculture, construction, and transportation is a larger problem. States have the regulatory responsibility for these non-point sources.[9] Livestock waste and dangerous pesticides and herbicides make agriculture one of the worst polluters of water. For example, Atrazine has been banned in most of Europe (without negative impacts on crop yields) but is used heavily by corn farmers in our Midwest and contaminates the natural well water (Ackerman 2008, see Chapter 5). Researchers find little benefit for this high cost. "Although pesticides are generally profitable, their use does not always decrease crop losses. For example, even with the tenfold increase in insecticide use in the United States from 1945 to 1989, total crop losses from insect damage have nearly doubled" (Pimentel et al. 1992, 750).

Making more drinkable water available for residential use requires changing from the industrial agricultural model that has been dominant since the 1970s.[10] Federal subsidies and programs have supported the industrialization of agriculture, but state and local policies have also played a role. The net result has been damage to water quality as well as profound effects on landscapes, wildlife habitat, and species diversity.[11] County agricultural extension units and state agricultural universities could help in the transition to more sustainable methods; however, this requires that they have more independence from fertilizer, seed, equipment, and pesticide companies that have interests in maintaining the current model.

Construction activity is another major source of pollution to streams and lakes. Wider roads and bigger parking lots along with more commercial and residential buildings increase impermeable surfaces and the risks of flooding. State and local governments can require certain kinds of building materials and techniques and prohibit others. In addition, they can vary the level of taxes levied on materials or properties based on their pollutants. Along with ensuring that water supplies are clean and safe, just making sure that there *is* enough water looms as major issue for many states and localities.

Water: Doesn't It Just Come from the Tap?

Water has been called "the new oil."[12] There is increasing competition for water in every region of the United States, including the Great Lakes area (Krantzberg 2009). In coastal areas, such as the Atlantic and Gulf coast plains and the Pacific Northwest, more pumping for domestic water use has depleted groundwater to such low levels that saline water has moved inland, affecting soil fertility and stability.[13] With looming shortages, new subdivisions now compete with water-intensive livestock and farming practices. Even though water cycles through the atmosphere and is "renewable" on a global scale, having clean, drinkable water available is not so simple. Access to potable water has become an issue across the United States (and much of the world)—even in areas with plenty of rainfall.[14] Climate change is likely to intensify droughts in the American West as well as in other parts of the world (Sachs 2006). Without serious conservation efforts to lower use by residences, agriculture, and industry, population growth will require more water.

The economies of scale that lowered per capita costs of water development when populations grew are largely gone. Federal water subsidies that lowered costs in many areas are also being phased out.[15] New water will be added from higher-cost sources than existing water comes from, which raises the average price to water customers. In some regions, ambitious and costly new sources of water have been proposed to deal with future needs. Many communities in California are turning to desalination of seawater.[16] For the Carlsbad project in San Diego County alone, $350 million in subsidies have been allocated (Associated Press, November 11, 2009) to the nine participating water districts. But environmental groups challenge whether water conservation techniques could make currently available water adequate with less energy used, also avoiding the harm desalination plants cause to marine life.

Another expensive source of water is trans-mountain diversion. Water is piped from the western slope of the Rocky Mountains over and through mountains to the eastern slope, where 80 percent of Colorado's population lives. Proposed new projects incur enormous legal costs to fight the smaller communities near the water source, as well as environmental groups. Continued growth depends not only on the success of legal battles, but on whether new commercial and residential developments are willing to pay sharply higher water prices for more water diversion.[17] A third source of water comes from drilling deeper into nonrenewable underground sources, such as the Ogallala Aquifer in the High Plains region of the central United States. This "prehistoric" water is nonrenewable, since it dates to the age of the dinosaurs. As with desalination and trans-mountain diversion, mining deep into the ground for water may be no more economically efficient than extremely deep drilling for oil would be. It is there, but it may not be cost-effective to use it.

Groundwater depletion is also happening in the Atlantic and Gulf coastal plains and the Pacific Northwest, where sources are renewable up to a point. With more pumping for domestic use, the water table falls and the land literally sinks in coastal areas. Stream flows are lower in other areas, and the quality of the water declines as salinity increases. There are similar problems on Long Island (New York), in the Ipswich River basin of Massachusetts, coastal counties in New Jersey, Hilton Head Island (South Carolina), Brunswick and Savannah (Georgia), and Jacksonville, Miami, and Tampa (Florida). Memphis, Tennessee, depends exclusively on groundwater for municipal supply, but it is also quite important to Baton Rouge (Louisiana) and the greater Houston (Texas) area, both of which have experienced significant declines (Cunningham, 2001). Potable water is scarce even in areas with high rainfall.

The demand for more urban water is not just a result of population growth. It is heavily dependent on land use and landscaping, both areas where local government can have a major impact. Local governments can approach this through a variety of solutions, some more compatible with quality of life and sustainable development than others. The first is more emphasis on renovation of existing properties and older neighborhoods, which requires less new spending on new distribution infrastructure but is likely to have only modest effects on water usage.[18] The second is cash rebates or mandates for water-efficient appliances and landscaping.

A third incentive could be tiered pricing, charging a low rate for normal in-house use but substantially more for the higher levels of use required for outdoor watering. This would encourage water conservation both in and outside the home. However, if prices are too high, they can result in unintended consequences, damaging the local green infrastructure of trees and landscaping during a drought.

A fourth method of water conservation targets new residential and commercial development. Higher tap fees on new buildings typically pay for new distribution infrastructure, but they could also be raised enough to cover development of new and more expensive water sources. These tap fees are likely to change behavior more quickly because build-ers still have some flexibility in regard to site location, permeable vs. non-permeable pavement, and types of landscaping whereas existing homeowners do not. Landscaping with native or other low-water usage plants initially costs more than a conventional lawn but is less costly over time where water is scarce and priced accordingly. This lower water use landscaping could be mandated for new homes or encour-aged by reducing other fees to participating builders. These subsidies may make economic sense (unlike location incentives) because the entire public benefits when the actions of new homeowners relieve the need to develop expensive new sources of water. Natural landscaping could also help conserve water and rebuild native bird habitats across the country.

Water conservation can be encouraged by a combination of these and other strategies. Otherwise, a lack of water planning may eventually im-pact the ability to meet other needs. Expensive new water sources along with water-treatment and water-distribution infrastructure can crowd out the ability to pay for other priorities in a city or county. However, local studies of the costs of growth often omit water and other utilities from their calculations (Chapter 7). It is only by recognizing the connection between different land use patterns and the use of resources such as water that future economic development strategies can support growth, quality of life, and sustainability. Let us turn to another area where local and state governments can have an impact on sustainable development, and that is with waste.

Recycling Waste into Resource

Each year billions of gallons of raw or poorly treated sewage flow through 600,000 miles of sewer pipes into U.S. rivers. This affects people, plant and wildlife, as well as farms and businesses downstream.[19] Local municipalities have substantial influence on the new development that sometimes outstrips processing capacity in local wastewater plants and storm water drains. Without adequate investment, storms cause existing facilities to overflow, spreading bacteria-laden water and risks of disease. Wastewater infrastructure in the United States has been graded as D for quite some time (American Society of Civil Engineers 2009). If cities are going to approve new development, then they need to make it sustainable in terms of the waste it generates and the infrastructure for dealing with that waste.

Taking natural resources and making products to be used and then later disposed as waste has been called the "take-make-waste" cycle.[20] In contrast, sustainability requires a continuous loop of resource recycling. The take-make-waste cycle has become so ingrained in the modern industrial system of production that it seems hard for communities to affect it much. However, they are heavily involved in the disposal step. Local governments manage or regulate waste disposal, landfills, and recycling processes. State taxes on products such as glass bottles with refunds for recycling can reduce the amount of waste going into landfills. These refundable taxes could be extended to other goods such as cell phones, computers, monitors, and televisions to increase recycling and reduce waste production even more.

Construction also creates an enormous amount of solid waste and produces more greenhouse gas (carbon dioxide) annually than the automobile. This is partly because homes built recently are twice the size of those built in 1950 and 50 percent larger than in 1990.[21] Along with the larger size of new homes, the materials used in them affect local waste disposal and landfills. Technologies currently available in construction (along with other areas), however, are not being fully utilized even though they would be profitable and more sustainable at the same time.[22] These ways to save money and nonrenewable resources are not new, unproven, or even expensive. They make perfect economic sense but are not the tried and true way of doing things.

This demonstrates how powerful habits are even for profit-oriented business managers. "Natural capitalism" refers to companies that recognize on their own the ways to be sustainable and profitable (Hawken, Lovins, and Lovins 1999). But the evidence shows that it is difficult for many businesses to adapt to new strategies on their own, even though these could be equally profitable. Local and state governments can play a role in stimulating this kind of environmental innovation by business. For example, Chattanooga, Tennessee, established an eco-industrial park where one company's waste becomes an input into another's production process (Portney 2003, 82–89).

There are many other examples of actions municipalities can take. Some have constructed wetlands to process sewage and at the same time restored stopovers for migratory birds that had been eliminated by past development. Some sewage treatment systems in Nevada, Texas, New York, New Hampshire, and Massachusetts are able to meet EPA drinking-water standards using hydroponically grown plants that consume nutrients and absorb many toxic substances. Municipalities of all sizes are also finding ways to provide their own power by utilizing local wastes. In Umea, Sweden, the oil-burning power plant was replaced by one fueled entirely by the city's own household and business waste, which has a higher energy value than most biomass fuels. The examples above are taken from *The Natural Step for Communities* (James and Lahti 2004), an excellent source for innovative changes possible at the local government level. We now address using sustainable energy sources for electricity and heating.

Sustainable Energy for Power Generation

The primary decisions about how to generate power are made through locally owned utilities or through private utilities regulated by states. Local or state governments could have a major impact on the global environment and sustainable economic development, through the type of energy and regulation people choose. Coal provides one-third of all electric power in the United States and appears to be a low-cost fuel to many people. However, when the spillover costs from mining coal and burning it are included, coal is actually an expensive way to provide energy. This is another example of how failure to include all costs in the price has distorted decision making. There are many alternatives to coal as a fuel, along with new methods of power generation from wind, geothermal, and solar energy. Below, we discuss ways to find fuel in waste and solve two problems at once.

Eskilstuna, a suburb of Stockholm, uses by-products of the timber and wood-processing industries in a state-of-the-art plant that captures 90 percent of the biomass fuel's energy, compared to a capture rate of less than 35 percent at most conventional oil, coal, or natural gas plants (James and Lahti 2004, 37–48). The Umea plant referenced earlier uses all wastes produced in the town to generate the power it needs. This not only deals with waste in a sustainable way, it reduces the dependence on fossil fuel (including oil and natural gas) that leaves communities vulnerable to international fuel price fluctuations and contributes to global warming.

In addition to making sustainable decisions about how to provide future power needs, local building and planning codes should be examined for how they effect the future demand for energy. It is cheaper now to continue to build homes and commercial buildings that waste energy, but they will be more expensive to operate over their lifecycle. A local economy may not be sustainable if future energy price increases make living there less affordable than in other areas that are less sensitive to price spikes. In contrast, if a community has more energy efficient public and private buildings, it will be economically resilient when energy prices rise.

A major concern for states and localities, however, is the cost of sustainable practices. Many fear that practicing environmentally sustainable development will drive away business and jobs, bankrupt local and state governments, or lower the standard of living of citizens. We next address the general question of cost.

The Costs of Sustainable Development

Just the word *sustainability* may raise the specter of high costs and a lower standard of living for some people. However, the potential for a better standard of living that is also sustainable is far from being an idealistic pipe dream. New materials and methods are developed daily to substitute for those that have caused problems in the past. The fear that environmental standards will drive businesses away appears largely unwarranted (Jaffe et al. 1995; Neumayer 2001). For example, environmental and safety-related shutdowns account for less than a tenth of a percent of major layoffs.[23] Some plants that have moved to Mexico emit less pollution there than competitors in the United States, probably because they are using newer technologies (Gallagher 2004). Many businesses have adjusted quite well to new environmental standards, making innovations and discovering new markets. Interface (carpet) and IKEA (furniture) are just two examples. At the local level, new "eco-niches," such as increased demand for locally produced foods and sustainably produced consumer products, are creating opportunities for small entrepreneurs and local businesses.[24]

This success seems hard to believe, since traditional economics implies that new regulations must hurt business profits or raise consumer prices. However, a growing body of evidence indicates that "business as usual" is not always based on the most cost-effective, or even the most profitable production methods (Porter and van der Linde 1995). For example, industry could profitably use *currently known* technologies to reduce energy use by 19–20 percent in the United States simply by recycling currently wasted steam, heat, and pressure.[25] Information and communications technologies could be used to reduce emissions by planning routes of delivery vehicles more efficiently and reducing unnecessary energy consumption in buildings.[26] Substantial moves toward more efficiency in use of water, fuels, and land are possible without lessening the standard of living at all. This is particularly true when the value that people place on environmental amenities (Chapter 3) and on avoiding environmental hazards is included in the standard of living.[27]

Although environmental sustainability can start by eliminating wasteful production and moving toward greater efficiency, it will also require some new methods that raise costs. But many of these costs are much lower than initial estimates anticipated (Ackerman 2008, 26). It is important to remember that doing nothing also imposes substantial costs on health, productivity, and quality of life over time. For example, today's toxic landfills are the legacy of past inaction and impose substantial environmental, economic, and social costs today. However, where there are costs, how can they be paid without decreasing the standard of living?

Over 20 percent of modern-day U.S. production currently covers the consequences of growth and waste (Hawken, Lovins, and Lovins 1999, 48–61). What are often called "defensive expenditures" (see Appendix 3.1) include environmental cleanup and treatments for lifestyle diseases such as type 2 diabetes.[28] Most of the increase in GDP in the past thirty years has been in these kinds of "uneconomic growth." Shifting production toward goods and services that improve health rather than diminishing it will not decrease the standard of living or eliminate jobs—it will simply change the kind of jobs we produce.[29]

While it is true that *any* spending creates jobs and income and tax revenues, the same number of jobs and levels of income can come from changing future spending patterns, as history has already shown. One hundred years ago, half of the U.S. labor force worked on farms, while only two percent do today. The twenty-first century economy will be based on energy conservation and environmental protection in ways that could not have been imagined in the past. This type of sustainable production can create new jobs for the unemployed and underemployed, and replace jobs from old industries. Less spending in areas that are "waste" can free up labor, capital, natural resources, creativity, and technology to invest in environmental sustainability. This is the familiar story of human and economic development through time—things change.[30] Technology changes, and values change. Ensuring that production is environmentally sustainable requires reexamining the value of defensive spending and of the competitive spending by consumers that we will discuss in Chapter 5.

But doing nothing because there will be costs incurred right now is not an option. Pretending that economic development can be sustainable without environmental sustainability ignores the reality that some aspects of nature are irreplaceable and cannot be substituted. Since the economy as a whole will *benefit* from sustainable development, flexible public and social institutions can smooth transitions to sustainable development. This does not mean that major lifestyle changes or difficult trade-offs will not be needed at some point, but rather that much could be done right now without major dislocation. This is especially true for rural communities that have always been primarily dependent on natural resources for their livelihood. We turn now to examining the particular costs of environmental sustainability on rural communities.

Rural Development and Changing Natural Resource Use

The history of many small towns and rural areas is an economic dependence on farming, ranching, mining, timber harvesting, or fishing. However, transportation to nearby cities, along with increased tourism and recreation, has changed the economic foundations of rural America today. Still, there is even more anxiety about how environmentally sustainable development will impact economic sustainability in rural America than in urban areas. People in small towns are concerned not just about their economic futures but about quality of life, including loss of community and opportunities for their children and grandchildren in the future.[31] This can result, however, in seeing the path to economic prosperity "through the rear view mirror" (Power 1996b, 9).

Just as there are limits on the sustainability of a resource (such as minerals to be mined), a local economy that depends too much on that resource is unsustainable. It goes through "boom and bust" along with mining, timber, or single-crop agriculture that supports the region's economy. Any commodity traded on the world market is subject to enormous price fluctuations, which is one reason why too much dependence on commodity businesses is not good for sustainable development. Modern industrial-style agriculture has high capital intensity and provides very few jobs to keep people in the community. It requires incurring high levels of debt to pay for equipment and commercial seeds and fertilizer. As a result, many formerly independent farmers have become corporate contractors or have abandoned farming entirely. Moving away from industrial agriculture to a more sustainable system could be more profitable, not less.

As consumer tastes continue to shift to locally and organically produced foods, there are new markets.[32] The number of organic farmers is growing rapidly, and organic sales are the fastest-growing segment in food (Organic Trade Association 2009; U.S. Department of Agriculture 2009). Many consumers are willing to pay more for fruits and vegetables, fresh eggs, and free-range chicken, pork, and beef that are local or organic (not always the same thing). Both are less environmentally damaging to soil and water than the dominant techniques used for wheat, corn, sugar, or soybeans.

Sustainable production (whether it is in mining, forestry, fishing, or farming) usually provides *more* local jobs, not fewer. For people who want to stay in rural communities and maintain that way of life, it may provide an adequate income when combined with the amenities and quality of life they prefer. Changing from the industrial model to a more local sustainable model could rejuvenate many small towns and rural areas. Rather than people fleeing these areas, as happened a century ago, a reverse migration is creating many rural renaissances. Changes in telecommunications, transportation, and the distribution of school funding are making small towns more attractive now than they were to past generations. In addition to sustainable agriculture, tourism can represent a new path for some rural communities.

Agriculture and tourism, however, can both be practiced in sustainable or unsustainable ways. Neither is universally "good" or "bad" for the environment, local economy, or community. Just as unsustainable agriculture drains the land and the vitality of small towns, industrial tourism can wreck the environment and local culture. Power observes:

> Most resort towns and recreational meccas in North America represent "industrial-grade" tourism—that is, a large-scale, high-volume industry that inundates communities and almost replaces them. However, tourism does not have to take place on this scale or in this manner. There is an alternative type of tourism that protects what is unique in an area by limiting and dispersing the impact of visitors (Power 1996b, 232).

Adventure travel, cultural and historical tourism, and eco-tourism are increasingly popular, especially with younger people. They represent real opportunities for many communities to develop sustainably, in contrast to industrial tourism or industrial agriculture. In Spain, a government-sponsored effort called *Agriturismo* links farmers and ranchers with people seeking rural experiences so that rural landholders can sustain their livelihood and remain in their homes. While many of the commodities traditionally produced in resource-dependent regions are in *oversupply* on the world market, the "new" tourism is in short supply. Looking in the rearview mirror makes the old extraction industries, including industrial agriculture, seem more economically important than the service industry of tourism. The facts suggest otherwise (Power 1996b, 236–46).

Competition between the needs of agriculture, mining, tourism, and residential development must be approached in new ways as quality of life and sustainability become increasingly important in economic development. True economic development ensures that change brings vitality and a better standard of living, rather than maintaining the status quo and attempting to fight all change. That is true in both rural and urban areas, but it is primarily in urban areas that communities have officially adopted commitments to sustainability. We look at some of them in the next section.

Sustainability Strategies for Local Governments

The word *sustainability* "has come to mean so many different things to so many different people that it probably does as much to promote confusion and cynicism as positive environmental change," wrote Kent Portney in *Taking Sustainable Cities Seriously* (2003, 3). In his review of thirty-one U.S. cities with a sustainability initiative, he finds three factors that are critical to making real progress. The first is to move beyond a

declaration or vision statement about sustainability to an officially recognized sustainability plan that includes strategies for its achievement.
The second important factor is to tie the sustainability plan to specific
indicators that are regularly used to judge effectiveness (as we discuss
in Chapter 8). Last, but not least, sustainability plans are more effective
in achieving their goals with active involvement of the mayor and city
council. In contrast, they are much less likely to succeed when assigned
to one or two departments without the involvement of top leadership.

Active involvement of key community leaders is also important,
because moving toward sustainability requires a new way of thinking
about economic development and urban planning. Chattanooga, called
the "worst polluted city in the United States" by the U.S. Department of
Health, Education and Welfare in 1969, was dependent on heavy industry
for jobs but had a terrible pollution problem as a result (Vey 2007). As
these jobs began to go away, economic development plans facilitated
creation of a company to produce hybrid and electric buses to be exported to other cities, as well as to be used in the Chattanooga bus system
(Portney 2003).[33] This helped the local economy and environment and
contributed to sustainable development beyond the region. An official
commitment to sustainability in the early 1990s was behind many of
these changes. It led to a Greenways program with a seventy-five-mile
network linking parks, recreational areas, and open space that made the
community more livable and attractive.

The Urban Land Institute's *Growing Cooler: the Evidence on Urban
Development and Climate Change* (2008) recommends similar changes
in states and localities to protect the green infrastructure of parks, open
spaces, and wetlands. A group of nature-friendly communities (including Baltimore County in Maryland, DeKalb County, the seat of Atlanta,
Georgia, and the Traverse Bay area in Michigan, along with some university towns[34]) have set new standards for development to protect the
natural resources they live with. They have revised zoning requirements
that encourage sprawl, established transfer of development or density
rights (TDRs) to allow flexibility in development patterns, and engaged
in public education on the issues (Duerksen and Snyder 2005).

Contrary to popular perception, sustainability is not a West Coast phenomenon in the United States or one for college towns or upper-income
enclaves. But what is the path for states and communities to become
more environmentally sustainable? Different strategies are appropriate
depending on the economy, geography, history, and local government

structure and community preferences. Chattanooga is an example of a city that was very concerned about economic development and found its future prosperity in being more environmentally aware. Several Swedish towns discussed earlier also embraced sustainable development as a way to reverse depressed economic circumstances and out-migration. Other communities begin from a quality of life or environmental responsibility stance.

Any community that makes a commitment to support adequate investments in all of the capital stocks can establish a sustainable development plan. There are many examples in the United States and around the world that can be adapted to local needs. Private nonprofit institutes such as the Rocky Mountain Institute and the Sonoran Institute focus on regionally specific problems. Local universities and colleges can also be resources for either the latest information, individualized consultations and service-learning projects of students.

Resources such as the Smart Growth Network (www.smartgrowth.org) the Council of State Governments, and the International City Managers Association (ICMA) are all providing more information every day on how to effectively practice more sustainable development in states and localities.

Conclusion

The conventional wisdom has been that economic growth will make protecting the environment more affordable (Friedman 2005). However, average incomes have more than tripled in the United States since the 1950s, after adjustment for inflation and population growth. This has not made the trade-off between low prices for consumer goods and environmental protection seem easier to most people. Clearly, it will take more than economic growth to create environmentally sustainable development. Moreover, some aspects of economic growth are environmentally unsustainable and require changes in how we do things. The future of true economic development will not be in location incentives to businesses, but rather in helping to create quality of life and sustainability where private actions cannot be profitable. Businesses can then develop the most appropriate technologies for sustainable development. But it helps to have broad public support for change, especially if it has costs up front. Community leaders should help to explain the links between costs, higher quality of life, and sustainability. State and local governments can help to "frame" choices in ways that encourage private behavior that supports sustainable development.[35] They also must play a role ensuring that their taxes, fees, and regulations help market prices reflect all the costs of production and consumption.

In this chapter, we emphasize that a twenty-first century approach to economic development must view the interactions of the economy, environment, and society differently than the old model did. The environment is not an input to the economy; the economy exists within society and within the environment. This new approach to economic development must consider the effects of decisions and policies on all capital stocks needed for sustainable development, including the unique role of certain kinds of natural capital. True sustainable development is about making choices and innovations to support the well-being of our children and grandchildren as well as ourselves. Rather than having to react when change happens, we can make choices now that try to anticipate future challenges.

While many decisions must and will be made at the national or international level, we have explored a variety of actions that states and localities can take and we will continue to do so throughout this book. Sustainable development requires consciously and carefully considering the inevitable trade-offs that must be made in ways that they have not been in past economic development.[36] We move next to what local communities can do to support development that fosters human and social capital and a sustainable society in Chapter 5.

APPENDIX **4.1**
When Markets Fail: The Role of Public Policies in Private Markets

Chapter 2 makes it clear that market forces work better than public decisions in signaling to businesses where to locate. If land or labor is not fully utilized in one location, it will look relatively inexpensive. This will attract businesses from other places where land and labor are relatively more expensive.[37] Price-value differences between cities and states send signals, an example of the workings of the "invisible hand" Adam Smith alluded to in *The Wealth of Nations*. Similarly, when energy is abundant and labor is scarce, low energy prices provide incentives to use technologies that "waste" energy but economize on labor. On the other hand, if energy becomes more expensive, the way to be efficient changes also. Rising energy prices should lead businesses to conserve, but since prices fluctuate so much, the effect may not be sufficiently long to change behavior.

Most businesses require strong and consistent price signals before investing in new technology or developing new products. If producers are able to avoid some costs (pollution, effects on global warming) by shifting them out of the market, then they can charge a price below the full and complete costs of production. (When a cost of production is shifted outside the original market, it is called an externality or "spillover cost.") Buyers will respond to this lower price, and more of the good or service will be produced than would be if its users were paying full cost. Market outcomes are therefore inefficient when there are significant spillovers.[38]

For example, disposal or recycling costs of cell phones, computer monitors, or refrigerators are invisible to the manufacturer, seller, and user. There is no price incentive to minimize disposal or recycling costs during manufacture to appeal to consumers. Instead, the incentive is to produce and sell a product that appears inexpensive, and to leave the solid waste to local landfills. If disposal or recycling costs were built into prices, consumers would know up front the full cost of what they bought. Manufacturers would have an incentive to make products more durable or more cheaply recycled to keep those costs and prices down.[39]

"Getting the prices right" is a major theme in environmental economics and in writings on natural capitalism. For example, damage to the ozone layer and increased global warming are likely to inflict much higher economic costs than was anticipated a decade ago (Stern 2006). Relying on market mechanisms to deal with the problem will not be sufficient, because it will result in too little action too late. This is due to an information problem and to the ability to shift costs to other parties. However, it is also caused by the very low present value of benefits in the future relative to costs incurred today when traditional financial discounting methods are used. These methods were developed to deal with time horizons of ten, twenty, or even forty years over which a capital investment would pay for itself. They are not suitable for handling time horizons of one or two hundred years over which extreme environmental damage may occur.

"Green" taxes can push the spillover costs back to the producer and consumer who are making the decisions, bringing the market price of a scarce or polluting resource up to full cost. They also discourage overuse of one resource by encouraging cheaper substitutes. Green taxes make much more economic sense than increasing sales taxes or property taxes, because the former is a tax on negative spillovers, or "bads." Heavy-metal leaks into lakes and canals have been cut by almost 50 percent in the Netherlands since 1976 with taxes on pollution (Journard 1999; Roodman 1998). These new taxes do not need to result in a higher tax burden, since the new revenue they generate can be offset by cuts in other less-efficient taxes, such as income, sales, or property taxes. Reducing more upstream sources of pollution leaves fewer toxic and solid waste problems for municipalities. A tax on landfill use in Denmark increased the reuse of construction materials from 12 to 82 percent in less than a decade, at a time when most other countries made only modest improvements in recycling (Gardner and Sampat 1998).

Part 2

Creating Sustainable Economic Development for States and Localities

5

Human Capital, Opportunity, and Economic Development

Our Rule #4 of economic development is that improvements in the standard of living must be broadly based. In this chapter, we explore the relationships between the standard of living and another important capital stock, human skills. Many people think of *human capital* as determined by education, but families are the first teachers. High rates of poverty among families with children can affect early human capital development. Windows out of poverty and low income come from what we call *opportunity* and the resulting move to a higher income level is called *mobility*. State and local governments can open these windows through changes in education and a host of other policies, as part of a broadly based economic development strategy.

While belief in the American dream continues, too many people have been left on the sidelines even during recent growth booms. We explain in this chapter how and why this has happened. *Inequality* refers to the size of the gaps between top, middle, and lower incomes. Increases in inequality create a "negative trickle-down" for middle- and low-income families that we later explore. The last half of the chapter covers how state and local actions can help to moderate inequality, create more opportunity, and even affect affordability. But first, we look at the relationships between economic growth and poverty.

Growth and Poverty

Growth should be like a "rising tide that lifts all boats" in the words attributed to President John F. Kennedy. Those words resonated with public experience from World War II through the mid-1970s as living standards rose for all groups. Expansions in educational, workplace, and financial opportunity fundamentally changed the economic landscape. They were an important part of more mobility, especially for women, African Americans, and other minority groups. With economic growth, many Americans whose parents and grandparents had very low incomes joined the middle class. Expansions in social security brought unprecedented numbers of older Americans out of poverty and ensured that fewer seniors are there today. The GI bill, FHA and VA home loans, civil rights and equal opportunity legislation were part of the upward mobility of younger Americans. States broadened opportunities by expanding higher education and schools added public kindergartens. Widespread gains in the standard of living during the post-World War II decades were the product of a strong economy *and* important public policies. Future improvements in the standard of living will require the right kind of growth and the right kind of policies.

The conventional wisdom says that achieving economic growth alone will bring widespread improvement in living standards. But there has been no consistent fall in poverty rates since the 1980s, in spite of substantial economic growth in the U.S. (Poverty for a family of four in 2007 was considered living on less than $20,000).[1] The working poor are a larger share of the population, even during boom times. Over the last several decades, it is children who have been most likely to be poor in America. The likelihood of mobility is shrinking for children of low-income parents, and it is much lower for black children than for whites.[2] Restoring opportunity and mobility for the middle class as well as the poor will require changes in education and in many laws and policies. We look next at changes in the distribution of income and wages to see why even many middle-class Americans are concerned about maintaining their standard of living.

Increasingly Concentrated Wages and Incomes

Differences in economic outcomes (such as income or wealth) between individuals or households in any year are called *inequality*.[3] Measures of inequality (such as the Gini coefficient or the ratio of highest incomes to median income) reflect the economic resources of people at all income levels, not just at the bottom. [4] A certain amount of difference in incomes is always expected, since people are in different parts of their economic life cycle (college student, worker, retiree). Individuals also have a variety of characteristics and skills that are rewarded quite differently in a market-based economy. They start from different backgrounds and they make different choices. But it is the increasing gap between top incomes and most of the population, rather than the presence of different economic outcomes, that affects both quality of life and economic sustainability in the United States today.

The failure of wages and incomes to grow more evenly comes primarily from national and international forces outside the control of state or local governments. Economists see a variety of factors at work that are concentrating income gains at the top. They include a shift from manufacturing to service jobs, rapid technological change that rewards education and skills, and increased trade and globalization. A sharp decline in union membership, changes in tax and regulatory policies, rising costs of worker benefits, urbanization, and other demographic shifts have also had an impact. But our focus in this chapter is on *what* has happened to relative incomes in the United States rather than *why* it happened. (There is a substantial literature about the causes of increasing inequality in the last few decades that we recommend to the interested reader in the endnotes).[5]

Income inequality increased in all rich nations during the past few decades for many of the reasons listed above. However, its *pace* was much more rapid in the United States, which now ranks third highest in income inequality—just below Mexico and Turkey (OECD 2009). The productivity growth that supported wage increases for the average American worker in the past now primarily fuels rapidly rising incomes for people already at the top. By 2005, over half of all income in the United States went to the richest 20 percent of the population, compared to 43.8 percent in 1981 (U.S. Census Bureau 2008).[6] To put this in perspective, if we had the same level of income inequality today as in the early Reagan-era the average American family would have over $4,000 more in income each year than it does now (Freeman 2007, 42). Instead, the wages of many workers did not rise by enough to keep up with inflation over the last few decades. Even with more family members working the income of a typical household rose very slowly. As a result, the affordability of housing, health care, and higher education are now concerns for all but the highest income families.

Growth with Inequality: Costs as Well as Benefits

Traditional economic thinking sees inequality as creating incentives to work, start small businesses, save for the future, and acquire skills and education (Forbes 2000; Partridge 1997).[7] All of these factors help to spur economic growth and the standard of living. Friedman (2005) argues that with the resulting economic growth, the better-off will be willing to pay higher taxes to help the less fortunate. However, rising inequality and lack of wage and income growth reduce incentives for low- and middle-income people. When workers see the benefits of growth going primarily to those at the top, it can have a negative effect on their work ethic or their desire to save for a better future. Inequality can reduce workplace efficiency if workers no longer believe that we are "all in this together" as decreased productivity and motivation raise costs to private business (Pressman, as quoted in Bernasek [2006]).

Some of the most negative effects of rising inequality fall on children and the human capital of the next generation. These costs will affect the entire economy and society, now and in the future. In the United States today, children's chances for success depend more on their parents' income and education than they did in the 1970s. African American children in our lowest income group are two and a half times as likely to stay there as white children (Harding et al. 2005; Mayer and Lopoo 2005).[8] But children of all races who are born into poverty today are finding it harder to climb out of poverty than it was a few decades before. Lower family incomes and fewer public expenditures result in low birth weights and higher rates of incarceration for youth (Rodriguez 2000). Academic achievement is also heavily affected by family income.[9] In contrast, mobility among income groups is currently much higher in Canada and many Western European countries than in the United States. One of the reasons for this difference in mobility is that public health and education programs compensate for more of the critical deficiencies in the lives of young children in these countries than in the United States (Mayer and Lopoo 2008).

Inequality also affects children and adults who are well above poverty incomes. It weakens important aspects of social capital through lower levels of community cohesion and trust and higher levels of crime and corruption (Glaeser, Scheinkman, and Shleifer 2003; You and Khagram 2005). Inequality has negative effects on health and other aspects of quality of life.[10] Inequality can stand in the way of sensible methods of conserving energy or protecting the environment, such as carbon or gasoline taxes, if a large share of the population cannot afford to pay them. It can become self-perpetuating, with political pressure for policies that redistribute wealth or income even more toward favored industries or those already at the top (Easterly 2001; Glaeser, Scheinkman, and Shleifer 2003; Johnson 2009). Many of these concerns are behind the local measures looking at inequality and affordability that we discuss in Chapter 8.[11]

In addition, both poverty and rising inequality impact the tax base of states and localities. It becomes harder to pay for infrastructure, education, public safety, and other services when so many citizens receive low incomes and therefore pay less in taxes. At the same time, the costs associated with crime (Morris and Tweeten 1971), social service, and at-risk education rise when there are more economically disadvantaged among the population. These all have large impacts on state and local government budgets. As the gaps between rich, middle class, and poor have increased, these costs have risen faster than the revenues from increased growth. Greater inequality affects even families whose incomes are above average and rising. More are finding it difficult to afford housing, health care and to send their children to college. When growth comes with rising inequality it leads to what we call "negative trickle down."

Rising Inequality and Negative Trickle Down

In the positive trickle down of the conventional wisdom, the benefits of growth may go first to the wealthy, but their spending creates jobs and opportunity for others. Even at high levels of inequality, economic growth will help all income groups as long as the distribution of income is stable. The increasing gap between the highest incomes and the rest of the population over the last few decades shows that the positive trickle has stopped. In its place is an additional squeeze even for many people whose income has risen in absolute terms. We call this a negative trickle down and identify three aspects. They are less availability of moderately priced housing, fewer public goods, and a change in the socially accepted "middle class" consumption standards.[12]

Declining real wages in the 1980s hurt many renters. But even during the late-1990s boom when incomes rose for almost every group, many saw rents increasing faster than their wages. Over half of poor households were spending more than half of their income on housing by the year 2000 (Gyourko and Tracy 1999). This was due in part to the profitable conversion of former rental properties to high-end town homes and the elimination of single-room occupancies in central business districts (Quigley and Raphael 2004). This housing trend is part of the negative trickle down that makes it more difficult to maintain living standards even at the same level of income. Some households do not share in the gains from rising productivity while others do, but they all compete for limited resources such as land and housing in booming areas (Matlack and Vigdor 2008).

A similar pattern showed up in construction of new housing. Investments in high-income residential or commercial properties became so profitable that few developers, contractors, or builders were interested in lower margin sales of smaller homes.[13] The growing market for "McMansions" and trophy homes resulted in little building at the afford-able level. It simply offered too small a profit margin to interest builders who were busy elsewhere. The limits on available land and building in a desirable area are also part of the negative trickle-down effect.

Many new homebuyers found that their incomes were rising, but not as fast as housing prices. An average family in 2000 had income 33 percent higher than their parents might have had in 1970, but median home prices grew by 83 percent.[14] With slow income growth and fewer people in the household, the size of homes (which had been increasing steadily since the 1950s) might have been expected to remain the same, or even to fall. Instead, the square footage of newly built homes rose almost 50 percent during the 1990s and into the following decade (2007 Characteristics of New Housing, U.S. Census Bureau). We move now to the second aspect of negative trickle down: the pressure of unequal income growth on publicly provided goods and services.

While income and wealth are used to calculate most inequality measures, full measures should also include access to the quantity and quality of public goods (Wolff and Zacharias 2007). Tax revolts held public spending in check even as the demand for many public services was increasing, leading to variations in spending on schools and public safety across communities. Widening differentials in levels of local public goods led to bidding wars, as families paid a premium for houses in the right zip code or right neighborhood, in order to gain access to a highly rated school district or low-crime area (Boustan 2007). Families with rapidly rising incomes could afford this, but many others had to increase their mortgage and credit card debt. We believe these are in part reflections of increasing inequality, as high income groups rely more on gated communities and private schools and the rest of the population feels increasingly squeezed (Greenwood and Holt 2010). This competi-tion over a declining share of state and local public goods is part of the negative trickle down from increased inequality.

For example, an important middle-class goal is sending children to college. However, a variety of factors has rapidly pushed tuition up far faster than costs have risen at both private and public universities. With rising demand from population growth and affluence, elite private uni-versities have experienced a sellers' market. This example of negative trickle down is similar to the demand for housing in highly regarded neighborhoods. But state universities have also become more expensive. Taxpayer-funded assistance to higher education funding began to shrink during the 1990s in many states, shifting more of the cost to students. Working more hours while in school has been one solution and bigger student loans have been another. But the interest rates on these loans are much higher due to less federal support. As a result, many students graduate with large debts simply to pay for a good education. This directly affects opportunity and mobility as well as the sustainability of human capital.

The third aspect of negative trickle down, labeled "conspicuous consumption" by Thorstein Veblen (1899), has economic consequences as much today as it did during the Gilded Age. Higher levels of discretionary income and consumer spending at the top create "expenditure cascades" (Frank and Levine 2006) that result in real economic and social pressures. These competitive expenditures by those who can afford them set new standards for many below who try to maintain them without the income to do so. The idealized houses of 1950s television sitcoms (where Wally and the Beaver shared a bedroom even though their father wore a suit to work and their mother kept her pearls on around the house) began to seem too small and lacking in amenities for families living the new American dream. Some who complain of inability to keep up have been tagged as envious and accused of class warfare. Not so, writes Robert Frank (1999). "Keeping up with the Joneses" is as much a response to social and workplace expectations as a desire for status. Getting or keeping a good job may be influenced by living in a highly regarded neighborhood and attending a prestigious (and expensive) school.

Frank (2007, 72) writes that "the tendency will be to steer expenditures in favor of consumption categories that signal high ability . . . items such as cars, clothing and jewelry." But just as it is impossible for everyone to be above average (except in Garrison Keillor's *Lake Wobegon*), not everyone can reach the top of the heap in consumer spending. Frank (2007, 3) calls this the equivalent of an "arms race" of consumption. He observes that competitive consumption diverts resources from public and private investments in quality of life and sustainability that do not have the same attraction as positional goods.

Along with housing affordability and competition over public goods, the pressure on consumption standards is likely to continue as long as the benefits of economic growth continue to be skewed to top income and wealth groups. And the increasing concentration of income comes primarily from national and international forces outside the control of state or local governments. Below we explore opportunity-oriented economic development for states and localities[15] that can help to moderate some of the effects of inequality and sustain the stock of human capital.

People-Centered Economic Development: Investing in Human Capital and Opportunity

Human capital refers to the accumulated skills that affect labor force productivity. These skills also contribute to social capital, as we discussed in Chapter 3. In today's rapidly changing world, a good education must prepare students to develop new skills and adjust to new knowledge if development is to be sustainable. However, health and habits are as important as skills for human capital development and sustainability. They depend on family and community as much as on education. Growing inequality affects whether children and youth receive the time and care they need to flourish. It makes increased opportunity—access to neighborhoods with good schools and safe streets—all the more important. However, even as racial segregation has decreased, greater economic segregation is creating new social and geographic barriers for many children and youth (Drier, Mollenkopf, and Swanstrom 2004). While the human capital investments made in school are important for sustainability, there is substantial evidence that they are not enough to close the inequality gap (Wolff 2006).[16]

Opportunity requires more than completing basic education. It depends on access to employment that provides on-the-job training for future advancement. It requires high-quality continuing education, both vocational and professional. State and local tax policy, worker-related legislation, and education funding and policies can substantially affect economic opportunities. In the next section of this chapter, we give examples of changes that help to create sustainable and broadly based economic development. The first of these areas is public education.

Education, Opportunity, and Mobility

Rapid and fundamental changes in the economy have made both formal education and "people skills" increasingly important in the workforce. A janitor today needs to read and write well enough to accurately complete things such as an Environmental Protection Agency hazardous-waste form.

Many low-paying jobs in retail, telemarketing, or services require a good voice and a pleasant demeanor. Workers without basic language and social skills are restricted to a limited number of low-wage jobs in general construction, meatpacking or food-processing plants, and even illegal garment and assembly work. This may explain part of why there is less mobility between income groups than there was in the past (Duncan et al. 1997).

The quality and availability of public goods and services also affect worker mobility. For example, other industrialized countries have had similar changes in job requirements but have higher mobility than the present-day United States (Sawhill and Morton 2007). These countries have all had universal health coverage for children since the 1960s, and many provide child subsidies and preschool education. Low-income children in the United States are more economically mobile in states that spend more on public education.[17] This is home-grown evidence that public policies can promote economic opportunity. We emphasize the economic development aspects of investment in K–12 education throughout this book. Here, we turn to other areas of public education that receive less attention from policymakers.

One of the best public investments is *high-quality* preschool programs for low-income children.[18] According to Nobel Prize–winning economist James Heckman, it yields a 12–14 percent return on the dollar (Carneiro and Heckman 2004; Heckman 2006). Every additional thousand dollars of well-targeted spending would result in an average future public savings of $1200–$1400. Much of the savings comes from lower public spending requirements during the K–12 years than is required for the education of most at-risk children. Children who complete a high-quality preschool program are also less likely to be involved in juvenile crime, and tend to have better future health and fewer teen pregnancies. Their improved academic achievement can also lead them to become taxpayers rather than recipients of public welfare.

The studies done by Heckman and others are based on data from children who attended a variety of types of early childhood education. Some of these programs did not yield much return at all, so it is important to stress that the investments must be in the right kind of programs. But when considering the financial return alone, which is as high as for extra dollars spent in K–12 or higher education, preschool education should be recognized as another path to economic development (Bartik 2005b). Expanding participation by low-income children in the small number of high quality programs currently available should be a top priority.

One reason that public preschool is not widely offered is because public school budgets are often under stress. Finding the funding is an obvious barrier. A second factor is that many of the returns (better health, less crime, lower welfare dependency) do not end up as cost savings to school districts but instead as savings for other local, state, or federal government agencies. Without cost-sharing from these groups, treating preschool as an investment with a high return does not make financial sense for the school district alone. In addition, since families with young children are often quite geographically mobile, a large part of the return to investment spills over to other cities and states. From a financial return perspective, it is the national government that should underwrite a large share of preschool costs.

However, even states that pay the entire bill to subsidize preschool for low-income children would see a positive net benefit over time. Lower costs of special education, low-income health care, and welfare would eventually outweigh program costs in almost all states, according to Lynch (2007). Higher future earnings of preschool students combined with lower social costs during their youth may be enough to make this a viable strategy even for some municipalities (Bartik 2005b). Investments in quality preschools for low-income children may turn out to be a better gamble for economic development than smokestack chasing. Along with these fiscal benefits, it is important to remember the positive effects of high-quality preschool on individual and social quality of life and sustainability.

Another area with potentially high returns but low investment is vocational training. Although only half of U.S. students graduating high school enter college,[19] vocational courses receive less attention than they did a generation or two ago. The emphasis on all youth going to college regardless of where their interests and abilities lie is counterproductive to economic development, in our opinion. In contrast, Germany provides high-quality vocational programs where students develop reading and writing skills related to their training and graduate with *better* mathematical, statistical, and computing skills, on average, than many students in the United States (Lerman 2008). A redesigned vocational curriculum could reduce the high-school dropout rate by providing reasons to stay in school for students who are "turned off" by college-prep classes. The ability to enter higher education later is a real strength of the U.S. educational system. It frees districts to provide more vocational training for students without limiting their opportunities to attend college later in life.

In the case of higher education, the direct impact on economic development is often as large as the effect of higher skills of graduates. Local universities and colleges bring new people, new ideas, and new dollars into a community. Graduates often stay because they like the local quality of life of university towns such as Austin (Texas), Ann Arbor (Michigan), and Cambridge (Massachusetts). New businesses that could rely on a readily available pool of talented workers sparked the high-tech and biotech sectors of these economies.[20] Another benefit is that faculty can provide analysis and fill information gaps to better inform local business development (Weiler 2000). However, in spite of the many positive roles of higher education in state and local development, it has received a shrinking share of most state budgets since the early 1990s. This is another area where smart economic development policy calls for a "U turn." If growing up in a family with the income to pay high tuition becomes more important than student ability and motivation[21] it will affect the future workforce and the sustainability of development. It also has negative impacts on incoming students and older workers who cannot return for coursework during their careers.

Economic vitality has much more to do with high-quality education *at every level* than with low tax rates or subsidies. Better-educated workers earn more money, pay more taxes, and support other local businesses. Education is an important part of the economic development picture because of its role in sustaining human capital.[22] But education is not just about job skills and higher income, as Adam Smith noted in *The Wealth of Nations*.[23] It is also an integral part of the social capital of communities. It improves the standard of living through increasing the ability of citizens to navigate complex consumer and voter decisions. It increases quality of life by enabling people to enjoy a greater range of music, art, travel, and culture. This improvement does not go away during economic downturns. Civic participation, volunteerism, and charitable giving are higher for people with more education.[24] They continue to be valuable to society whether or not the economy is thriving. And graduating from high school creates sustained positive effects on the health and educational achievement of the next generation of children, as well as making it less likely that they will engage in juvenile crime (Greenwood 1997).

Education is no longer enough to ensure opportunities for economic mobility because the links between education, skills, and income have weakened during the past few decades. Completing a high school or even a college education does not guarantee a good job as it did in the past.[25] Supporting human capital also depends on formal and informal institutions that foster opportunity after graduates are in the workplace. In the next sections, we address specific areas where state and local policies can help.

Moderating Inequality and Increasing Mobility

In contrast to economic development strategies built on location incentives or improving the business climate (see Chapter 2), twenty-first century development lies in the economic potential and quality of life of people. Rather than a tax break to a company in the hopes that it will create sustained employment at higher wages (a trickle-down approach) we suggest that public dollars should "percolate up." Investments for education, worker benefits, and other opportunity programs contribute to a higher quality workforce. This, in turn, creates more incoming tax revenues, and less spending on social services, crime, and at-risk education for the next generation. In the following sections, we address several areas where state or local policy can moderate growing inequality or increase opportunities for upward mobility and contribute to economic development. We begin with the effect that regressive tax systems have on the disposable income of low-wage workers.

Reducing Tax Burdens on the Poor

State and local tax systems now take a larger percentage of income from low-income households than from high-income households. Many "low-tax" states have low rates for the well-off, but much higher rates for the poor (Davis et al. 2009, 11). Changing tax policies to lower the tax burden on the poor would lessen the burden on low-income families. States could collect more of their revenue from income taxes with exemptions and graduated rates, and provide refundable child care and earned-income tax credits at the state in addition to the federal credits.

Many states with exemptions base them on the owners' age or how long they have lived in the property. Exemptions based instead on income level or property value would make property taxes less onerous at lower incomes. Despite being regressive, sales taxes seem to be a popular funding source with voters, who often see them as paid by visitors from elsewhere. However, the shoe is on the other foot when one travels and must pay the high sales taxes in other states and cities. Raising more revenue from income taxes would allow cuts in sales tax rates, again reducing the burden at lower incomes.

Worker-Oriented Opportunity Programs

In addition to policies that moderate inequality, states and cities can adopt specific programs and policies directed primarily toward increasing opportunities for workers. Many laws protecting the rights of workers are weaker than in other industrialized nations and than they were from the 1940s through the 1970s in this country. The conventional wisdom has been that worker protections interfere with the rights of private capital and are bad for the business climate. For example, collective bargaining is often seen as negative for business. However, while some workers' rights undoubtedly limit management flexibility, they also increase worker health, economic well-being, and satisfaction—all of which contribute to a higher standard of living.

States with higher rates of unionization and stronger labor laws actually have higher average incomes than those that do not. As we said in Chapter 2, the direction of cause and effect between higher incomes and union activity may run either way, but this provides evidence that unions can be compatible with a strong economy. That is good to know, because although union membership has declined sharply over the last thirty years, a recent survey of American workers indicates that 32 percent of non-union private sector workers would like to have union representation and do not. Support for a worker organization that was not involved in collective bargaining but could discuss workplace issues with management was 78 percent (Freeman 2007, 83).

Worker-oriented legislation and programs fall into two groups: those broadly directed at people with many levels of income and education and others targeted toward workers with specific employment barriers. Many of the policies we discuss below help children as well as their working parents, making them long-term investments in human capital as well as short-term help for workers. We turn first to general policies to help all workers.

Today's worker is much more likely to have a sequence of different employers and periodic spells of unemployment than workers in the past. For that reason alone, decoupling health insurance from employment is increasingly important to worker well-being and to labor market flexibility. In addition, "job lock" from preexisting health conditions is cited by many workers as a major reason for staying in their job when better opportunities exist. There are also some state policies that discourage labor force mobility. Workers who voluntarily leave for a better job and lose it within the first year do not qualify for full unemployment insurance coverage in many states. Limiting benefits in ways like this keeps rates low to businesses but this costs workers who strive for better opportunities.[26]

Businesses also pay the premiums that fund workers' compensation payments for injuries or death. Since premiums are risk-rated, fewer fatalities and injuries reduce business insurance costs. But instead of using this as an incentive to employers to maintain a safe workplace, some states have kept premiums artificially low by capping compensation to injured workers and surviving families.[27] Along with this, safety standards are often not adequately enforced.[28] The combination of these policies reduces incentives for safety by businesses and increases the costs to injured workers and their families and to social service and health care programs.

One way to encourage work is to pay a good wage. States with a higher minimum wage than the federal requirement encourage work when their minimum is adjusted to account for the local inflation rate.[29] The conventional wisdom has been that a minimum wage creates unemployment, especially among teenagers and the least skilled workers. However, comparing employment changes in states that raised their minimum wage with those that did not shows little or no difference in job creation (Card and Krueger 1995; Neumark et al. 2004). Still, there remains a concern that an increased minimum will hurt small businesses or raise prices to consumers. Along with recognizing that the effects in both cases tend to be quite small, it is important to remember that wages are not only costs to business. On the other side of the ledger, wages support families, generate consumer spending, and are used to pay taxes.[30] This is all part of a "percolate up" strategy for economic development that also improves the average standard of living.

Opponents of minimum-wage increases often advocate earned-income tax credits as an alternative way to help low wage workers. We agree that these are a useful tool within limits. However, the credits are taxpayer paid subsidies that allow employers to continue receiving worker services at low wages. And unlike a higher minimum wage they do not provide an incentive for employers to use labor more efficiently. Finding the appropriate mix of earned income tax credits and wage increases is an important part of an opportunity-oriented economic development policy.

Continuing education for adults is also an important part of an opportunity-oriented economic development policy as technology and institutional arrangements change rapidly. Affordable access to community colleges and four-year and graduate-degree programs can help workers adapt to new jobs and new careers with certificate programs and degrees. We turn now to workers who depend on self-employment rather than wages.

Opportunities through Self-Employment and Small Business

Sustainable economic development should also focus on policies that are friendly toward start-ups and genuinely small businesses[31] as well as toward workers. Self-employment is much more important in the economy today than it was for recent generations. It is the preferred option for many workers who want more flexibility and independence as well as the default option when companies downsize. State or local governments can play an important role in providing help for individuals who are starting up a business, through small business incubators or the economic gardening programs discussed in Chapter 2. Enhancing options for the self-employed is another part of broadening workplace opportunity.

Purchasing health insurance on their own, especially if they have a family, is a real barrier to workers who want to become consultants or self-employed contractors. Expansion from self-employment into a small business is limited by the costs of covering workers with health insurance. If major health care reform at the national level is insufficient, states need to continue to move forward in this area (see Burtless 2007). The initial costs of unemployment insurance and workers compensation coverage can also be very high until a new business has established a good experience rating. This makes it harder for the self-employed to expand by hiring other workers. Creative rethinking at the state level about the rates charged to new businesses with no employment history could make it easier for new businesses to hire their first workers.

At the local level, some of the greatest barriers to self-employment and small business come from zoning and building codes. Some do not allow home offices in residential neighborhoods. Cities and counties interested in increasing opportunities need to revisit these codes and regulations and examine the costs and benefits of each. These are all ways to encourage self-employment and be small-business friendly. We next consider the second group of opportunity-oriented policies, those that affect workers with specific barriers or challenges.

Opportunity for Workers with Specific Challenges

For single-parent or two-worker families, being a good worker and a good parent is a real challenge, with fewer extended families and neighbors than in earlier generations. "Family-friendly" employment policies increase the likelihood that workers with children will remain at their jobs and move up job ladders to better paying positions (Waldfogel 2007). Allowing working parents to use their own "sick days" to care for ill children is good for public health and for worker retention as well as for children. Quality of life improves when parents can get release time from work for school conferences and when good child care is available at the job site. Studies of former welfare recipients during the late 1990s found that financial assistance with child care was a critical factor for many in keeping their new jobs. This costs money, but if communities are serious about wanting to expand opportunity and provide good role models for children in all families, it may be a wise investment.

Disabled workers are another group with a special challenge and are an increasing share of the low-income population. They benefit when permitted to work under restricted hours or conditions to supplement the low financial and medical assistance most receive. Many can still make major contributions to the economy and society if there is a way to accommodate their disabilities. But particularly for small business employers, some subsidies may be needed/appropriate in order to cover the cost of these accommodations.

Along with physical disabilities, drug or alcohol abuse and mental illness are major barriers to success on the job. Dealing with substance abuse and mental health issues is primarily a state and local responsibility, although federal and nonprofit dollars provide some financial support. In many states, offenders have to pay for their own rehabilitation. This effectively restricts judges to ordering very low-cost programs, even if they are far less effective per dollar than others available. However, effective monitoring and treatment of mental illness and drug and alcohol dependency could bring important increases in labor force productivity and lower dependency rates of the individuals and their families.

Another group that represents a growing share of the low-income population is former prisoners (Raphael 2008). Their families often rely on public assistance once they enter prison. After release, a felony record now permanently bars most from occupational licenses in many states. Former prisoners are also ineligible for the increased number of jobs that require security clearance. With more nonviolent crimes classified as felonies than in the past, the prison population has grown very rapidly.[32] Sustainable development requires planning for what this predominantly young population will do when they exit prison. Bringing former felons who have served their time into the workforce in ways that are safe and appropriate for the rest of society can potentially increase productivity and avoid future re-imprisonment costs. It also helps the quality of life of their families and the future prospects of their children.

Low-wage workers not connected to the welfare system can benefit from the same kinds of assistance given to welfare recipients. Continued access to job and career counseling is as important as formal training in ensuring their success (Clymer et al. 2001). Workers with transportation barriers due to disability, low income, or loss of driving privileges can be helped by more alternatives to the automobile, as we discuss in Chapter 6. This is all part of economic development: some people currently dependent on government programs can become less dependent, and others can become net taxpayers. The "percolate up" approach increases incomes, with the added bonus that it does not create the strains on the environment or infrastructure of population growth (a subject we address in the next two chapters).

Changes in urban design and transportation planning affect opportunity through walking, biking, and public transit routes to work and to school. These are particularly important for younger and low-income workers, who are often parents of young children. Urban design also affects the availability of affordable housing, an important part of mobility and opportunity as well as the standard of living. We close this chapter with thoughts about how housing fits into an affordable lifestyle that improves the quality of life and sustainability of development in any town or city.

Increasing Opportunity: Affordable Housing or Affordable Lifestyle?

To sustain a good standard of living, an *affordable lifestyle* takes account of the costs of all basic necessities, not just the size of rent or mortgage payments. Yet housing does play a central role, because the shelter of a home is a basic necessity of life. Purchasing a home remains the most important way to save and accumulate wealth in most households. A subsequent home equity gain makes it possible to afford college tuition, finance small business start-up costs, and have security in retirement. In addition, home location determines school and neighborhood quality for most children and ease of access to groceries and other retail. [33]

The central role of housing in the middle-class American dream has made its affordability an increasing concern over the past thirty-five years, as prices rose more rapidly than the incomes of most of the population. As the words "affordable housing" became almost a mantra, the methods used to increase opportunity to achieve the American dream became increasingly convoluted during the 1990s and into the first decade of the twenty-first century. As we outline below, these methods actually sabotage true economic development because they create spending patterns that are neither economically nor environmentally sustainable and do not increase quality of life.

Initially, many blamed growth management for shortages of affordable housing.[34] Oregon established one of the earliest urban-growth boundaries in 1979 and received heavy criticism. But housing expert Anthony Downs (2002) concludes that the Portland boundary had little effect on median home prices. Prices of homes actually rose *less rapidly* there than elsewhere after it was established, until waves of in-migration from California in the early 1990s. By the end of that decade, housing price increases in Portland once again slowed to less than they were in many other parts of the West.[35]

Sprawling development (further addressed in Chapter 6) was touted as a solution to affording a larger home with more amenities when middle-class incomes did not keep up with increases in housing prices. Lower prices for housing in Las Vegas, Phoenix, Denver, and Houston seemed to provide evidence that sprawl was an equalizing force.[36] But sprawl also increases spending on second (or third) cars, along with gasoline, maintenance, and auto insurance costs.[37] Approximately 57 percent of the income of the average household went to pay combined housing and transportation costs (Lipman 2006). The proportions for housing costs vs. transportation costs varied considerably by urban area and were higher for lower-than middle-income families.[38] Transportation spending began to outstrip spending on housing in several metropolitan areas (e.g., Houston and Indianapolis) even before gasoline prices rose in 2007 and 2008. Affordable housing did not always lead to an affordable lifestyle.

Along with housing and transportation, another part of an affordable lifestyle is the level of local taxes. Property taxes in newly developed areas look low to new homebuyers when they are based on a pre-suburban (usually rural) level of development. Along with cheaper land, there is little infrastructure and there are few amenities. To pay for new roads, parks, schools, sewer systems, and fire and police stations, there must be tax increases. In many states, local districts raise rates sharply to cover the new infrastructure—in others the burdens are shared with existing homeowners, who then see their tax bills rise.[39] At the same time, older roads, schools, sewer systems, fire and police stations, and parks are often abandoned or underutilized. This pattern of abandoning old infrastructure and building more in new areas is part of the reason for the rising pressures on state and local governments.

Sprawl failed to deliver on an affordable lifestyle, as we outline further in Chapters 6 and 7. However, it was eventually joined by a second strategy for bringing bigger and more elaborate homes and cars to workers who did not share in the productivity bonanza of the 1990s.

This second method of reconciling higher income inequality with higher standards for middle-class consumption came through credit. Normally, slow wage growth would limit demand and dampen housing price increases. By the 1980s, families with an additional wage-earner could count both incomes toward qualifying for a mortgage. When even that became insufficient, guidelines changed to accommodate more spending. Larger proportions of gross income (from 25 percent to 30 percent and eventually 40 percent) were counted as available for mortgage payments. Eventually even these higher debt-to-income thresholds were not enough to sell higher-priced homes.

It was time for a new strategy. New kinds of mortgages (no down payment, interest only, adjustable rate, and subprime) came into play. They were purported to help middle- and low-income families buy the home of their dreams, even while the incomes of 90 percent or more were lagging.[40] And they did bolster demand from low- and middle-income households and (temporarily) allow them to accumulate more wealth. But the evidence indicates that creative financing was tied to new building more than to affordability concerns. Most sub-prime mortgages were in rapidly growing areas, although economic need was just as much in the Northeast or Midwest (Mayer and Pence 2008). Equally dangerous "Alt-A" jumbo mortgages fueled the market for higher-income buyers in prime real estate locations. More lower-middle-income and near-poor families were able to move into better housing via subprime mortgages (Jargowsky 2005) but that was unsustainable for many. What seemed a quick fix for many problems at once—making housing affordable, creating local jobs in construction and real estate, and providing profitable investment opportunities for banks and other investors—was actually a giant transfer of wealth that did nothing for long-term economic development. In the short term, more people could afford a lifestyle beyond their means. But eventually many of them lost their investment and their chance to build real estate wealth. Communities that staked their prosperity on a continuing housing boom also suffered from the ensuing bust.

This brings us to a very important point about housing, quality of life, and sustainable economic development. The primary purpose for home ownership is to increase the quality of life of individuals, families and communities through greater stability. Buying a home also provides a mechanism for saving over the life-cycle. Working families can make mortgage payments at relatively low interest rates and acquire a capital asset that is a hedge against inflation. Borrowing against that asset may be a way to finance a start-up business or college education for children. For most retirees, mortgages have been fully paid and their homes cost only the maintenance, insurance, and property taxes. At that point, reverse mortgages allow older homeowners to borrow against their equity to finance necessary medical or care expenses. Investing in housing provides many ways to improve the standard of living when approached from this standpoint.

When housing is instead treated as an "engine of economic growth" to create jobs or stimulate the economy, the problems begin. Residential construction is historically a cyclical business dependent on population and economic growth. As a highly durable good, homes do not need to be replaced on a regular basis like many goods and services. Without more population (which is growing very slowly in the United States except for immigration), there is little need for more than housing upgrades and maintenance on a net basis (Akerlof and Schiller 2009). As parts of the population become more affluent and they want to buy new and more expensive houses, they still require a buyer for their old house. Increasing the total housing stock more rapidly than the number of households is growing can never be a sustainable source of jobs and demand for long periods.

Conclusion

We began this book by differentiating economic growth from economic development. Economic development is sustainable and broadly based, with improvement in the overall standard of living. When growth leaves too many people behind, it is not sustainable and does not improve the overall quality of life. Investments in quality of life and sustainability must start with people, but rising inequality and decreasing opportunities undermine this. Some costs from rising inequality are borne by those who miss out on higher wages and incomes. But negative trickle down also affects many people whose incomes rise. The competition becomes intense and unaffordable for goods and services with a limited supply (housing or the "best" schools) even for many in the middle class. They may also have less access to or lower quality of public goods and services. Income and poverty measures do not fully capture all these effects.

Economic development must increase opportunity and affordability to deliver broadly based benefits. We see the presence of opportunity and inequality measures in local indicators as demonstrating increased recognition of these costs at the grass-roots level. More important than low taxes, affordable housing, or low gasoline prices—each only a part of household costs—is how they fit together into an *affordable lifestyle*. The popular media and politicians compete to frame the debate in terms of low taxes or affordable housing or quality schools. However, neither people nor businesses are looking for any one of these in isolation. They want a "value package" of services per dollar of taxes paid regardless of the level of taxes. They also want attractive and reasonably priced housing and transportation, good wages, and quality of life. They want it all, but they settle for a reasonable balance compared to what is found in other communities.

Moving away from the old economic development of the past fifty years to one centered on what helps people will create many economic benefits. In addition to better living standards and long-term investment in children, it can encourage more local retail and a broader tax base. Investing in human capital is only part of the story of increasing access and opportunity. In this chapter, we looked at how states, cities, and counties can support opportunity and mobility with their laws and policies as well as with their taxes and expenditures. In addition, they can encourage community and urban design that supports an affordable lifestyle, increased health and outdoor experiences, transportation options, and opportunities for both children and adults to develop their full human potential. We turn to this in the next chapter.

6

Sprawl, Infrastructure, and Sustainable Development

A central thesis of this book is that growth—whether in population, land use, or even income—often brings unanticipated increases in both private and social costs along with its benefits. When communities grow or change shape, local governments are expected to provide public goods and services to meet the new demands.[1] They must invest sufficiently in infrastructure for sustainable development, but it is also important that it be the *right type* of infrastructure for a twenty-first-century society. The shape of a community—its neighborhoods, commercial districts, transportation networks, schools, public buildings, and parks—contributes to its character and attractiveness as well as to the cost of living and doing business there. Public and private land uses determine that shape, and both are influenced by state and local policies. They can have major effects on sustainable economic development and quality of life.

The conventional wisdom is that growth automatically generates enough revenue to cover new costs associated with that growth. However, the predominant land use patterns of the past fifty years in the United States—often called "sprawl"—have brought higher costs to local governments. They have also had many negative effects on quality of life and environmental sustainability. For all these reasons, sprawl is unsustainable in many communities (Drier, Mollenkopf, and Swanstrom 2004). Communities locked into these urban design models will have trouble competing on both attractiveness and cost in the future. Quality of life and sustainable development are becoming more important not just for attracting and keeping people, but also for keeping the costs of local government low relative to the level of services provided.[2] Undoubtedly, many people will continue to want traditional suburban development, and we are not arguing that such developments should come to an end. But they are not the direction for most communities to be pursuing with new development in the twenty-first century.

In this chapter, we first define the term "sprawl" and the benefits that made it attractive and dominant for half a century. We then look at the costs of sprawl: financial, social, and environmental. Next, we explore how schools and transportation, as examples of public goods and infrastructure, relate to land use and in turn how each affects other aspects of quality of life and sustainability of development. We then move to looking at "smart growth" and "new urbanism" models that attempt to integrate quality of life and sustainability with economic development. We close the chapter by looking at barriers to their implementation and some solutions to these.

Defining Sprawl

Definitions of sprawl are as many and as broad as its place in the American landscape.[3] The simplest definition is that sprawl exists where new land is developed more rapidly than population grows.[4] By this criterion, 94 percent of metropolitan areas in the United States are sprawling, including rust-belt cities with declining populations and other areas with high population growth (Fulton et al. 2001). One definition of sprawl that we like is a "combination of a decrease in population density, an expansion of developed land area, and an emptying out of the center in favor of the periphery" (McGuire and Sjoquist 2007, 304). A U.S. Department of Agriculture survey of the literature finds the following elements in most definitions: "low-density development that is dispersed and uses a lot of land; geographic separation of essential places such as work, homes, schools, and shopping; and almost complete dependence on automobiles for travel."[5] Other noted land use experts add fragmented planning by local governments and leapfrog development to the characteristics that comprise sprawl (Burchell et al. 2005, 12). With these definitions in mind, let us now explore why the pattern of development called sprawl has become so widespread in the United States.[6]

The Benefits of Sprawl

To better understand why sprawl has become the dominant pattern of land use today, we look briefly at changes in the United States since the early part of the past century. The United States developed from a primarily rural nation to one with relatively dense cities (although never as densely built as those in Europe). Getting away from dirty industry in these cities was a major impetus to the early "streetcar suburbs" that are now part of urban living. Planners in the early and mid-twentieth century believed in separating residences from work as a way to increase health and quality of life. During that time, indirect subsidies and many zoning and planning policies directly encouraged sprawl.[7]

After World War II greater affluence increased the demand for larger homes with trees, gardens, and a grass-covered lawn (Margo 1992).The spread of automobiles made sprawling development possible at the edge of metropolitan areas, in many smaller towns and cities, and even in rural areas. Along with changes in transportation, communication technology made location (spatial proximity) less important for economic development. Larger homes could be built on larger lots at less cost, and traffic congestion appeared to be less than in cities. Concern for clean air, isolation from urban problems of crime, schools, and lower property taxes all attracted homebuyers to new suburbs and bedroom communities. People seemed to be voting with their feet and their pocketbooks.

Since the family home is the largest portion of wealth in middle-income groups, moving to the suburbs was a way to protect that wealth as long as price appreciation was strong. People sought more opportunities for "small-town" style participation than there were in urban living, along with services tailored to middle- and upper-income households. For families with children, very real concerns about school and neighborhood safety as well as education often drive relocation. Even for many home buyers without children, being in a school district with higher average test scores is important to perceived home value (Kane, Staiger, and Samms 2003).[8] The cheapest way to acquire these amenities seems to be moving to a new suburb. Some see the primary cause of sprawl in the pull of suburban amenities and others in the push of declining schools and neighborhoods and "white flight."[9] However, better public schools actually have more to do with income and educational levels within the neighborhood than with urban or suburban status. The same is true for levels of crime and many other urban problems people attempt to flee (Burchell et al. 2005).

People of different economic status used to live in much greater proximity to each other, as well as to their jobs. The zoning movement of the 1920s led to the separation of land use in most cities today. The fragmented local governments often associated with suburban sprawl are well designed for "fiscal zoning." Establishing a large minimum lot size makes it less affordable for middle-income families to live in a community, thus the term "fiscal zoning." Explicitly "exclusionary zoning" was ruled illegal in the Mt. Laurel decisions (New Jersey Law Library

2009), but many zoning systems come close to the line. As mentioned, the initial motive was to separate residences from industry (dirty and polluting) and even from retail and light commercial businesses. Many suburban neighborhoods were planned subdivisions that fit this model. However, this new pattern of development required new infrastructure. Even as local governments saw the costs of infrastructure rising, they continued to charge homes in sprawling areas the average price for new infrastructure. Suburban development therefore appeared much less expensive to developers and new homebuyers than it really was in terms of total costs. Twenty years ago a report commissioned by the state of Florida to study costs of development said:

> That many people prefer suburban or rural residential locations removed from urban congestion is not a contested issue. . . . However . . . such preferences are often partially subsidized by revenues paid from other area residents and businesses, and from intergovernmental fund transfers. Developments in these locations do not always pay their full share of the costs for providing their off-site public facilities and services (Duncan 1989, 25).

Clearly, sprawling development has provided many people with things that they want. This leads us to look more carefully at the financial, social, and environmental costs from sprawl.

The Costs of Sprawl: Financial, Social, and Environmental

Sprawl has seemed a way to make housing more affordable, yet it has resulted in *higher* total household costs once commuting and other expenses are included (Lipman 2006).[10] In addition, increasing numbers of people are saying that they are unhappy with the costs of sprawling development or the impact that it has on quality of life.[11] By looking at the financial costs of sprawl to communities and individuals, it is clear that moving to new development models that emphasize better quality of life and sustainability will not *necessarily* cost more. This is actually likely to save money.

Development costs are affected primarily by lot width, municipal improvement standards, characteristics of occupancy, contiguity of development, distance to central facilities, and size of urban area, according to the Urban Land Institute's comprehensive study of land use.[12] With sprawl, each of these elements drives costs higher. For example, roads are 25 percent more expensive, utilities 15 percent more, and school capital costs 5–7 percent higher as compared with other land use patterns. (Frank, J.E., 1989) When the same land—whether a parking lot, school, or a storefront with residential apartment above—is shared by several uses at different times, it is less costly to build the infrastructure. Sometimes it is also less costly to operate.

With sprawling development, homes are often harder for police, firefighters, and ambulances to find and reach. This requires building more fire and police stations unless response times to emergency calls are going to be longer. Wastewater services cost more not only because there are more miles of hookups, but also because impervious surfaces make storm water run rapidly into rivers and streams. Large parking lots and wider roads, along with bigger rooftops, contribute to less water absorption capacity in an urban landscape. If storm water could be absorbed into the ground, also recharging the local water supply, the demands on wastewater infrastructure would be less (National Resources Defense Council 1998). In *Sprawl Costs: Economic Impacts of Unchecked Development* (Burchell et al. 2005), the authors conclude that more compact development can provide the amenities people want while saving an average of 11 percent on total development costs. They reference a study for the Los Angeles area that shows as high as a 25 percent cost reduction.

Along with financial costs from sprawl, there are many costs to quality of life. The link between urban design and lack of exercise has caught the attention of *The American Journal of Public Health*. In 2003, it devoted a whole issue to the relationship between the built landscape and increasing obesity, high blood pressure, and other health problems.[13] It is more than laziness that leads many Americans to avoid exercise—it's also danger! Cyclists and pedestrians on the road in the United States were two to six times more likely to be killed than those in Germany or Holland, according to research by Pucher and Buehler (2008). They attribute this primarily to the transportation design that accompanies sprawl and point to the traffic-calming and car-free central city zones in Europe that allow bicycling without building special lanes.[14] Simple widening of roads for faster traffic flow will only make roads more dangerous to cyclists and pedestrians (Burchell et al. 2005, 110–12).

Sprawl leads to less engagement between people, wrote William Whyte in *The Social Life of Small Urban Spaces,* in part because of fewer public spaces and buildings in which people can meet.[15] It lacks the effect of "eyes on the street" both day and night, weekend and weekday, in maintaining public safety, as pointed out by Jane Jacobs in *The Death and Life of Great American Cities*. The urban vitality that so many people find missing in planned suburbia comes from a mix of different ages, heights, and types of buildings and a multiplicity of uses for those buildings. The ethnic restaurants or small repair shops that can afford space in older buildings sandwiched between the new are squeezed out by high rents in new or recently remodeled structures (Jacobs 1961).

In addition to less opportunity for small businesses, increased separation between central city and suburban areas has a number of negative economic and social effects. Sprawl is "both a cause and consequence of economic restructuring and emerging social inequalities" according to Squires (2002, 18), who calls sprawl more than a spatial phenomenon. Dramatic increases in economic segregation between 1970 and 1990 came from rising income inequality (Mayer 2001; Watson 2006) and suburban sprawl (Massey and Fischer 2003, Jargowsky 1996).[16] This isolation impedes the upward mobility of the poor (Jargowsky 2002). Education is to be the great equalizer, but it is very dependent on where one lives. Access to other public goods as well as to groceries and retail is diminished (Swanstrom, Dreier, and Mollenkopf 2002). Economic segregation lowers the access of workers living in the central city to the 70 percent of jobs that are located in the suburbs (Kasarda 1995). If inner city parents do commute long hours to a job in the suburbs, they are likely to have less time to interact with their children or be part of their own neighborhoods.

Economic segregation has some of the same negative effects as racial segregation (which began to decline after 1970). Both lessen the long-term social capital of the larger community by isolating groups with differences from learning about each other. When sprawl accompanies rapid population growth in a metropolitan area, the economic segregation is much less than when sprawl occurred with little population growth (Watson 2009). Racial segregation also occurs less in rapidly growing areas than in those with slow growth. We note here that more diversity and less economic and racial segregation are benefits that rapid in-migration brings to an area, along with the costs discussed earlier.

Sprawl also hurts environmental sustainability in many ways, as we discussed in Chapter 3. Its biggest cost is loss of land for wildlife habitat, agriculture, watersheds, or as scenic open space. The annual loss is estimated at 2.2 million acres (U.S. Environmental Protection Agency 2001). Private open space between households cannot replace many of the environmental roles that public open space plays, such as providing bird and wildlife habitat.

Habitat destruction is the major threat to 80 percent of endangered species, and less sprawl would make an important difference, according to the EPA report. Air pollution is also significantly higher with sprawl due to greater automobile use. Water use increases because of the landscaping associated with sprawl. Large new homes use substantial amounts of resources in their building and in their heating and cooling, as well as generate more waste and wastewater.

Last but not least, sprawl is often criticized for destroying historic buildings as well as landscapes, and replacing them with bland or ugly structures. The wider roads and larger parking lots associated with sprawl do often lead to demolition of existing structures. However, new buildings can be attractive or unattractive, regardless of whether they are part of sprawl. The industrial model of development associated with sprawl tends to focus on short-term cost and replication. Builders like development that can be "reproduced anywhere with predictable results, thus reducing risk to developers and the banks that finance them" (Burchell et al. 2005, 13).[17] When the same design and orientation are used for office buildings, stores, or restaurants without regard to location, it can be hard to know where you are in America once you enter a suburban retail district. Concern for quality and diversity of the built environment where one lives is reflected in some local indicator projects that we review in Chapter 8, reflecting its importance in quality of life.

The charges against sprawl are many—higher infrastructure costs, impacts on human health, social disconnectedness, economic segregation, environmental damage, and loss of unique sense of place. Yet many people see benefits to the development pattern called sprawl and resist the call for new forms of urban and suburban design. We believe that people in their communities should make choices of the type of land use and environment they wish to live with. Our point is that citizens need to be aware of the full costs associated with their land-use policies. Many people might prefer a new Lexus or Land Rover to an economy car. But they don't expect the rest of society will subsidize their preference. Similarly, both fairness and economic efficiency dictate that people pay the bill for the kind of urban development they want just as they pay when the car they want costs more. The short-term private costs of sprawl have been low, leading it to be a popular choice. But when the full public costs are totaled up over a longer period, they are more than most people can actually afford in private costs or in tax levies.

Not only are environmental and social costs high, sprawl has consequences for the delivery and cost of other public goods and services. For example, school transportation depends on density levels, neighborhood design, school setting, and how pedestrian- and bicycle-friendly streets are. Yet school districts are rarely major players in planning decisions that determine land use. Below we explore the consequences of sprawl for schools, children, and economic development.

School Construction and Local Economic Development

Good public schools are important to developing long-term human capital (Chapter 5) as well as to attracting and retaining companies with good jobs and benefits. Good schools also have a direct effect on the property values of all homes, whether or not there are school-age children present, as mentioned earlier. Moreover, the tradition of local control over schools in the United States means that much of what is important in a child's education is determined at the state or local, rather than on the federal level. All of this makes schools a key area where local decisions can have a large impact on sustainable community development and quality of life.

School facilities affect the communities they serve "not only in terms of the quality of education, but also the economy, the environment, public health, transportation, social equity, community cohesion, and local finance" according to a recent report linking schools and patterns of growth (ICMA 2008). The report concludes that the status quo in school construction has encouraged both sprawl and disinvestment in older neighborhoods. Average school size has grown considerably since the 1960s, and schools have become increasingly distant from the students who attend them. Almost half of all children walked or biked to school in 1969, but by 2001 less than 15 percent did.[18] Either the students lived too far away or walking was too dangerous because of traffic conditions (U.S. CDC 2005). More walking is an inexpensive way to reduce youth obesity.

Larger schools are not always cheaper but have still been encouraged by many city or county development rules, state funding formulas or mandates, and other school policies.[19] Formulas may specify that when renovation or expansion costs are more than a third of the costs of a new building the state will not provide matching funds for revamping an older building. However, these formulas rarely consider all of the costs involved. In addition to new construction, there are site acquisition expenses and costs to maintain or dispose of the existing facility.

In many cases, cost estimates do not include additional roads or sewer and water lines required to support a new school. They rarely include the increased transportation costs of students from a larger service area, or higher maintenance and operation costs of a larger building. But "the unquantifiable value of the role that the existing facility may play in the life of the community is part of the quality of life" (ICMA 2008).

Financial considerations are allowed to predominate over the human and social costs of large schools relative to small neighborhood schools in most decisions today. This has an unfortunate effect on quality of life because schools that are safe for children to walk or bike to encourage exercise and reduce traffic. They can also serve as a focal point and meeting place for a community. An article in the *American School Board Journal* (McCann and Beaumont 2003) finds that smaller grade schools provide a higher-quality education. Smaller high schools have substantially higher graduation rates than large ones. A recent study by the Annie E. Casey Foundation (2008, 2) finds that "community schools can improve student learning, increase parent participation, give teachers more time to focus on instruction, and contribute to making schools and communities safer." It is unfortunate that they are deemed inefficient by the limited model used in decision making today.

When local governments approve large scale residential developments they create demand for new schools. However, school districts may face a financial crunch finding the capital to build facilities before new property taxes begin to flow. In one Michigan district, the new schools helped attract many young families from central city neighborhoods to affordable homes in new developments. But within ten years, rapidly rising home prices and property taxes led many of them to leave and school enrollment to decline. In the meantime, school closures in older established areas had hurt property values, local businesses, and the tax base (ICMA 2008). This is an example of the need for better cooperation between the gatekeepers of development and school districts.

The costly practice of abandoning old schools and building new ones is also driven by neighborhoods that have less diversity of age groups today. A new subdivision is often first occupied by families with young children who attend the newly built school. When the children grow up and leave but the parents stay, neighborhood schools may be closed and the few students left bussed to schools much farther away. Eventually the parents (now older) move away from the neighborhood. The houses may then be purchased by new families with young children who want a school nearby.

This cycle of building schools, closing schools, and then building new schools and its destabilizing of neighborhood home values could be broken if buildings and spaces were designed to accommodate a variety of public uses over the years. Half-empty schools could be used jointly with other educational or civic groups. When neighborhood schools are closed, they could be temporarily converted for public health or nonprofit activities, senior services, and assisted living, and then retrofitted as schools later. This could save taxpayer dollars, help to preserve neighborhoods, and serve students better than the current practice of abandonment and rebuilding. However, it is another change requiring more cooperation between schools and local governments. In some states, enabling legislation would be required for a school building to be used for any other purpose. Working together may save school districts capital and transportation money in the long run, as well as keep neighborhoods from declining.

Sometimes the initiative for preserving neighborhood schools comes from a state legislature. South Carolina and Rhode Island eliminated minimum acreage requirements, and Maine mandated *maximum* site sizes for public schools. Local governments can also lead the initiative for new policies that fit the future quality of local development citizens want. For example, through the efforts of the city of Casper, Wyoming laws that affected school planning were amended to better serve the needs of Casper students and the larger community. We turn now to transportation and how it affects the sustainability of development and the quality of life.

Roads and Traffic

Transportation has always been a critical factor in economic development, linking export businesses to the outside world as well as enhancing the mobility of workers and consumers within an area. Building more roads has been the dominant solution to improving U.S. transportation since the 1950s. With the exception of a few highly dense urban cores in the United States, walking and mass transit have not been serious components of the transportation network. Alternatives such as biking are often treated by local governments as a form of recreation (almost like swimming or skateboarding!) that raises quality of life but is unrelated to economic development. In contrast, much of northern Europe began to give a priority to bicycling when fuel prices rose in the 1970s. Bicycling became a mainstream mode of transportation for both men and women, and for all age groups (Pucher and Buehler 2008).

Automobiles have reigned supreme partly because they give freedom and flexibility, but also because drivers pay more attention to operating costs rather than total costs. In addition to the price of buying an auto-mobile, insurance, registration, and maintenance make the total cost about three times the costs of fuel. Providing space for parking has costs, which are primarily paid by retail stores, public buildings, and employers rather than drivers. (Of course, this cost is passed on to the consumer and taxpayer.) Automobile drivers pay a direct charge for parking on only 1 percent of all auto trips in the U.S.[20] The result is that once a person has purchased an automobile and paid for insurance and registration, the additional cost of making a trip is very low.

With more trips per person, traffic jams have been worsening and ac-cident rates rising. This happens not only where there is growth in popu-lation, but also when there is more sprawl without population growth. Traffic jams and slower traffic impose costs on drivers, both on personal and business trips. Annual hours of delay per traveler tripled between 1982 and 2005 (Texas Transportation Institute 2007). More population, more cars per person, increased urban sprawl, gasoline prices that are still cheap by world standards, and lack of public transport are all cul-prits. Economist Robert Frank sees yet another factor at work: increased traffic congestion is also related to the growing inequality in income and wealth that we discussed in Chapter 5. Frank calls the basic mechanism at work the "Aspen effect" and warns that much of the United States is becoming more like greater Aspen, Colorado:

> Wealthy residents have long since bid up real estate prices in Aspen and other exclusive resort communities to levels that virtually exclude middle- and low-income families. Most of the people who provide services in these communities—teachers, policemen, firemen, laundry and restaurant workers—must therefore commute, often at considerable distance. As a result, all roads into Aspen are clogged morning and night with commut-ers, many of whom come from several hours away. "Greater Aspen" now has a radius of more than fifty miles. (Frank 2001)

Automobiles give great freedom and comfort and are clearly valued as part of the American lifestyle. However, 7–11 percent of non-commuting vehicle trips during peak morning traffic are solely for taking children to school, excluding drop-offs on the way to work or other destinations (U.S. Department of Transportation 2008). Might the quality of life be higher and the cost of living lower in a world that had more short walkable trips, more biking to work and other activities, and more use of mass transit? Parents ferrying children to school and activities is a familiar story and one that rarely adds to quality of life. In a world less dependent on the automobile and more on alternative transportation, cars could be used when necessary and for pleasure. Families could reduce their living expenses substantially by owning one rather than two or three cars.

What we described above seems a pipe dream because it requires a different kind of urban design than what we have in place now. However, it is possible to require new development to be built in a transit-friendly style, even before transit has enough ridership to be economically feasible. The way building and development occur today will determine how easily they can accommodate the needs of the future. Multimodal transportation, including walking and biking along with buses, automobiles, and trains, is now recognized as a key part of both sustainability of development and quality of life. Federal transportation planning currently requires communities to work together and to plan for transportation modes other than the automobile, partly to deal with congestion problems across the United States.

Public transportation systems are most cost effective and user friendly at high levels of density on grid-style urban streets. Both of these also encourage frequent ridership, which keeps average fares down. But even in the best of cases, all public transit systems require some subsidy to operate at a price that will attract riders.[21] It makes sense for non-riders to help to pay that subsidy. Every rider on alternative transit reduces traffic and congestion for the remaining drivers, creating a spillover benefit. It can actually be more cost effective for taxpayers to subsidize transit than to pay for building more roads (in addition to being more environmentally friendly). Popular opposition to transit subsidies seems to be based on the assumption that automobiles "pay their way" through the gasoline tax and their drivers should not be asked to do more. In fact, as cars have become more fuel-efficient, the revenues from the gasoline tax have declined in many states even as miles per driver have increased. Automobiles do not pay their own way, just as public transit cannot. Many of the benefits of transit don't go to the rider, but to the rest of society.

There are also many environmental and social costs from the automobile that the gasoline tax was never designed to cover. Air pollution is a widely known example of an environmental problem related to automobile use. Social costs come from the increased separation of residential and commercial areas, along with economic segregation. This requires many workers to have a car to get to their low-wage job. Some of these workers have transitioned from welfare to work, helping county budgets in other areas. If expanding opportunity through more work is an important community value, as we discussed in Chapter 5, then both our land use and our transportation systems need to support that value. Subsidizing transit is a way to help low-wage workers.

The dispute over transit gets to the heart of how our view of twenty-first century economic development differs from the traditional one. Economic development is not just about tax breaks for businesses to support private capital. It includes constructing an infrastructure within which workers can get to their jobs and support themselves and their families. State and local governments with a new vision of economic development can shape land use and transportation to create more opportunity and better health and fitness. They set the framework for many private business decisions about location and expansion. Planning decisions that serve a community well take all costs and all benefits—financial and non-financial—into account and explore the various tools at hand for dealing with them. Only then can economic development be sustainable and consistent with improved quality of life.

We turn now to some new approaches that give a more active role to state and local governments. These have been labeled "smart growth" and "new urbanism." Both reflect increased preferences for the amenities that contribute to quality of life as well as for efficiently delivered public services.

Smart Growth and New Urbanism: Land Use, Transportation, and Schools

Today's new urbanism reflects a return to mixed use, walkability, and transit options—a pendulum swing from the dominant planning mode in the United States for most of the past century. Advocates of smart growth and new urbanism argue that alternative patterns of land development can better protect and enhance natural, human, and social capital, with lower costs to local governments. They see increased density of development combined with greater proximity of residential and compatible commercial properties contributing to a more walkable and transit-friendly environment. Smart growth should also permit preservation of key historic and cultural features as well as open space and natural environment in the areas that are not developed.

Smart growth promotes "mixed land use, directing development toward existing communities, using compact building design, and preserving open space and farmland . . . [as well as encouraging] a range of housing and transportation choices, walkable communities, and a strong sense of place" (as defined by Burchell et al. 2005, 18). It represents the latest wave of comprehensive land use reform, which began at the state level in Oregon (early 1970s), followed by Florida (1985), Maine, Rhode Island, and Vermont (1988), and New Jersey, Georgia, and Maryland (1990s). Despite a recent backlash to these reforms in both Oregon and Florida, the net effect of comprehensive planning is positive, according to DeGrove (2005). Many early efforts, including California's and North Carolina's coastal protection plans, stemmed primarily from a desire to protect valuable environmental resources.[22]

Costs of infrastructure began to be a reason to favor smart growth in the 1980s and 1990s. Comprehensive planning came to be seen as part of an economic development strategy. The smart growth movement of the late 1990s and first part of the twenty-first century also includes more focus on quality of life and sense of community. Smart growth and the new urbanism are no longer considered barriers to economic development, but ways to move toward a new and better future, at least by some groups. Replacing the traditional zoning practice of checking "one size fits all" boxes with zoning that is flexible and performance oriented would create more livable cities and neighborhoods (Elliott 2008). An example of this is "complete streets" policies that require all new streets to be constructed as complete transportation corridors with sidewalks and bike lanes included in the design (Burchell et al. 2005, 162). As streets undergo major repair, they would be retrofitted to meet new standards. This would add substantially to safety for pedestrians and cyclists as well as enhance transportation options.

Smart growth and the new urbanism are *not* the gentrification that has displaced low- and middle-income families in some urban neighborhoods. Growth restrictions and zoning can be exclusionary, but truly *smart* growth must expand opportunity. For example, rezoning existing areas to allow accessory apartments in single-family homes could accomplish two goals. It would make these homes more affordable to their owners, as well as provide more low-cost rentals. As buildings providing single-room occupancies are either torn down or converted to condominiums, new low-cost rental options must be made available. Without them, the number of homeless persons increases. Improving transit systems—including bike paths and lanes, and pedestrian walkways—increases transportation access for many young and lower income families. Just as it incorporates the ability to live and work without an automobile, smart growth emphasizes proximity to schools and parks and to basic retail goods and services. We turn now to how planning and zoning can contribute to a better quality of life and sustainable development.

Planning and Zoning Should Increase the Standard of Living Rather than Creating Barriers

Smart growth that serves people includes easy access to grocery stores and other retail shopping, even without an automobile. A neighborhood with limited availability of nutritious food can have lifetime and even intergenerational impacts on the health of residents. The movement of smaller grocery stores out of older neighborhoods to areas where they can build mega stores has created what one community council calls a "food desert" (*Chattanooga Times Free Press,* March 28, 2006). With increasing attention to this aspect of quality of life around the nation, the American Planning Association has now added a food track to its national meetings to address this issue.

A shortage of grocery stores is just one example. Many urban neighborhoods do not have adequate access to retail shopping and must travel to spend their dollars in other neighborhoods or municipalities. Stores leave established neighborhoods for many reasons, even when there are enough shoppers with buying power. Single-use residential zoning may "grandfather in" a corner grocery store, but then not allow it to be enlarged or even sold for a new use. For decades, the standards of the American Planning Association and most communities opposed building new neighborhoods that included small retail businesses. Shopping and recreation were deliberately separated, creating the need for multiple automobiles and more roads. Communities also adopted many codes that made it difficult for individuals to retrofit and restore homes and small businesses in neighborhoods that already had sidewalks, parks, and access to stores and restaurants. Zoning restrictions were designed to protect homeowners and property values, but new conversations with residents might reveal that what they want in the twenty-first century requires a differrent model from the reforms of sixty or seventy years past.

Today's highly complex zoning laws are the result of one kind of zoning overlaid on another, along with a host of variances and exceptions that are both confusing and contradictory (Elliott 2008).[23] Setting the bar too high on standards for renovating older buildings makes it cheaper and easier to build anew on cheaper land. Code requirements for parking can also make urban locations impractical. Renovation and adequate parking are both laudable goals, but there must be a balance between them and what is necessary and affordable in an older location. It is time for many cities to take a fresh look at their zoning codes and approval process. Otherwise, these unintentionally create incentives to relocate and discourage the revitalization of older neighborhoods and retail areas.

Is It Smart Growth or Sprawl that People Really Want?

Supporters of current development patterns argue that people have voted with their feet and their pocketbooks for suburban sprawl. A 1999 survey by the National Association of Homebuilders showed that 83 percent of households chose a larger home in an outlying area over a similarly priced town home with greater access to urban amenities and public transportation (Burchell et al. 2005, 127). But homes in suburban developments have been priced at an artificially low level relative to their total cost. Many costs were shifted to the general public through environmental damage and degradation of public services (or increases in taxes) rather than being paid by the homebuyer. We do not know what buyers would have chosen if home prices had reflected more of the true costs. But certainly there would have been less sprawl than there is today, because people do respond to higher prices.

In addition, most people choose from homes that are available for purchase, rather than designing and building the home of their dreams. "If you build it, they will come," describes the dilemma of many families relocating to an unfamiliar city. They have limited time to buy a new home, get settled in a new job, and start children in a new school. The easiest way to do that is not to research the quality of older neighborhoods and schools, but to buy into a new subdivision. These same developments often give prizes or bonuses to realtors who sell a certain number of their homes, an incentive that individual sellers around the rest of the city cannot match. Buyers lack good information if they are not familiar with a community, so their decisions may reflect constraints as much as preferences.

Long-time members of a community can make more informed choices because they have better information than new residents. In addition to expressing their values and preferences through where they live, shop, and attend school, they can regularly let them be known through the voting process. But that process does not capture the complexities of what people want or allow for all the public debate needed. Elections are about candidates or specific issues and rarely pose clear choices about development strategies. Many sensible solutions may not even be on the table. In Chapter 8, we suggest another way to match public choices with community preferences.

Accurate information about preferences requires that buyers, builders, and citizens have better information on the spillover effects (costs and benefits) of particular forms of land use and development. Without widely available and reliable information of the effects on quality of life and the average tax burden, it is disingenuous to attribute the current land development patterns to "what people want." State and local governments are best positioned to fill the role of providing information on spillover costs and benefits. Instead, many follow a "don't ask, don't tell" policy when it comes to the affordability of different patterns of growth. Since state and local policies establish many of the conditions within which people make choices they have an enormous influence on the built environment, the natural environment and the overall shape of the community. To help make growth truly "smart," policy makers should have objective and reliable studies on the effects of alternative development patterns.

Of course, not everyone thinks smart growth is smart. Land use planning affects too many pocketbooks and too many sensibilities to avoid eliciting some strong and varying opinions. For example, a Los Angeles County supervisor writes that his city's latest plan to become denser is "development run amok" that will ruin city neighborhoods with a "one-size-fits-all" approach. He suggests that demolition and conversion of apartments to luxury condominiums are greater impediments to adequate affordable housing than current zoning laws.[24] (Of course, they may be major impediments but it could still be a good idea to revamp the zoning laws.) Other opponents of smart growth, such as the Thoreau Institute and the Cato Institute, oppose planning in general as an abridgment of basic freedoms. However, urban living comes with benefits and costs. One cost is that property rights may be limited due to negative effects on others. The issue is where to strike the balance, and this is rightly a subject for periodic debate.

In the end, any growth that is "smart" must fit both the priorities and the pocketbooks of local citizens today and in the future. That is why citizen involvement in setting goals is important. Unless new growth increases quality of life in a way that citizens are willing and able to pay for, it is not "smart growth." Unless new development is sustainable over time, it will not result in a vibrant community. This sustainability must encompass all of the capital stocks we have talked about throughout this book—natural capital, private business capital, public infrastructure, human, and social capital. We turn now to barriers to sustainable development and some proposed solutions.

Smart Growth and Sustainable Development: Barriers and Solutions

Goals that incorporate economic growth, sustainability, and quality of life are the most efficient way to approach economic development. Coordination needs to happen within each unit of government in addition to cooperation among different governments in the same area. However, lack of trust, time constraints, and failure to communicate and understand each other's goals limit collaboration among local governments, state government, and school districts in many places.[25] One way to encourage more cooperation is for states to establish grant pools that can be applied for only by collaborating units. This is most applicable where states have an important role in funding (for example, school districts, counties, colleges, and universities). For example, the federal requirement that transportation funding be regional has created mechanisms that require local government cooperation in regions of each state. These may be the building blocks for wider dialogue and collaboration.

Beyond lack of cooperation, there are other barriers to smart growth. They include the objections of neighboring property owners and the environmental problems of brownfields (discussed in Chapter 4). Developers who do renovation or infill development find it much more cumbersome than new development on former farm or ranchland. The Smart Growth Network and Burchell and colleagues (2005) have excellent recommendations for how local governments can work better with developers to change the shape of the community. For example, grouping small parcels of infill land, removing any pollutants, and then expediting zoning and project plan approvals from various agencies has worked well in some cities. Local government can also take a role in developing methods for early public involvement. States or counties can allow transfer of development rights (TDRs) to raise densities on some land while preserving other land as open space. *Managing Growth in America's Communities* (Porter 2008) also presents very concrete suggestions about how and where to grow, how to manage infrastructure development, and how to preserve community character and quality of life.

A major barrier to smart growth comes from the preferences and incentives given to new big-box stores with the idea that they will create "economic development" through new sales tax revenue. New store locations may simply shift purchases from one part of the city (or county) to another with little net gain in activity or jobs for the area. That movement may happen on its own as market forces satisfy changing consumer demands, but taxpayers do not need to give incentives to encourage it. If the move of retail stores away from existing neighborhoods does not fit the total picture of what citizens want for their future, then encouraging it is not good economic development policy.

Subsidies to land development at the fringe of cities create a similar problem, whether direct or indirect. Building new roads and providing other amenities with taxes paid by people in existing neighborhoods is a subsidy. Guaranteeing higher–cost water by charging current ratepayers more for new water rights acquisition is a subsidy. Charging the full price for development at the fringe would change the balance developers currently face. As we mentioned earlier, these subsidies make it less likely that developers will choose infill projects that would keep public costs down. Yet a variety of interest groups are successful in keeping these subsidies that raise the values of land they own or produce lucrative construction contracts. Logan and Molotch (1987) use the term "growth machine" to describe the process that controls many local governments.

> Current urban arrangements . . . are not there simply because they maximize efficiency. . . . Instead, they represent the physical and social consequences of cumulative strivings by capitalists bent on profit, renters seeking property returns, and neighborhood groups striving for use values from place. Each group, within its limits, has left no stone unturned in the attempt to mobilize and manipulate every political, cultural, and economic institution on its behalf. The city, the meeting ground of these activities, is the result of all this work and will be modified, transformed, or undone through similar efforts in the future (Logan and Molotch 1987, 292).

Many smart growth ideas and initiatives across the nation have probably failed to reshape development as much as they could because they typically have few incentives and little teeth behind them. Until we change incentives that go in the wrong direction—such as having lax standards in rural areas transitioning to suburban areas—calls for smart growth will have little impact on development. The controversy over transitioning to higher density development in Los Angeles is just one of many examples that shows how important it is that new strategies fit community values and constraints.

Incorporating Land Use into Local Economic Development Plans

Ensuring that land use supports sustainable development, quality of life, and increased opportunity will require a shift in most communities' economic development plans and public sector priorities.[26] The plans have been oriented toward supporting growth and assuming it will bring quality of life and be sustainable. Many zoning and land-use plans are based on outdated models that do not give enough consideration to environmental and human costs, or to taxpayer costs. Giving the maximum freedom to landowners is based on a long tradition of upholding private property rights.[27] However, just as industry must now modify techniques in order to produce fewer pollutants that affect others, development patterns must take account of the social and environmental costs of land use and transportation. Only then are they part of a true economic development that increases quality of life and is sustainable over time.

State and local governments' capital improvement plans should evaluate whether any new public building meets broad community goals and design standards (ICMA 2008). In addition, they must consider more than the needs of private companies and property owners when they make land-use decisions. Rather than an *increase* in public spending, a *change* in both spending patterns and land use planning is needed. Many public-sector costs can actually decline on a per capita basis with changes in the design of neighborhoods and cities. The future of local economic development lies not in seeing conflicts between quality of life, sustainability, and economic development, but in pursuing them jointly in an integrated fashion.

When trade-offs are necessary, they should be acknowledged up front rather than dealt with later in a piecemeal fashion. We argue that local governments do not serve their "consumers" well by being passive or making separate decisions about land use, schools, water, or transportation. Too often boards or commissions that make decisions about one area are not aware of or coordinating with other groups about how their decisions affect the overall growth, quality of life, and sustainability of communities. Decision makers should be conscious of the great leverage they have in the development of human, social, and natural capital important for sustainability and the importance of making wise and coordinated decisions for true economic development.

What is the model for communities that want to use the tools they have to work toward sustainable development and higher quality of life? The capital stocks framework outlined in Chapter 1 provides a way to look at the impacts on sustainable economic development and quality of life of actions taken by individuals, organizations/businesses, and local governments. The traditional model of economic development (described above as a "growth machine") focused largely on serving the needs of private capital (i.e., business and large landowners). In that model, the next priority after private owners is public infrastructure that fits the needs of the "growth machine." In contrast, taking account of the effects of public spending, regulation, and taxes on natural, social, and human capital is at the foundation of a truly "smart growth" strategy that will lead to higher quality of life and economic development that is sustainable.

In *Taking Sustainable Cities Seriously* (2003), Kent Portney points out that while cities may adopt green building codes, growth boundaries, smart growth, or eco-industrial parks, it is unlikely that they will be seriously addressed without establishing local indicators. If smart growth is to reflect community preferences given the constraints of the tax base, the natural environment, and other historical and institutional forces specific to each community, we believe that local indicators (see Chapter 8) should also be taken into account. We conclude this chapter with a summary of how local and state governments can use their influence in land use, transportation, and schools to improve economic development, quality of life, and sustainability.

Conclusion: Sprawl vs. Smart Growth?

As we have outlined in this chapter, private land use patterns have costs and benefits beyond the ones that their owners see. Some costs affect other businesses or individuals as well as local governments and schools. If more costs than benefits are spilling over, this subtracts from community quality of life and the sustainability of local economic development. It is up to states and communities to balance short-term profitability of land use with broader, long-term social costs and benefits. The issue is how to set policies around land development that preserve as many rights of private ownership as possible while also asserting the public interest in quality of life and sustainability.

Whether cities are still "building out" their land area or redeveloping blighted areas, they need comprehensive plans that reflect community visions. If these plans and visions are to be more than empty rhetoric sitting on a shelf, they must incorporate indicators that policy choices can use as benchmarks. Strategic or comprehensive plans that are "wish lists" reflect high-minded aspirations without recognizing potential conflicts. If the plans are to be living documents that actually shape current and future quality of life, all budget and regulatory decisions must factor in the likely effects on goals and indicators from the plans. Many local governments use performance indicators, but these are generally limited to measures that local governments can control (such as response time for the fire department or number of street miles repaired). A serious commitment to increased quality of life and sustainability must consider the effects of government policies on broader measures beyond the control of local government.

For example, city zoning can have effects on vehicle miles traveled or time in traffic that were not part of the original intention. Contracting out for municipal services can save dollars in the city budget but result in former workers' going to the city hospital's emergency room because they no longer have health insurance. Budget choices between spending on public safety and parks, to use another example, should be made in full consideration of how these choices impact goals in the comprehensive plan or vision for the city.

Inevitably, goals and values will conflict with each other at times and require tough decisions. Linking these decisions to indicators demands official recognition that public safety is given a higher priority than mobility or environmental quality in a particular decision. This requires political maturity of both elected officials and the public and an end to the "you can have it all" promises popular in campaigns. There will be revisions to any plan as economic, political, and social realities change. Nevertheless, if the debate about conflicting priorities is out in the open, full awareness of costs and benefits is more likely to happen when it can make a difference rather than after decisions are locked in place.

Smart growth and the new urbanism are strategies to make housing and transportation more affordable, through more effective land use that also enhances quality of life. Smart growth encourages infill and more compact development for several reasons. One is environmental, another aesthetic, and a third is to make housing, utilities, transportation, and other infrastructure more affordable. Contrary to being exclusionary or elitist, smart growth policies generally stress mixed-use and transit-friendly development styles that more easily accommodate low and moderate incomes and the elderly. This kind of development can *reduce* some costs to private citizens as well as the public sector, depending on the shape it takes.

Genuinely smart growth can be an economic development strategy as well as a tool for preserving quality of life (Muro and Puentes 2003). There is strong evidence that smart growth can save local governments money in the long run, but what about the short run and the effect on balancing the budget next year? In the next chapter, we discuss the tax and revenue aspects of fiscally sustainable development. State and local tax laws and policies can have different fiscal impacts depending on the shape of development.

7

The Effects of Growth on Fiscal Sustainability

Along with sustaining natural, human, and physical capital stocks, state and local governments must also be *fiscally sustainable*. Otherwise, quality of life declines as infrastructure and service levels deteriorate, or higher tax rates are required just to maintain the status quo. This chapter focuses on the effects of different growth patterns and tax structures on state and local government budgets. By tax structure, we mean the combination of fees and income, property, sales, and excise taxes that raises revenue. The mix of taxes is important because it affects the cyclical and long-term revenue stability as well as gives incentives for different patterns of land development.[1] States have very different tax structures including the division of taxing and spending authority between state government and localities. Local actions in land use directly affect revenues as well as expenses at the local level in some states. In others, most revenue goes to the state and then is allocated to localities.

Regardless of the mix, taxes and spending have risen much faster at the state and local level than at the national for several decades. There are a number of reasons for this increase, as we explore below, but new patterns of land use seem to be one important factor. If people prefer sprawling development, one solution to fiscal sustainability is to make taxes and fees reflect its true cost rather than shifting costs to the rest of the taxpayers. In the last chapter, we said that truly smart growth must reflect what people want. However, they must also be willing and able to pay for what they want. Otherwise, it is not fiscally sustainable in the long run.

In this chapter, we define fiscal sustainability and then explore how it might be affected by various kinds of growth. Several illustrations of growth, some that are fiscally sustainable and others that are not, are presented. Although our initial focus is on growth patterns, tax structure is at least as important to ensuring fiscal sustainability when there is growth. The chapter concludes with suggestions of how local and state governments can change their tax structure, land use, and infrastructure planning to move toward fiscal sustainability. In Appendix 7.1, we briefly review state and local tax systems, which vary considerably across the United States. In Appendix 7.2, we discuss tax and tax-expenditure limitations.

Defining Fiscal Sustainability

Fiscal sustainability means being able to continue the same level of public services and investments in infrastructure within the existing tax structure. (Of course, new taxes or higher rates may be necessary at times for new or improved programs or services.) When *revenues per person* from the existing system of taxes and fees grow at approximately the same rate as the growth in *per capita costs,* growth is fiscally sustainable. In the popular parlance, it "pays for itself," if growth is not fiscally sustainable, taxes must be raised to cover costs. Otherwise infrastructure and service levels will decline, and schools and roads will become overcrowded. Water and wastewater systems may not be able to keep up with population growth, with resulting harm to the environment and to public safety. Community centers and parks that have contributed to the sense of place may not be adequately maintained. In all these cases, costs are incurred by the community even though taxes are not increased.

Temporary shortfalls due to economic downturns do not indicate a mismatch between tax structure or level and cost patterns, because they will be eliminated when the economy recovers. Long-term gaps that require continual budget cuts or tax increases to provide the same level of services do indicate a mismatch. They are a signal for a state or community to look at the *value delivered per dollar of taxes*. Recall from Chapter 2 that this value per dollar is much more important for economic development than the *level of taxes or spending*. Higher taxes for higher services or better infrastructure or education may help economic development. However, when taxes or fees must be increased simply to get back to the old level of services, this is a negative for both economic development and the standard of living. Value per dollar has fallen.

There are two major reasons why growth in population or land use may not be fiscally sustainable over time for a community or even a state. The first comes primarily from the revenue side, when declining economic prosperity shrinks the tax base. This may be due to a temporary downturn in the economy that is regional or national and beyond the control of state or local government. In these cases, a budget stabilization or "rainy day" fund requires saving up during boom times to be able to cover expenses when revenue is temporarily low. In other cases, per capita revenue falls because of job loss in key economic sectors—natural resources, a particular industry, tourism, or a military base. A forward-looking economic development plan should strive for a diversified economic base that is more likely to be sustainable over time than one too dependent on any one economic sector (see Chapter 2).

A second reason for lack of fiscal sustainability comes when the local economy is growing but there is a mismatch between spending and revenue. Of course, total costs will grow when there are more people but there should also be more taxpayers to increase total revenue. It is when costs rise more rapidly than revenues that there is a problem. To better understand the forces driving state and local government spending, we look at three reasons for rising costs per capita. The first applies whether there is growth or not, the second applies to income growth, and the third to growth in developed land area.

Rising Costs Per Capita in Local and State Governments: Cost of Services

The first contributor to rising state and local government costs is the large share of their budgets that pays for labor costs. Around 80 percent of most state and local budgets pays salaries and benefits (including rapidly rising health care costs). Costs of services rose more rapidly than average costs across all sectors of the economy. State and local governments are primarily "service businesses."[2] Teaching, policing, and social work are examples of services that require people-to-people contact. While many manufactured goods have fallen in price due to labor-saving technology or lower labor costs abroad, these savings are often not possible in a service business. As a result, the index measuring price increases for state and local government purchases rose more rapidly than the consumer price index (CPI) in almost all years since 1999 as shown in Figure 7.1. (In contrast, during the late 1980s state and local government costs increased less than consumer prices). When outside analyses of government spending use the CPI as a proxy for increases in government costs, they might as well be comparing apples and oranges. In some time periods, one goes up faster than the other and vice versa. We next explore the second reason for pressures on state and local government.

Rising Budget Pressures: The Effects of Affluence on the Demand for Services

The second reason for rising pressures on budgets is that income growth (even without more population) usually creates more demand for public-

Figure 7.1 **The Consumer Price Index and the State and Local Government Expenditure Index**

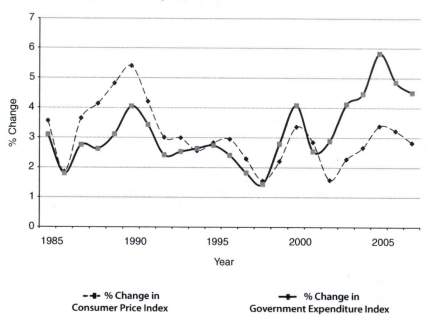

sector goods. More affluent citizens want better public schools along with more access to higher education. They ask for amenities such as parks and open space, recreational and cultural facilities, local events, and museums. However, increasing taxes for new services that raise quality of life is fundamentally different from increasing taxes to maintain the same or fewer services.

If people are willing to pay more taxes for more or better-quality services and infrastructure, then increased taxes and spending can be perfectly sustainable. Later in the chapter, we illustrate this in Figure 7.2 (see page 125). Line A shows a community willing to pay higher levels of taxes for higher levels of services relative to line B. The important point is that demands for public services and infrastructure match the ability and willingness to pay taxes to support them. Both are examples of fiscal sustainability because in each case the tax level and structure accommodate demands for more amenities, services, or infrastructure. We turn now to a third reason for budget pressures. It comes from growth in real per capita costs due to sprawling patterns of land use.

Rising Costs: Growth in Population or Land Area

Private sector land use often has unanticipated impacts on public costs, as we reviewed in Chapter 6. These spillover costs (see Appendix 4.1) shift away from the consumer or decision maker, and impose costs on third parties. (Of course, there can also be spillover benefits, but few complain about those!) While no individual new house and few commercial buildings require a new road or more efficient waste treatment facility, the cumulative effect of more houses or buildings will make these expenditures necessary. More building on scenic hillsides vs. level ground and the use of non-grid street systems (including cul-de-sacs) raises the cost of roads, flood control, and road maintenance per residence. It may also raise the cost of police and firefighter services if locations are more difficult to reach or more prone to fire danger. Large new schools built to capture economies of scale often have higher costs of transportation, administration, maintenance, and security than do smaller, more centrally located schools. In addition to higher infrastructure costs, there are other reasons why population growth or less density of land use raises costs.

When there is more pressure on the environment, additional urban and suburban amenities are required just to maintain the same quality of life. Larger lot sizes might appear to reduce environmental impact, but the evidence is that the need for roads, power lines, and water and wastewater pipes cancels that out. Where agricultural or vacant land formerly provided environmental services such as fresh air and wildlife habitat (see Chapter 4), land may now need to be purchased for parks or greenbelts to serve the same purposes. In addition, growth is likely to generate new demands for public safety, since crime rates often increase with population growth and more anonymity. Costs of services studies by the American Farmland Trust indicate that the higher taxes paid by commercial or residential development relative to agricultural land are more than offset by higher costs of the development (Theobald 2001). The informal support networks of extended family, church, and neighborhood may erode as social capital diminishes with urban sprawl. Formal networks of county extension agents and social service workers that require new tax dollars take their place. All of the economic, environmental, and social pressures of growth lead to demands for more services, and this requires more tax dollars per person.

In Chapter 6, we referred to a series of studies that found substantial cost differentials between sprawling development and more compact and contiguous "smart growth." There is a developing consensus that smart growth or new urbanism saves 10 percent for cities and counties on infrastructure (Burchell et al. 2005) and 5 percent for schools (J. Frank 1989). McGuire and Sjoquist (2003) cite other studies where road and utility costs may be reduced as much as 20–33 percent.

These higher costs come *at least as much* from land use patterns as from simple population growth. Larger houses and vehicles (not only automobiles but also trucks and fire engines) require more land, which contributes to higher rates of land use per person. Not only are there more parking lots and roads, they must also be bigger and wider just to accommodate the same number of vehicles. Cities and states with relatively stable populations also experience these costs of growth especially if there is increased affluence. In many parts of the country (the Midwest and Northeast in particular) there was little to no population increase, but people moved from central cities to exclusively zoned outlying areas (Swanstrom et al. 2006). When this happens, existing infrastructure is underutilized at the same time that new infrastructure is being built. Without population increases, it is hard to see how the additional costs could be paid without higher tax revenues. We now turn to how different kinds of tax and fee structures can affect fiscal sustainability.

Tax Structures and Fiscal Sustainability

By tax structure, we refer to the *mix* of different taxes and fees, and the exemptions built into each, rather than the *level* of taxes. In most areas, the tax structure is primarily a historical accident inherited from an earlier era that has had only piecemeal modifications. In almost every state, commercial enterprises pay higher rates of property tax than residences, and agricultural land pays the lowest rates. Residences tend to bring more costs of services, especially schools, although, of course, these students are the children of workers in some local businesses. Nevertheless, from the viewpoint of any one locality, whoever gets the commercial property wins and whoever gets the residential property loses from a fiscal perspective. The underlying tax structure can affect whether new growth "pays for itself" as much as changes in the costs of services.

Almost everyone agrees that taxes should be structured in a way that is fair, transparent, and easy to administer. They should also provide adequate revenue as a community grows, to prevent surprise requests for new or higher tax rates to fill spending backlogs. Unless a community knows up front what effects different patterns of growth—sprawl vs. density, new development vs. infill, gentrification, or brownfield redevelopment—will have on costs, they cannot make informed decisions about the future. The tax structure also provides incentives for the patterns of growth that citizens decide they want and are willing to pay for. In this section, we concentrate on how the incentives in many current tax systems encourage sprawl. We save a larger discussion of different types of taxes and their potential revenues for Appendix 7.1.

Heavy reliance on local sales taxes relative to property taxes provides a reason for counties or municipalities to give incentives to malls and big-box stores to lure shoppers (and sales tax dollars) from neighboring jurisdictions. They pay much lower property taxes than industrial development but generate lots of sales. On the other hand, reliance on property taxes for a large share of revenues gives incentives for sprawling development (Brueckner 2001; Nechyba 1998). This is because property taxes on an identical house or business property are generally lower in outlying areas where land is cheaper. One solution is to charge development or impact fees when costs of private development to the public sector are higher than average.

Charging For High-Cost Development Patterns

Traditionally, costs of infrastructure for new development were shared by all property taxpayers. As long as the average cost of new infrastructure is relatively similar to the cost of the old (adjusted for inflation), this seems a reasonable way to spread costs over time. But the evidence is that sprawling development patterns have much higher costs than the traditional style. The existing population may not want to pay for this new and more costly form of land development. Land exactions or impact fees can be charged to developers and largely will pass on in higher new home prices (Yinger 1998). Still, many developers oppose these fees or charges because they dampen demand for new homes in high-cost areas.[3] You can almost hear Homer Simpson saying, "Well, d'oh!" If new styles of development cost more, then it's not so surprising that buyers would have to pay more and some would shop elsewhere.

From an economic point of view, higher impact fees are an appropriate market signal of true costs in that location, not a violation of affordable housing principles. But impact fees are generally calculated from *average* costs of infrastructure, not the higher costs in sprawling developments.[4] Reflecting differences in incremental service or infrastructure cost would provide better market signals (McGuire and Sjoquist 2003). These costs vary among geographic locations (hillsides, flood plains) relative to others. Stormwater and drainage costs also vary with construction design and materials. Impact fees could be used to encourage development in lower cost areas first, if they reflected these cost differences. Including a share of expected future infrastructure costs in impact fees or land-exaction charges would increase this incentive.

Taxes must bring in sufficient revenue for growth to be sustainable. However, the same taxes also create incentives for where to locate new houses, offices, stores, and factories, and how to build them. Land taxes, advocated by Henry George a century ago, tax the value of raw land rather than its improvements. A tax on land has fewer distortions to behavior than the standard property tax and encourages less sprawling development. In Pittsburgh, the only U.S. city that combines a standard property tax with a pure land tax, the tax structure has provided less incentive to sprawl (Oates and Schwab 1997).

To help clarify the impacts that growth can have on fiscal sustainability, we now look at a variety of ways that spending and revenues might be equal to each other, or diverge with growth. When they diverge, it is because revenues from the existing tax structure increase at a different rate (more slowly or faster) than costs per resident.

Putting It All Together: Fiscal Sustainability Means Incoming Revenues = Expenses

Fiscal Situation #1: Service Needs = Level of Revenues at All Population Levels

When population grows due to in-migration, it should create a larger tax base as well as new service needs. On the other hand, when population is stable but per capita income increases rapidly, this may increase the demand for amenities and higher quality services but it should also enlarge the tax base. Figure 7.2 illustrates the neutral case where both costs and revenues per person increase at a constant rate with growth in total personal income (either from population or per capita income growth). [5] We begin with Figure 7.2 because it is the simplest example

Figure 7.2   **Tax Revenues Equal Expenditures with Growth**

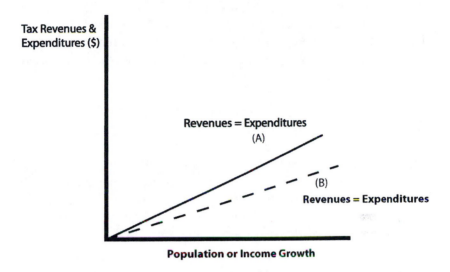

and also reflects the expectations of many taxpayers of how state and local government's costs and revenues correspond.

The *level* of tax revenue and expenditure per person is considerably higher in some states or localities than in others (line A vs. line B), but this reflects different voter preferences for public versus private goods and services. At any time, they can change those preferences up or down. However, in neither case will revenues fall short of expenditures as long as taxes are structured to reflect gains in income and population. In cities and counties, the population in new subdivisions pays for new roads, schools, parks, and pools needed through the taxes they pay, without having to raise tax rates for the population in general. For states, if population or per capita income growth results in more students wanting to enroll in state universities, there are more tax dollars going into total revenues to cover the state subsidy. Despite the inherent appeal of this model, the real world is often quite different.

To begin with, the neutral assumption in Figure 7.2 can be strictly true in the short term only for operating budgets because of "carrying capacity" and the lumpiness of infrastructure investments that we discussed earlier. One new house or business does not create a need for any new infrastructure. Road miles are not added every time someone moves to town; schools do not add parts of classrooms for every new child.

However, in a fiscally sustainable system, the trend reflected in Figure 7.2 will still be true over time. New infrastructure costs will eventually be covered by new revenues that are automatically generated without raising tax rates. We now look at cases where revenues and expenditures per person diverge persistently. First, we take the more optimistic fiscal situation often painted by advocates of growth.

Fiscal Situation #2: Increasing the Tax Base with Population or Per Capita Income Growth

Many economic development efforts have the explicit goal of increasing the tax base, as shown in Figure 7.3. Total personal income can rise either through population growth or higher per capita income. An increased tax base under the existing structure of taxes and rates will be able to cover the costs of growth. It can even yield a "growth dividend" *if costs per resident rise more slowly than new revenues.* New programs and facilities are then affordable without increasing tax rates, or tax rates can be lowered to yield the same revenue and still maintain the same level of services.

States that have a progressively structured income tax with higher rates for higher incomes, or have property taxes that increase considerably with higher market values, may realize a revenue benefit from growth. In contrast, if sales taxes are the primary revenue source, revenues will not be as responsive to either population or income growth (see Appendix 7.1.). Communities that are sales-tax dependent often compete for retail malls and big-box stores to bring customers from other areas. If they are successful at attracting enough of these shoppers, this could still attain the optimistic case depicted in Figure 7.3. However, other jurisdictions nearby bear the costs of residential development for the workers and customers at the stores even though the community getting the sales tax revenues does not. This is a zero-sum game for the region or state as a whole.

Localities that depend on property taxes are in better shape to benefit from growth, especially if they have large industrial or commercial enterprises also paying taxes. Residential property taxes alone can cover costs on their own only in very affluent communities where the properties are large and expensive. However, large numbers of exemptions to businesses, nonprofits, or seniors can erode revenues from property tax. Low caps on property tax (California and Colo-

Figure 7.3   **An Increasing Tax Base**

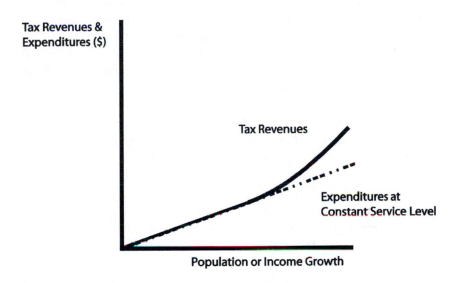

rado, for example) also can result in insufficient revenues to keep up with growth.

To summarize, depending on the structure of taxes, they may rise more quickly than population or income growth. If costs per person are rising less rapidly than tax revenues, there is a fiscal dividend. We next explore another way to get a fiscal dividend.

Fiscal Situation #3: Declining Average Costs per Capita as Population Grows

Even if tax revenues rise only at a constant rate, declining costs per person could still result in a growth dividend. This is shown in Figure 7.4. There are three different ways to have declining average costs. The first is by taking advantage of any overcapacity in schools, roads and transit systems, and water and wastewater plants. Then, new residents will be new taxpayers but will have little effect on service or capital costs. Recall from Chapter 2 that communities with overcapacity can have a net financial benefit from location incentives. The second case comes from economies of scale that cause average per capita costs to decline with growth in population. Larger power and water plants are often more efficient, so a small community may find that average costs decline with growth. More specialists can be hired in city or county government to deliver services more efficiently. Increased density of development can also contribute to cost savings in distribution and delivering of certain services. However, as size increases, governments (or school districts) must also create more information systems and bureaucratic structures that begin to offset economies of scale.

The third way to lower average costs per person is through fiscal zoning.[6] Restricting lot size and the building of properties affordable to low-income families effectively excludes residents who will not pay much in property taxes. Many of these are families with children, whose education takes a big bite of the property tax dollar. If fiscal zoning is successful, costs per person will be lower and revenues per person higher, again creating a dividend (see Figure 7.4). However, of the three options discussed above, none may be realistic or acceptable. Moreover, while fiscal zoning benefits some residents, it harms quality of life and sustainability in the larger community or state through negative impacts on nearby communities. We turn now to two situations where costs rise faster than revenues and there is no fiscal sustainability with growth.

Figure 7.4   **Falling Per Capita Costs**

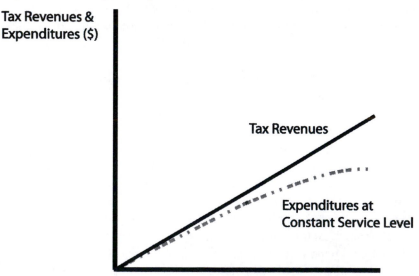

Tax Revenues & Expenditures ($)

Tax Revenues

Expenditures at Constant Service Level

Population or Income Growth

Fiscal Situation #4: Costs Rise While Tax Revenues per Capita Are Constant

Rather than costs per person declining with population growth, they often rise. Large lots and noncontiguous development, two of the key elements of sprawl, have been shown to raise infrastructure and service costs (Burchell et al. 2005). Costs may also rise because more families with children move into an area, or because there are more low-income residents who use certain government services more intensively. Any of these factors can create a gap between the existing tax structure and maintenance of service levels (Figure 7.5), which makes continued growth fiscally unsustainable. In this case, a state or locality cannot "grow its way" out of the gap between tax revenues and spending because typical new residents cost local government more than they pay in taxes. We turn now to the last and worst case example.

Figure 7.5 **Rising Per Capita Costs**

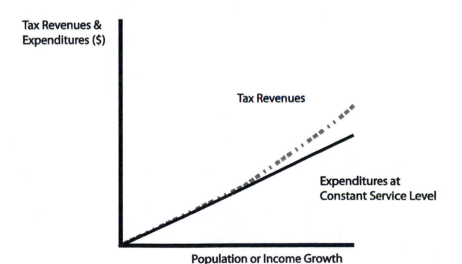

Figure 7.6   **The Worst-Case Scenario**

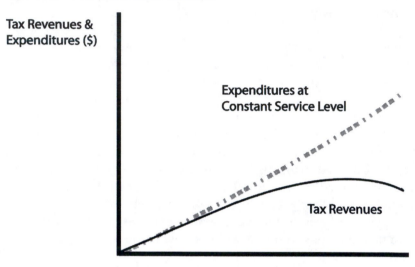

Population or Income Growth

Fiscal Situation #5: Costs Rise Rapidly and Tax Revenues per Capita Fall

When revenues grow less rapidly than population or income while costs increase faster, there are ever-widening gaps between needs and revenues, as in Figure 7.6. Tax revenues per person may be declining due to the reliance on sales taxes or too many exemptions and caps on the property tax that make revenues less responsive to income growth. There may be tax or spending limits that do not respond to economic growth and the higher service levels people expect as they become more affluent.

If costs per person are rising while tax revenues per person are declining states or localities face a "perfect storm." Either tax structures or rising costs must be tackled to restore fiscal sustainability in the future. While taxpayer revolts have focused on the size of government and the increases in taxes, we think there is a link between inefficient patterns of growth and rising taxes. The next section summarizes barriers to fiscal sustainability, with or without economic growth, and how to achieve it.

Fiscal Sustainability with Growth

Fiscal sustainability requires a system where the average taxes paid per new resident equal the average costs per new resident (including some share of future infrastructure) as long as service levels remain the same. A series of calls for higher tax levels in order to maintain *existing* levels of any service (road quality, police or fire protection, class size in schools) indicates that growth is probably not fiscally sustainable.[7] To keep tax rates from increasing, budgets are cut in other areas (parks, recreation, and so forth). This suggests the same problem—the current tax structure does not accommodate the costs of growth. The tax and budget problems that many states and localities faced during the boom of the 1990s and the housing bubble of the early twenty-first century indicate that either Figure 7.5 or 7.6 describes their situation fairly accurately. We look first at the evidence on the cost side before considering the revenue side of the sustainability equation.

Getting accurate measurements of the net fiscal impact of population growth on local and state governments is difficult for a number of reasons. *Actual* government spending cannot be reliably used as a measure of costs when some of the "cost" of new population growth is paid through declining quality of life. Overcrowding or less access to schools, parks, roads, and other public facilities and slower response times to fire, police, and medical emergency calls are all examples. This makes attention to quality-of-life factors especially important during periods of rapid growth.

On the tax side, location incentives to businesses may erode the tax base by more than they add to existing revenues from new business activity. In addition, property taxes or fees that are based on average cost of services do not fully capture the higher costs in new subdivisions so they may not bring enough revenue to cover new costs (McGuire and Sjoquist 2003). Many new developments are in areas with fragmented local governments that shift costs to nearby localities through fiscal zoning. Others depend on special taxing districts set up to finance infrastructure or services (see Table 7.1A in Appendix 7.1). When the problems from reliance on sales taxes and the complications of tax and tax-expenditure limits are added to the mix, it is not surprising that there are perennial revenue problems in many state and local governments. However, the critical question is whether current revenue systems encourage and accommodate the kinds of growth and quality of life that people want in the twenty-first century.

On the spending side, there must be a new vision of efficiency in government. It is more than stopping the traditional "waste, fraud, and abuse" and making sure that government employees put in a full day's work. Land-use regulations and incentives from the tax structure must be used to lower costs and increase efficiencies, along with improving quality of life and sustainable development. Many people prefer a lifestyle that uses land differently, but public policies should ensure that they pay the full cost of this choice. Subsidizing suburban development does not have the positive spillover benefits that education does. In fact, if the negative spillover costs to the environment were added to the costs of sprawl calculations made by planning experts, the true costs would be even higher.

Planning efficient use of land and infrastructure is part of being a responsible steward of the tax dollar. More local governments do use some kind of fiscal impact analysis, but it is often based on historical average cost per person and generally deals only with the impacts to one unit of government. Future costs may rise by more than inflation if the incremental costs per person are higher with more sprawl. And the record shows that many costs do spill over to other units of government (and vice versa).

State and local governments have tools to ensure that these costs are paid through fees or taxes that vary with the pattern of development, and through congestion fees on drivers. Unless the appropriate level and type of taxes or fees are charged, other costs will spill over to the rest of the community. In sum, fiscal sustainability depends on aligning the tax structure and land planning so that increased land use or population growth pay for themselves with new revenues generated by the system.

However, a fragmented system of local governments with (sometimes) high degrees of autonomy of spending, taxing, and regulation is a barrier to better planning for growth and its fiscal consequences. In Table 7.1, we show the states that have more than the average units of government relative to their population. Some of these units are cities, counties, and school districts, but many are special districts formed to tax and provide infrastructure and services in newly developed areas.

It is in the American tradition to have many small units of government so as to restrict the power of any one unit. This also allows more choices among types and levels of government (the "Tiebout effect"), presumably increasing overall quality of life.[8] However, the fragmentation of local governments also makes it easier for businesses and developers to

Table 7.1

States with Above Average Units of Government per 1,000 People

States	All government units	Government units per 1,000	Special district, % of total
United States	*87,525*	*0.30*	*0.40*
Ohio	3,636	0.32	0.17
Mississippi	1,000	0.35	0.46
Kentucky	1,439	0.35	0.50
West Virginia	686	0.38	0.50
Pennsylvania	5,031	0.41	0.37
Oregon	1,439	0.41	0.64
Delaware	339	0.42	0.77
Colorado	1,928	0.43	0.73
New Hampshire	559	0.44	0.26
New Mexico	858	0.46	0.73
Indiana	3,085	0.50	0.36
Oklahoma	1,798	0.52	0.31
Illinois	6,903	0.55	0.46
Wisconsin	3,048	0.56	0.22
Arkansas	1,588	0.59	0.44
Missouri	3,422	0.60	0.44
Maine	826	0.64	0.27
Iowa	1,975	0.67	0.27
Minnesota	3,482	0.69	0.12
Idaho	1,158	0.86	0.69
Vermont	733	1.19	0.21
Montana	1,127	1.24	0.53
Kansas	3,887	1.43	0.39
Wyoming	722	1.45	0.76
Nebraska	2,791	1.62	0.41
South Dakota	1,866	2.46	0.20
North Dakota	2,735	4.31	0.28

Source: Compiled from the *Statistical Abstract of the United States: 2006. The National Data Book.* U.S. Department of Commerce. Economics and Statistics Administration. U.S. Census Bureau.

shop around for more lax regulations. It leads to tax competition, such as fiscal zoning and excessive location incentives that may not always be in the interests of quality of life or sustainable development. It makes cooperation on regional issues more difficult. As a result, decentralization may not always be more efficient or sustainable.[9] To overcome this, the different units of local government must work at collaborating and taking greater account of their effects on each other.

We close this chapter with a summary of ways that local government can support economic development that is centered around people. After all, they often serve the same voters and taxpayers!

Conclusion

One critical question is whether current revenue systems encourage and accommodate the kinds of growth and quality of life that people want in the twenty-first century. We have discussed many factors in this chapter that have contributed to lack of fiscal sustainability (and added fuel to the tax revolt, we believe). We focused on three that state and local governments have some ability to control. The first is the high cost of sprawling land-use patterns. The second is the incentives the tax structure may give for this kind of development. The third is the responsiveness of the tax structure to economic or population growth required for fiscal sustainability. Keeping all of these healthy will support the innovations in society and the economy and the flexible institutions necessary for sustainable development. A city that approves development without taking account of the costs and benefits to the private sector or the financial costs to adjacent school districts, cities, and counties is likely to have unhappy citizens even when its own fiscal house is in order. Children from new homes will show up at the schoolhouse door almost immediately. Taxes on newly developed properties (vs. the lower taxes on vacant or agricultural land) can take up to two years or more under state laws to yield more school revenue by reflecting the value of improvements.

A county that looks only at its own bottom line rather than the impact on cities within its borders needs to be reminded that city residents are county voters and taxpayers also. Few people think much about the different layers of government—they just know the total property tax bill went up or the sales tax is higher. Tax-sharing arrangements or equalization of taxes over larger regions could end some of the tax and zoning competition between localities.

Fiscal impact analysis should be broadened to include nearby govern-ments and school districts, and it should include reasonable estimates of future costs to reflect sustainability. In addition, a full economic analysis of costs and benefits should include the impacts on citizens of growth management decisions and resulting environmental effects. This means considering the impacts on quality of life and all capital stocks involved in the economic development process—natural capital, social capital, and human capital, as well as private business and public sector infrastructure. To do all this, it is very useful to have community indicators as part of the planning process. We turn to those in Chapter 8.

Appendix 7.1
State and Local Government Tax Structures

Traditionally, state and local governments in the United States have relied on the "three-legged stool" of income, sales, and property taxes for their revenues, with income taxes generally only at the state level. There are six major issues with tax structure. We dealt with the first, the transparency of tax incentives, in Chapter 2. A second was the effect of different taxes on low- and middle-income families relative to high income (Chapter 5). The flexibility that states allow their localities in taxing and spending (Barrett and Greene 2008) is a third that we have only alluded to in this book. We have focused in the last two chapters on a fourth issue—the incentives (often unintended) that the tax structure gives for particular growth patterns—and a fifth—how well the tax structure will accom-modate costs of growth. We turn now to the sixth issue, the stability of revenue from different taxes.

Revenue stability is very important for local and state governments because they must balance budgets annually and most have limits on debt financing even for infrastructure. Sales taxes have become an increasing share of local government funding in many areas but provide a less stable revenue stream than property taxes because so many big purchases such as automobiles, appliances, and building materials are discretionary. Depend-ing on the degree of progressivity built into the income tax,[10] revenues will increase more or less rapidly in an economic boom and fall in a downturn. However, they will be considerably more responsive to a changing eco-nomic situation than sales or property taxes. Diversifying revenue sources with a mix of different types of taxes creates more stability, since each has different patterns over the business cycle. Each tax base also responds differently to other economic and demographic changes.

Sales taxes have two problems as a revenue source. First, they are more variable over the business cycle than property taxes because they apply to so many discretionary consumer goods. While the tax base (the items to which the tax applies) varies considerably from state to state and sometimes between localities in a state, the sales tax is more a tax on goods than on services (see Table 7.1A, page 137–138). It brings in less additional revenue as average incomes increase with economic growth because an increasing portion of that new income will be spent on services rather than goods. For example, auto maintenance is not taxed while auto supplies are, cleaning services are not taxed but cleaning equipment is, and so on. As a result, the share of income that goes to sales taxes falls over time if services are not included. In economic terms, the sales tax is less *elastic,* or responsive, to income growth than some other taxes, like property and income.

Only six states—Hawaii, New Mexico, Delaware, Washington, South Dakota, and West Virginia—apply the sales tax to a wide range of services, as we show in Table 7.1A. In half of the states, cable TV is taxed, and in slightly fewer than half, satellite TV is taxed. The move to expand the sales tax base has slowed considerably since the widely unpopular attempts in Florida and Massachusetts twenty years ago.

A second major problem with sales tax as a revenue generator is the net leakage of sales tax dollars from one jurisdiction to others. More people commute—for business or pleasure—across city, county, and state lines on a regular basis than was the case fifty or even twenty years ago. As part of this lifestyle, it is sometimes more convenient to buy during the lunch hour or right after work while outside the boundaries of "home." Vacations and long weekends provide even more opportunities for shopping away from home. In addition, the growth of Internet sales further weakens the connection between place of residence and consumer purchase. All of these factors work together to make sales-tax revenues rise less rapidly than incomes unless a community finds a way to attract dollars from nonresidents. (Tourism, malls, and big-box stores are all potential ways to do just that, as discussed earlier.)

When local governments rely too heavily on sales taxes there are three very negative consequences. First, they have big swings in tax revenues when consumer spending fluctuates. Automobile sales and new building

Table 7.1A

Taxation of Services by States

State	No. of services taxed	State	No. of services taxed
Alabama	37	Oregon	0
Alaska	1	Alaska	1
Arizona	58	New Hampshire	11
Arkansas	72	Colorado	14
California	23	Nevada	15
Colorado	14	Illinois	17
Connecticut	80	Virginia	18
Delaware	143	Massachusetts	19
Washington, DC	70	Montana	19
Florida	64	California	23
Georgia	36	Indiana	23
Hawaii	160	Maine	24
Idaho	30	Michigan	26
Illinois	17	North Dakota	27
Indiana	23	Missouri	28
Iowa	94	Kentucky	29
Kansas	71	Rhode Island	29
Kentucky	29	Vermont	29
Louisiana	55	Idaho	30
Maine	24	North Carolina	30
Maryland	39	Oklahoma	32
Massachusetts	19	South Carolina	34
Michigan	26	Georgia	36
Minnesota	67	Alabama	37
Mississippi	74	Maryland	39
Missouri	28	Louisiana	55
Montana	19	New Jersey	55
Nebraska	76	Pennsylvania	55
Nevada	15	New York	56
New Hampshire	11	Utah	57
New Jersey	55	Arizona	58
New Mexico	156	Wyoming	62
New York	56	Florida	64
North Carolina	30	Minnesota	67
North Dakota	27	Tennessee	67

(continued)

Table 7.1A *(continued)*

State	No. of services taxed	State	No. of services taxed
Ohio	68	Ohio	68
Oklahoma	32	Washington, DC	70
Oregon	0	Kansas	71
Pennsylvania	55	Arkansas	72
Rhode Island	29	Mississippi	74
South Carolina	34	Wisconsin	74
South Dakota	146	Nebraska	76
Tennessee	67	Connecticut	80
Texas	81	Texas	81
Utah	57	Iowa	94
Vermont	29	West Virginia	110
Virginia	18	Delaware	143
Washington	157	South Dakota	146
West Virginia	110	New Mexico	156
Wisconsin	74	Washington	157
Wyoming	62	Hawaii	160
Average	**55.25490196**	**Median**	**55**

Source: Tax Administrators News 69, no. 5 (May 2005).

represent a big share of these taxes, and they are both quite discretionary and sensitive to economic conditions. Second, revenue over time will not keep up with personal income in the area because of leakage and the trend toward purchase of services. Third, heavy reliance on sales taxes for revenue leads to the pursuit of shopping malls and megastores by cities and counties—with the hope that nonresidents' retail purchases will bring in new tax dollars and local residents will not stray elsewhere. The hunger for short-term revenues may overshadow the long-term costs associated with new development, as we discussed in both Chapter 6 and this chapter.

Putting More Fairness into Local Taxes

A lot of the popular concern with taxes is more about fairness than the efficiency aspects that concern economists. How equitable is the income tax relative to the property tax? Is the sales tax fairer than the property tax? How about special excise taxes on gasoline, cigarettes, or hotel stays? Are there people who do not pay their fair share of taxes? Former Senator Russell Long (Louisiana) is reputed to have once said during a heated Congressional debate over tax reform: "I'll tell you what fairness is . . . it means don't tax you, don't tax me, tax that fellow behind the tree!"

In all seriousness, fairness can be judged by ability to pay or by benefits received. The income tax reflects the ability-to-pay view of fairness. Property taxes reflect the benefits-received principle (Fischel 2001) because they pay for local services and infrastructure that raise the value of local property.[11] They also reflect the amount of wealth potential in the property, which has an element of ability to pay. A major public criticism of the property tax is that retirees with moderate amounts of real estate wealth may have low cash income. However, "circuit breaker" provisions for low-income seniors that exempt a certain level of property from taxes can take care of this problem without eliminating the entire property tax. Reverse mortgages and other financial instruments are also available to seniors if their property has appreciated to substantial amounts and is generating high tax bills. Yet while the property tax is a more stable revenue source and reasonably fair in terms of benefits received, it may encourage sprawling development, as we referenced earlier.

Sales taxes seem more fair to many because they are perceived as related to discretionary purchases (especially when food and prescription drugs are exempted from the tax), and therefore to ability to pay. Many people like the fact that out-of-town visitors pay sales taxes, thus paying for the benefits of visiting their fair city. But as we discussed in Chapter 5, sales taxes violate the ability-to-pay criteria and are the most regressive tax. They collect a much higher percentage of income from low-income people than from middle-income, and from middle-income than from high-income (Davis et al. 2009). This is partly because services and so many other items that high-income people spend money on are exempt. Sales taxes are not as directly related to benefits received as the property tax. They are probably popular with state and local governments because retailers do the job of collecting them. Perhaps because taxpayers pay them little by little they seem less painful than income or property taxes.

Taxes of some kind are a necessary evil to pay for the goods and services that must be provided publicly, so every community needs to choose a reasonable mix of different types. Although no tax is ever viewed as completely fair by everyone, inequities in the total tax burden are fewer when there is less reliance on any one tax.[12] That is why the majority of states have a combination of income, sales, and property taxes. One reason economists worry about high tax rates is that virtually all taxes distort private market signals and can affect how efficiently resources are used. There are fewer distortions to resource allocation when revenue is raised through a range of taxes, since each tax can have a lower rate than would be the case if one tax was used to collect all the revenue. When goods with negative spillovers (like pollution or other harmful activities) are taxed, this actually makes private decisions *more* efficient rather than less. Perhaps someday our whole tax system will have shifted to taxing "bads" rather than goods. For now, we turn in the next section of the appendix to a review of the tax limitation movement and its impact on state and local government.

Appendix 7.2
Property Tax Limits and Tax-Expenditure Limits

Modern movements to limit taxes began in the 1870s in Alabama, Missouri, and Texas with property tax limits.[13] Many more states joined the trend during the Great Depression (O'Sullivan 2001). There was little tax limitation activity in the first three decades after World War II. Then in 1978 California's Proposition 13 passed.[14] Real (inflation-adjusted) taxes per capita fell in California by more than fifty percent by 1995 (Sexton, Sheffrin, and O'Sullivan 1999). Though the tax revolt was associated with middle-class frustrations, the largest cuts actually went to low- and high-income households (Chernick and Reschovsky 1982). Proposition 13 was effectively a "tax" on mobility because it shifted more of the property tax burden to new buyers and discouraged empty-nesters and retirees from moving to smaller housing (Danziger 1980). It increased affordability for existing homeowners but made housing *less affordable* for new buyers. It also resulted in substantial cuts in school funding in California (Silva and Sonstelie 1995). Massachusetts and Michigan were among the many states that followed soon after with their own property tax limits. Illinois established limits in suburban counties surrounding Chicago in 1991.

Did the passage of tax limits show that people thought government was getting too big? Or did they believe that government was operating inefficiently and wasting money? Thirty-eight percent of Californians believed revenues could be sharply cut without cutting services (Citrin 1979). Eighty-two percent of supporters of the Massachusetts limits and 75 percent of supporters of the Michigan amendment also believed service quality could be maintained (Courant, Gramlich, and Rubinfeld 1980). Several factors seem to make voters especially receptive to tax limits. The first and most obvious is increased tax bills at any one level of government. However, there may be other economic problems that squeeze middle- and low-income households, or general lack of trust in government and disagreement with how it is spending. Some public finance experts also see the Supreme Court's school-funding equalization decisions as effectively converting a local property tax into a statewide revenue source, thereby breaking the benefit link between local taxpayers and local schools (Fischel 1989). This may be part of the reason voters seem more ready to accept new sales taxes than new property taxes, even in areas where the property tax is quite low.

Where property values rose very rapidly and property tax bills mushroomed, many people rebelled against what probably seemed unfair taxation. Their income had not increased rapidly, and their benefits received did not either. However, the early 1980s were also the time when the federal government shifted away from revenue-sharing with state and local governments. This federal money had subsidized many local public goods like roads, community development, and public safety. To keep the same level of services, more revenue had to come from somewhere. We move now to the broader tax limits that encompass all types of taxes and all levels of state and local government.

While many states have had statutory restrictions on their spending for decades, comprehensive tax expenditure limits (TELs), such as Colorado's 1992 Taxpayers Bill of Rights (TABOR), are far stricter than limits were historically. They restrict spending at *all* levels of government (state, county, city, school district, and so on) as well as increases in all types of taxes—income, sales, or property. An expenditure limit effectively prevents state governments from circumventing tax limits by raising tuition, changing the cost of hunting and fishing permits, motor vehicle licenses, or other fees to provide more revenue. Similarly, cities or counties cannot increase parking fines or building permits to bring in revenue above the expenditure limit. Total revenues for any level of government cannot increase faster than population plus inflation no matter where the money comes from (federal funds are an exception). If they do, they must be refunded to taxpayers at the end of the fiscal year.

In states that have the initiative and referendum process, these are often voter-approved amendments to the state constitution. When the limits interact with existing laws and other constitutional provisions in ways that most voters have not anticipated, there is no legislative "fix."

Just as in California, the effects of the first TEL (Colorado's TABOR) on school funding were not visible at first but soon became substantial. Several years later, voters approved still another constitutional amendment to increase per pupil funding one percent above inflation for the next ten years, with the TABOR spending limit still on the books. Since the two could not work together a budget crisis loomed in the middle of prosperity. For several years there were refunds to taxpayers at the same time that budgets were slashed. Eventually, a massive statewide campaign for modifications was led by many business groups that had earlier supported TABOR. This shows how difficult it is to make sensible tax and fiscal policy when it is set in general elections and especially in constitutional amendments. In contrast, the legislative process allows for deliberation of unintended consequences and for modifications.

The effects of a TEL go far beyond lowering taxes and shrinking government. Strong TELs that affect local as well as state government give incentives for particular types of land use. Some formulas count annexations and new building as a proxy for local population growth. This means that the spending limit increases when there are annexations and new building while it would not for urban redevelopment. The limits may then bias local government in favor of land development that allows them to keep new revenues versus infill that does not fit the formula. The complexity and variability of the TELs (Brown 2001; Resnick 2008) cause their impact on economic growth and development to vary across the business cycle with the local economic base and with the structure of the TEL in any particular state.

From an economic development perspective, TELs such as TABOR make it impossible to use economic growth to increase the tax base. The limits on spending increase with population growth and inflation, but they do not increase when there is real economic growth (increases in per capita income).[15] In contrast, spending limits in some states are based on growth in per capita income, which allows growth to pay for itself or yield a fiscal surplus as long as governments are keeping per capita costs under control. However, all TELs—regardless of the formula they use to calculate limits—discourage the kinds of public investment that make a state or city an attractive place to live and do business.

Tax reform also becomes more difficult under a TEL because tax cuts are allowed but tax increases to create alternative revenue are not. For example, cutting the sales tax rate would be allowed, but increasing the mill levy or the income tax rate to make up the difference would not be. This holds even if the effect is revenue-neutral (i.e., bringing in the same amount of revenue that the old tax did) or yields a net tax cut. A greater focus on tax reform and the *structure* of taxes could be much more productive in aligning willingness to pay with quality of life and sustainable development, but once a TEL is passed that is very difficult (Resnick 2008).

Efforts to pass these strict limits in states that do not have a TEL (or have a more flexible version) were weakened by the approval of the major modification to Colorado's TABOR discussed above. However, it is likely that the anti-tax movement will continue, albeit with mixed success, as it has in Minnesota, Michigan, New Jersey, Oklahoma, Washington, and Wisconsin in recent years. For a discussion of the effects of initiatives in general on state and local finances, see Mullins (2003).

8

Indicators and Plans for Sustainable Economic Development

Integrating quality of life and sustainability into economic development requires incorporating them into the planning process of cities, counties, and states. Since governments (like businesses) tend to pay more attention to the "bottom line" of what can be measured, communities need new benchmarks for a new direction. However, as we have observed throughout this book, these traditional indicators (job and income growth, retail sales, and housing starts) do not begin to incorporate all aspects of true economic development. Sustainable development requires measures of education and health, housing and opportunity, as well as environmental and cultural resources.

In this chapter, we first define what we mean by "comprehensive" indicators and how they differ from performance indicators. We then explain why it is better to choose many of these indicators locally. We follow with a brief review of several comprehensive indicator projects from around the United States and examples of the indicators they use. We discuss common challenges that these local projects face and recommendations for overcoming these challenges. We focus on going beyond providing information to using it to improve decision making about land use planning, taxes, and spending in local governments.

In the final section of the chapter, we summarize ten myths of economic development that negatively influence quality of life and sustainability of development. We counter by returning to our four rules of economic development first stated in Chapter 1, giving examples of how they can be translated into truths about economic development. First, we define and explain comprehensive indicators.

What Are Comprehensive Indicators and Why Do We Need Them?

By comprehensive indicators, we mean indicators that encompass many aspects of the economy, environment, and society. They have a much larger scope than traditional economic indicators or internal performance indicators. In contract performance indicators measure only inputs or outcomes that public departments or agencies control. This is all well and good, but it misses many aspects of quality of life and sustainability that most people care about. Traditional economic indicators reflect the old view of business as the sole catalyst for growth and innovation, assuming that a higher standard of living will automatically follow when businesses thrive (see Chapter 2). However, growth and technological change depend on more than business investment. Economic development is better predicted by measures that reflect innovation (in technical progress and institutions), the resilience of natural, human, and social capital, and the distribution and sustainability of all capital stocks.

Sustainable development depends on maintaining and investing in capital stocks—human, social, natural, and manufactured capital (private business and infrastructure).[1] Protecting and investing in these capital stocks would be easier if adequate information about them was systematically gathered for public planning. Most currently-used indicators measure flows rather than stocks—for example, the number of housing starts in a period rather than the percentage of the housing stock affordable to the average family. Comprehensive indicators should measure these, even if it is only possible to use proxies.

Traditional economic development emphasizes low taxes or special incentives for business, often at the cost of other capital stocks. The new view recognizes the role of all capital stocks as well as their interrelationships—both synergies and trade-offs—in sustainable development. Comprehensive indicators should stimulate new thinking about investments in *both* the private and public sectors. For example, the large amounts of waste currently produced along with goods and services means that we need *new kinds of infrastructure* that protect the natural capital stock of nonrenewable inputs and environmental services. (This means being cost-effective over the long run, since public buildings or transportation networks that waste energy unnecessarily will not be competitive as the twenty-first century unfolds.) The new view emphasizes using indicators from evidence-based research to overcome the myths of folk economics. This means integrating solid information about what works for economic development, education, crime prevention, resource vulnerability, and a host of other areas into quality-of-life and sustainability indicators (Brugmann 1997).

Strictly speaking, quality-of-life indicators should focus on current aspects of the standard of living not covered by income, such as air and water quality, public education, and safety. Sustainability indicators should focus on the depletion or enhancement of capital stocks, so that the standard of living (income and quality of life) can at least be maintained in the future. In practice, communities do not make a distinction and include both kinds of indicators regardless of how the project is labeled (Greenwood 2004; Portney 2003; Smolko, Strange, and Venetoulis 2006).

We turn now to the question of why comprehensive indicators should be developed locally when there are excellent national systems for collecting economic and environmental data. First, local indicators can include categories of interest beyond what the federal government collects (population without health insurance or acres of impervious surface). Second, they can also explain linkages among different kinds of data (air quality and hospital admissions). Below, we explore additional reasons such as the diversity of communities, differing preferences and priorities, the benefits of the indicator process for local "social capital," and the need for certain actions to be taken locally. We begin with the diverse nature of communities across the United States.

Why Collect New Indicator Data Locally?

Communities across the nation and within each state are different, and that is good. Each community has unique aspects of quality of life and challenges to the sustainability of its development along with the issues it shares with other communities. Conversion of farmland to development raises different issues in different parts of the country. The spawning of salmon has a cultural importance to residents of the Pacific Northwest as well as being an environmental indicator. Communities in other areas would choose a different measure as an environmental bellwether. Locally chosen indicators can account for these unique characteristics and what investments are needed to sustain them. The information in many non-economic indicators (air and water quality, open space or park land, outdoor recreation opportunities, and exposure to environmental hazards) is better measured in connection with place or community rather than with the individual.

Community-based measures are more appropriate for public safety and for measures of trust or neighborliness.[2] Educational performance varies so much among schools and districts that local measurements are important.[3] Cultural and recreational activities are specific to a community. The art museum and the baseball team reflect both opportunities for residents and the character of the community. Communities with indicators to measure these cultural and recreational activities want measures of their social environment as well as their natural environment.

In today's mobile society, people have been increasingly "sorting" themselves into communities with lower taxes and lower services and into those with higher taxes and higher levels of services (Gyourko and Tracy 1991; Tiebout 1956).[4] Even at the same tax level, priorities on how to spend the tax dollar differ widely because quality of life means different things to different people. People with similar values cluster together creating communities with a particular range of values and priorities. While almost everyone says they value education, quality schools are clearly a higher priority in some areas than others. Retirees and empty nesters are likely to concentrate more of the dollar on public safety compared to localities with many children. Creating access to bike paths is a priority in some suburbs while preserving access to hunting may be more important in rural areas. Regulatory priorities also vary. Some communities strive to preserve single-family homes on large lots, while others welcome the density that permits transit options or cultural variety. The information provided in locally chosen indicators reflects these different priorities in a way that state or national indicators cannot. In addition, developing locally based indicators seems to increase the social capital of a community.

The identification and selection process for quality-of-life or sustainability indicators provides an opportunity to build community support for a broader economic development process. An early guide for development of community indicators says, "By convening citizens to consider how to measure their overall well-being, the community as a whole is spurred to create new visions of the future, develop new working relationships across old boundaries, and define its assets, problems, and opportunities in new ways" (Tyler Norris Associates et al. 1997, 1). At their best, community indicators increase engagement and provide a mechanism for accountability of decision makers to act in line with these goals.

For example, Oregon Benchmarks was a response to environmental issues and rapid population growth. It may have led to passage of urban growth boundary legislation for Portland. In Nevada, the pattern was the reverse. Growth management legislation led to an indicators project for Reno so that growth patterns could be compared to target variables before policy changes were considered. The Boston Indicators Project was a response to a high-tech boom that had benefitted many people but resulted in fewer opportunities for others. The rapid increase in housing prices was pushing many young people to move away from the Boston area.

Many aspects of quality of life and sustainability of development are local, and public dissatisfaction in these areas suggests a need for more information and more action. Locally chosen indicators may help to focus energies where states and localities can make a difference (e.g., education, land use, transportation, and water) and away from national and global economic conditions where there is less local influence.[5] Although there has been significant fiscal and regulatory devolution to states and cities, even most "local" indicators are still chosen and collected by federal agencies. This provides standardization and continuity of collection, which are both valuable. However, it does not address specific problems that need to be dealt with locally. Below, we review what led several cities or regions to develop comprehensive indicators and the processes they used.

Local Indicator Projects: Some Examples

Only a few states have attempted comprehensive indicators, while most projects are at the county or metropolitan area level. We use several local indicator projects from around the United States as examples of how they develop and are maintained.[6] They are the quality-of-life indicators of Jacksonville (Duval County, Florida), the sustainability indicators of Seattle (King County, Washington) and greater Austin (central Texas), along with Boston Indicators (Massachusetts). As expected, some priorities differ between these very different areas, but there is also a surprising consistency in the measures chosen. Portney (2003) applauds these cities for collecting indicators and for also using them to inform decisions.

In the 1980s, the city of Jacksonville in northeast Florida was the first to collect and track data on *quality of life*. Their effort was motivated by two concerns. The first was a need for traditional economic development; the second was high rates of poverty in a population with a large share of African Americans. The nonprofit Jacksonville Community Council partnered with the local chamber of commerce to develop a set of indicators. They first convened over one hundred volunteers to establish priorities and make decisions. Five years later, the consolidated city/county government of Jacksonville joined the partnership. The

Jacksonville quality-of-life indicators (www.jcci.org) have been updated annually since 1989 and are the longest continuous set of locally chosen indicators in the United States. Sustainability came into the picture in Jacksonville later, but is now a local initiative.

The first set of comprehensive *sustainability indicators* was developed in Seattle in 1993 by a network of volunteer groups with local corporate and foundation funding. Sustainable Seattle (www.sustainableseattle. org) recieved substantial national, and even international, recognition for this effort. However, a period of very low funding and little staff then followed. As King County became the primary locus for indicators,[7] Sustainable Seattle shifted its emphasis to school workshops, neighborhood forums, and studies on the impact of "buy local" strategies on local business districts (Sustainable Seattle *Sustainability Report 2006*). In 2004, the nonprofit organization received a grant from the Sloan Foundation to measure quality of life at the neighborhood level. Sustainable Seattle has joined with another local nonprofit, Communities Count (www.communitiescount.org) to look at indicators for smaller cities in the area. Sustainable Seattle seems to have been one of the catalysts for a long series of projects that culminated in one of the most integrated sustainability projects in the nation in King County, Washington.

The second catalyst was the state of Washington's growth management legislation in the early 1990s. Its new requirements for local governments provided a focus and a reason to collaborate in new ways. King County had already adopted internal performance indicators for its departments. Then after growth management legislation was passed, city and county leaders began identifying benchmarks to reflect community priorities. The county began with an existing citizen budget priorities process. Using additional community forums and focus groups, they identified what information residents most wanted and the format that would make it easily accessible. A Government Performance Reporting Trailblazer grant from the National Center for Civic Innovation helped to fund this. The next step was to link the external sustainability and quality-of-life indicators that people cared about with internal performance indicators.[8] The result was King County AIMS High (see Annual Indicators and Measures at http://your.kingcounty.gov/aimshigh/index.asp/). Just as in Nevada, growth management legislation in Washington State spurred community development of local indicators.

Another set of sustainability indicators began for somewhat different reasons in the metropolitan statistical area around Austin, Texas. Rapid growth during the 1990s in the high-tech area along with sprawling development led to concerns about the sustainability of water and land use and quality of life. Central Texas Indicators[9] began in the City of Austin planning department with initial guidance from the University of Texas Graduate Program in Community and Regional Planning. Local print and electronic media and other businesses contributed in-kind resources toward completion of the project. Responsibility for annual updates (available at www.centex-indicators.org) rests with an executive director and an otherwise volunteer organization of regional community leaders. This includes representatives from the City of Austin, participating counties, the State of Texas, United Way, and several other nonprofit organizations.

The last project we discuss is Boston Indicators, a joint effort of the Boston Foundation, the City of Boston, and the Metropolitan Area Planning Council. Just as in Austin, this began in the late 1990s in response to a booming economy. This was very good for "knowledge workers," but residents in the Boston area with less education were becoming worse off economically. The first report (2000) focused on economic disparities while the second (2002) was about housing affordability and the outmigration of young people. The Boston Indicators program provides a central clearinghouse where indicators and research from different groups and agencies can be easily available to all. However, the Boston sustainability project is the responsibility of the Department of the Environment rather than part of the overall economic development plan. Portney cites this as an example of how governmental structure can drive the emphasis of an indicator project (2003, 225).

Recent reports from Boston Indicators provide many kinds of information regarding the risks of coastal inundation from global warming and emphasize local strategies for sustainability. The Web site provides information about how the Zip Car and MIT's stackable, foldable car can be paired with greater use of mass transit to reduce local energy use, congestion, and pollution.[10] Boston Indicators now includes a Web site (www.tbf.org/IndicatorsProject) where new data and reports are posted with on-line data-mapping and a data portal leading to other sites. It sponsors leadership forums tied to issues highlighted in its indicator reports and seminars for new and emerging leaders.

These examples show some of the different ways that community-based indicator projects can begin and evolve over time. Some are the result of a depressed economy and others of a growth boom. Some begin with environmental concerns and others with social concerns. All are based on the recognition that traditional income gains, job growth, or retail sales strength are not enough to measure sustainable economic development and quality of life. Each project began with certain local issues and varied its approaches to fit local views and needs.

Examples of Comprehensive Indicators

In the six tables below we provide examples of indicators chosen by the groups above and explain how they attempt to measure (sometimes by proxy) the quality of life or the sustainability of capital stocks. In the first column of each table we name the indicator. In the second we describe whether it is measuring quality of life or sustainability of a capital stock. While the line between these is blurry (affordability is clearly an issue of quality of life, but also may affect future sustainability), we classify indicators by their primary function.[11] Some measures clearly serve in both capacities, particularly those focused on children or young adults. They help to predict future human and social capital as well as indicate current quality of life.

We begin with supplementary economic indicators in Table 8.1. They reflect a more diverse group of interests and values in the community than is seen in traditional economic indicators. The measures go beyond per capita or median income to include poverty rates as well as estimates of how many children live without basic needs being met. Some communities have survey data for this. Others track the percentage of schoolchildren receiving free or reduced-price lunches, to include many living 50 percent or more above official poverty levels. Supplementary economic indicators also include measurements of diversification of the job base and of new patents granted in high-tech economies. These both measure sustainability of the private economy but encompass aspects of the economy not that are in traditional economic indicators.

Environmental and land use quality indicators (Table 8.2) go beyond the federally collected data available for all communities. Rather than measuring "climate" as popular quality-of-life indicators often do, these indicators look at the ways in which human beings and their local decisions relate to the environment. This is an example of a global problem in which the actions of communities spill over to each other. The quality of daily life and health depend on air and water quality as well as proximity to parks or open space. Daily life is affected less directly by

Table 8.1

Supplementary Economic Indicators

Indicator	Capital stock or quality of life (QOL)
Poverty rate	Distribution around per capita income → QOL
% of children in free/reduced school lunch program	Children: sustainability indicator for human capital
% able to buy median-priced home or afford apartment	Affordability of rents, how many can afford average home in → QOL
% change in median income/% change in CPI	How does local income growth compare to local inflation rates? → QOL
New patents granted per capita	Private capital and vitality
% of jobs in largest companies, largest industries	Private capital and diversification/stability

Table 8.2

Environmental and Land Use Quality Indicators

Indicator	Capital stock or quality of life (QOL)
Toxins released in lbs., annually	Sustainability, QOL, health
Solid waste generated per capita per day or recycled per capita	Sustainability of natural capital
Good air quality days or water bodies meeting state standards (%)	QOL, health, visibility, natural capital
Open space/park acreage per 1,000	Sustainability, QOL, natural capital
% living near urban open space	QOL, natural capital
% of land surface impervious to water	Sustainability of land use/landscaping/ flood prevention, natural capital

solid waste, per capita water consumption, and impervious surfaces. We classify these as sustainability indicators because they indicate what is happening to natural capital over time.

Many environmental indicators affect public health, so they are sometimes classified with health indicators. This highlights how interrelated these different aspects of life in a community are. Different communities choose to group indicators in various ways that will not always follow the tables we use here. Indicators of health and public safety in Table 8.3 begin with measures of quality of life and sustainability for human capital. The first two measures are the percentage with no health insurance and the number of nonemergency cases in hospital emergency rooms. Both function as

Table 8.3

Health and Public Safety Indicators

Indicator	Capital stock or quality of life (QOL)
% with no health insurance	QOL: supplements income and employment status as indicator of security
Emergency room use for nonemergencies	QOL: no insurance or family doctor; sustainability: infrastructure utilization
% of babies born at low birth weight	Human capital
Infant mortality rate per 1,000	QOL: low income, drug or alcohol use, lack of prenatal care, or early teen mother
% of youth (12–17) reporting alcohol use	QOL: indicator of youth problems; sustainability: indicator of future alcohol abuse
Packs of cigarettes sold per person	Human capital, QOL
Lung cancer deaths per 100,000	QOL: retrospective of past tobacco use or occupational hazards
% feeling safe walking at night	QOL: Indicator of perceived public safety, sense of neighborhood, social capital
Indexed crime rate per 100,000	QOL: Indicator of public safety, social capital
Family violence or child abuse reports per 1,000	Social capital

measures of health insurance affordability. Since better jobs generally carry health insurance, the percentage with no health insurance is also an indicator of job quality in a community. Emergency room use is also an indicator of local infrastructure utilization since more subsidized clinics are likely to cause less inappropriate use of the emergency room.

The percentage of people who feel safe walking at night could be considered a public-safety indicator or one for social capital. Civic and social participation indicators chosen by communities in Table 8.4 vary based on community issues and whether surveys are available or administrative records are used.[12] While racism is a quality-of-life issue, it also affects the sustainability of human and social capital, particularly in relation to youth and children. Most of these indicators track both quality of life and sustainability of social capital into the future.

Table 8.5 shows a sample of cultural and educational indicators that focus on both availability and use of these resources, as well as attainment. High school graduation rates are indicators of both quality of life and sustainability. They measure where youth in the community are currently, as well as indicating their future prospects and their longer-term

Table 8.4

Civic and Social Participation Indicators

Indicator	Capital stock or quality of life (QOL)
% of registered voters voting in local (vs. presidential) elections	Involvement of citizens in local government, social capital
% reporting trust in city leaders or city government	Social capital
% perceiving local racism or disparities in juvenile courts	Social capital
Suicides per 100,000	QOL, social capital
% volunteering time without pay	Citizen involvement, social capital
% who know or help neighbors	QOL, social capital

Table 8.5

Cultural and Educational Indicators

Indicator	Capital stock or quality of life (QOL)
High school graduation rate	QOL, human capital
% of students at or above grade level according to state test	Better human capital indicator, also QOL
% of licensed child care workers replaced annually	QOL, possible human capital
% attending artistic or cultural activities during past year	QOL: access to and participation in local arts and culture
Library circulation per capita	QOL

impact on the community. Testing at grade level during the earlier years of schooling provides an advance indicator of high school graduation and future job quality, so is an even better sustainability indicator. Turnover among licensed child care workers may be the only readily available proxy for measuring the quality of life for children in day care. Given the importance of good preschool education to future educational attainment, health, and income (Chapter 5), child care is an area where more and better indicators are needed for sustainability measures.

Transportation and mobility indicators are shown in Table 8.6. Accident rates could be classified as an indicator of public safety, but they also indicate transportation quality. Commuting time reflects road congestion, sprawl, or access of residential neighborhoods to commercial centers. Bike lanes and sidewalks indicate the opportunities for alternative transit

Table 8.6

Transportation and Mobility Indicators

Indicator	Capital stock or quality of life (QOL)
Average commute or % commuting <25 minutes	QOL, infrastructure
Vehicle miles per capita (daily)	Land use patterns as well as distance from job or school, QOL, infrastructure
Vehicle accidents per 1,000	QOL, infrastructure
% street miles with sidewalks or bike lanes	QOL, infrastructure
Direct air flight destinations daily; Bus or light rail service	Business and tourism access, QOL Infrastructure, mobility options, QOL

as well as for health through outdoor exercise. Direct air flights show the connectivity of smaller cities to larger commercial centers, which can be quite important for tourism and for business travel. Public transit options such as bus and light rail relieve congestion but also provide mobility options for youth, the elderly, and those with a disability or medical conditions that preclude driving.

Many of the indicators in these tables emphasize elements of quality of life and sustainability that benefit existing residents as well as those that would attract visitors or new residents. Some of the indicators give advance warning of actions that are unsustainable. Linking sustainability indicators to their effect on specific capital stocks (water supply, tree coverage, and educational resources) could help to bridge the gap between indicators that resonate with the public and indicators that align policy and decisions with long-term sustainability. Below, we examine some of the real challenges to communities that want to follow these examples and to others around the nation and the world.

Challenges and Recommendations for Local Indicator Projects

There are many challenges to successful indicator projects. This probably explains the relatively small group of successful ones compared to the many communities that have started them. The challenges include: 1) identifying the reason for the project and its goals and focus, 2) choosing key indicators that are useful and that resonate with people, 3) collecting the data and sustaining this over time, and 4) using indicators to evaluate policy choices even when there are difficult trade-offs.[13] We address each below, along with recommendations for overcoming it. We begin with some reasons communities start indicator projects and how this affects the usefulness of the project.

Some indicator projects have the unstated goal of gathering positive evidence to use in recruiting businesses or jobs (Rogerson 1999). If the reason for indicators is primarily to promote how "good" the community already is then indicators likely to reveal problems may be omitted. This interferes with indicator use as a tool to improve over the long term. A second reason that communities start an indicator project is in reaction to a shock to the local economy. This might be a major plant closure but could also be an influx of new residents. Once the shock has been weathered the community or its leaders may lose interest and fail to support continued data collection, analysis, and reporting.

To be successful the reason for the project needs to be more than short term, since choice of indicators and data collection takes time. A third reason for many indicator projects may be concerns in one area, such as health, the environment, the local economy, or children's well-being. These narrower areas generally have stronger constituencies than comprehensive indicator projects because they relate directly to the concerns of certain groups. However, these projects are less likely to lead to the kinds of changes we advocate in this book because they do not address the interrelationships between environment, economy, and society.

After meeting the first challenge of deciding the scope and goals of the indicator project, the second challenge is choosing measures to match the goal. Very general survey questions such as "How would you rate your quality of life?" are popular but not very useful since they tend to be answered as "good" or "excellent" by the overwhelming majority of people in any community. This says less about community characteristics than about people's attitudes toward their own lives. Any local indicator project must choose from many available measures from federal sources, state and local administrative records, and nonprofit organizations. These may be familiar, and their availability lowers the costs of collection. However, the data that is most readily available is not necessarily the data most relevant for policy decisions. It is important to commit to measurement of some (but not too many) key areas where there is no current data.

We recommend considering indicators that other communities have used before going into the process of developing whatever unique indicators will be measured locally. It is also important to be able to sustain collection of this additional data to track changes over time. However, data collection requires a serious commitment of resources along with the patience to wait for results. Lack of funding, internal community conflicts, and shifting interests are often responsible for projects that die on the vine.

Competing interests will surface with different opinions about what to measure. Controversial choices will displease some people. There may also be "tension between scientific rigor and public values and perceptions" (Brugmann 1997, 63). At this point, an intensive educational process may be required to explain why some measures are more reliable or more appropriate than others. For example, if the public is concerned about rising juvenile crime rates, it needs to know the research on effectiveness of community policing versus intervention with at-risk youth and families versus passage of tough new laws. Otherwise, the indicators that should be measured along with the actual rate of juvenile crime may be the wrong ones.

Indicators can also create a frame of reference in which policy decisions are made, since their very existence implies certain priorities. Probably as difficult as selecting indicators or sustaining their collection is getting people to acknowledge that there are trade-offs. It is easy to get people to agree that they want *more* of everything good and *less* of everything bad. The lack of explicit trade-offs in indicator projects is one of the most important criticisms from an economic perspective. Of course, one should start with any "win-win" improvements that can be made, but there will only be so many. Not everyone recognizes that more of one infrastructure (roads) will create less of another (open space and flood absorption capacity) until indicators are used to help make a decision about a proposed new road. Dealing with trade-offs is never politically popular.

However, good indicator projects make explicit the interdependence of economy, environment, and society and the trade-offs that often occur between these groups as well as within them. At some point, improving public education is likely to cost more tax money. A policy that is good for conserving water (the environment) may make it more expensive to maintain lawns and parks (green infrastructure). A decision that is good for economic growth (bringing in a large new industry) may have costs to the environment and sense of local community.

Developing a community consensus, choosing the right set of key indicators, maintaining their collection and publication over time, and using these indicators in decisions that may require difficult trade-offs, demands the involvement of a broad spectrum of the community, an issue that we address next. Indicators reflect community values more accurately if the selection process is widely advertised and involves a wide range of local stakeholders. Indicators chosen primarily by government staff or by local economic development groups or foundations are less effective in facilitating dialogue and change than those developed from a broader base. While being inclusive may appear cumbersome and time-consuming, examples of how to proceed already exist (see Hart 1999; Portney 2003, ch. 2; Redefining Progress 2006).

Clarity and reliability of each indicator can be improved by "test runs" before stakeholder and citizen groups. Including enough experts helps ensure that the measures chosen are reliable and policy relevant (see Brugmann 1997). This is a delicate balance, since the process should not be overly controlled by experts and insiders. Public participation and education must be more than mere public relations. Without broad public support, changes in individual behavior necessary to improve quality of life and sustainability of development will be much slower. Translating findings into action requires broad public acceptance of relationships, such as fuel consumption and increased pollution, or preschool education and better socialization. This is why the educational component is such an important part of both the selection process and later presentation.

Presentation that is accessible, accurate, and readable is important. Sustainable Seattle used a very easily understood format with a one-page summary chart that provided a quick overview. The supporting document contained more detail. Arrows showed either improvement ↑, worsening ↓, or no change ↔ for each individual indicator. Full-page discussions for each indicator explained 1) its importance and why it was chosen; 2) how the indicator was affected by other factors; 3) the effects of changes in the indicator on quality of life or sustainability; and 4) the source of the data and any measurement issues. Several indicators were collected in each group (environment, population and resources, economy, youth and education, health and community). Each of these groups also received a directional arrow reflecting overall level and degree of change.

Use of Web pages has revolutionized the local indicator process just as it has many other areas of modern life. But local media still have an important role in bringing public attention regularly (not just for one annual report a year!) to the indicators and the trends and relationships the indicator reports demonstrate.[14] It is important that the presentation go beyond providing information to link changes in indicators to the actions of individuals, businesses, nonprofits, and government. This linkage is the first step in using indicators to shape policy and improve accountability in states and localities.

Integrating the indicators into accountability tools and using them to inform key policy decisions is critical to whether they lead to real changes in sustainability and quality of life. This fourth challenge is so important that we devote a special section to using comprehensive indicators. They can improve the accountability of state and local governments and help in setting policies and budgets that are in line with public preferences and real world constraints.

Using Indicators to Set Policies: Long-Term Planning and Budgets

Many states and localities already use performance indicators to measure internal variables such as police response time or cost per mile of road resurfacing. In contrast to performance indicators, community indicators relate to the end results people care about—safety, traffic delays and congestion, economic and cultural vitality—and the outside forces driving them. King County, Washington, is now linking performance indicators to comprehensive community indicators to influence policy. Oregon Benchmarks, the City of Santa Monica's Sustainable Development Plan, and Sustainable Portland are examples of other indicator projects that have helped to integrate comprehensive indicators into planning processes.

Indicators can be used to precisely define the meaning of broad goals—such as "increase economic well-being" or "preserve quality of life"—for elected officials and government departments. If affordable housing, less traffic congestion, and preservation of open space are all goals than this points to certain kinds of infrastructure development and zoning and building policies and it is appropriate to invest in that direction. Along with considering the *fiscal* impact of regulations and policies (including effects on school districts, colleges, and other local governments), the impact on the local economy and quality of life should be carefully evaluated rather than assumed.

Moving beyond performance indicators to broader indicators puts the burden on decision makers to examine how their actions and policies reflect specific community goals. This can help guard against several pitfalls. First, it is generally easiest to keep on doing things in the "obviously correct" way that they have always been done. Second, governments are always likely to be more responsive to special-interest pleadings because they hear from these groups more regularly than they hear from the average citizen. Third, many elected officials and staff are frustrated by inconsistent voter demands, such as "cut my taxes" but at the same time "increase spending on education" or "improve our roads."

Indicators can provide a mechanism for the accountability of local decision makers. Zoning and other regulations, budgets, and tax structures should all be consistent with the quality-of-life and sustainability goals expressed by citizens to achieve economic development that fits community needs and aspirations. Otherwise, economic growth will be unsustainable or will bring problems that cancel out its benefits. The accountability aspect of indicators can also help to guard against the first two of these pitfalls—doing it the same old way and giving priority to special pleaders. The trade-off aspect of indicators can help in explaining to the public what the tough choices are.

Concluding Remarks: What *Can* Make a Difference in Local Economic Development?

We began in Chapter 1 by calling for a new path for local economic development that incorporates quality of life and sustainability with economic growth. We are not the first to note the inefficiency in both dollars and results of pursuing economic development, environmental protection, and community quality of life separately (see, in particular, Deller, Lledo, and Marcouiller 2008). A joint strategy can pursue them simultaneously rather than expecting that growth will produce quality of life or make environmental protection affordable.

Chapter 2, for example, emphasized the many reasons that tax incentives for business location or expansion are neither cost effective nor the best way to improve a local economy. In addition to the fact that investments in private capital are best made as private decisions rather than by government, these incentives come at the expense of investing in other capital stocks. Traditional economic development has focused on helping private business, sometimes looking backward to try to restore days gone by. This is the "rear view mirror" that Thomas Power (1996b) talks about.

Chapter 3 considered how important social capital is to both the economy and quality of life and how public policies can inadvertently enhance or weaken it. Achieving the right mix of stability and flexibility to encourage innovation and creativity is not a function of any single policy but of a larger atmosphere in which schools, businesses, and government operate. Chapter 4 focused on essential natural resources, such as water and how water scarcity can undermine economic development plans. It suggested finding new resources in what has long been discarded as "waste."

Chapter 5 took some new perspectives on human capital, outlining the relationship of state and local decisions to opportunity and an affordable lifestyle. This is "percolate up" economic development that improves earnings and quality of life for the workers and provides returns for local government as well. Attracting more highly educated people to a community boosts human capital levels in the short-term, but can also increase economic and social divisions. Broadly-based improvements in local education will be needed to sustain higher human capital and to benefit the entire community.

Chapter 6 concentrated on the effects of sprawling development for transportation, affordability, quality of life, and sustainability. Chapter 7 examined their effects on the ways in which growth impacts local government budgets. Whether there is a fiscal dividend or a budget shortfall may depend on local land use and transportation decisions along with tax and fee structures. The predominant view of state and local governments, including their planning departments, seems to be "growth is good as well as inevitable." What is called growth management most often tries to accommodate existing preferences in growth patterns, with occasional efforts to minimize negative environmental or social impacts (Warner and Molotch 2000). We think it no accident that rising costs in housing and transportation followed a radical shift to auto-oriented development patterns that use more and more land per person, and a period of high economic growth.

The tax revolt, along with increasing concerns about quality of life and sustainability, shows that it is time for a new path. Traditional methods of economic development such as business incentives have wasted untold dollars of taxpayer money. The emphasis on business climate, especially national ratings that pit one state or city against another, has often come at the expense of quality of life and sustainability of development. State and local governments have often worked at cross-purposes in pursuing economic development and quality of life. The result has been lack of fiscal sustainability along with unsustainable behavior in regard to natural resources and other capital stocks. A new model will produce better results and probably save tax dollars in the long run.

By definition, not everything can be a priority at the same time. When communities develop strategic plans that claim this is possible they may satisfy a broad group of constituents but they have not prepared a tool that will be useful for difficult policy choices. A top priority for one area inevitably means that other areas will be second priority at best. We have found that the traditional model of putting growth first and assuming that it will create quality of life and sustainability has not delivered. Instead, using much more specific information about citizen priorities and the linkages between them can provide a sustainable economic development for the twenty-first century that integrates quality of life.

Since income alone is not a satisfactory measure of the standard of living, pursuing higher paying jobs or higher community incomes will not always increase nonmarket elements of quality of life. Many environmental or social aspects may be damaged by economic growth. The future of local economic development lies in areas where state and local governments can make a difference in the standard of living: land use (including urban design), transportation and education, and preservation of water, wildlife, and scenic beauty. Truly smart growth must be growth that citizens are willing to pay for over time and growth that maintains or increases their quality of life.

Local governments have limited control over economic patterns but a greater ability to influence the path of economic *development,* since so many aspects of quality of life are partially in their control. Public safety, education, social services, parks and open space, cultural activities, and transportation are largely state and local functions. There is substantial discretion over the level and composition of spending. Local governments shape land-use patterns with their control over infrastructure, water, and wastewater, and their provision of public safety and public schools, not to mention zoning. The quality of air and water, the preservation of land from toxic wastes, and the sustainability of local agriculture and other natural resource industries are dependent in part on local decisions. Local decisions shape the formation and sustenance of social capital, the "glue" that holds communities together and fosters the development of healthy youth for the next generation. This requires not just a good educational system but broad access to health care, child protection, and many other aspects often thought of as "social services" that support a sustainable economic system over time. Transportation options, including commuter bike trails, affect health and job options as well as the environment and land values. Local actions and decisions also have ripple effects on global sustainability.

We close with ten myths discussed throughout the book that have often led economic development efforts in the wrong direction:

1. Job growth or population growth will always create higher average incomes and quality of life.
2. The economy and the environment are separate entities that compete with each other.
3. If incentives can encourage other public policies goals (recycling or attending college), it makes sense to use them to bring in new businesses.
4. Economic growth creates the financial resources for environmental protection.
5. "Growth pays for itself," i.e., can solve fiscal problems in states or local communities.
6. Science and technology can create substitutes to deal with any damages from growth.
7. Economic growth always creates upward mobility and reduces poverty.
8. Industrial agriculture improves the standard of living by bringing food prices down.
9. Since officials are democratically elected and accountable, there is no need to develop additional indicators of public values and priorities.
10. Markets respond well to changing consumer demand, so they will also do a great job in environmental protection, public education, and improving quality of life.

Myths are myths because they have hardened in people's minds. We hope that our book has given good reasons to seriously question these and other myths. In place of them, we go back to the beginning of this book with our four rules for economic development:

1. Economic growth alone is not economic development.
2. The standard of living is more than income; it includes many nonmonetary aspects of quality of life.
3. True economic development must be sustainable over time rather than be based on resources that will be needed by future generations.
4. Fourth, improvements in the standard of living must be broadly based, reaching the overwhelming majority of the population.

We hope this book has persuaded you of the importance of these rules in setting practice and policy. Using them as guidelines, we believe that communities can achieve economic development that fits their values and is also compatible with the quality of life they wish for themselves and their children.

Notes

Chapter 1

1. While we believe the principles we use in this book are universal, the examples here apply primarily to the United States.

2. See Adkisson (2009a), Deller et al. (2008), Green et al. (2005), and Shaffer et al. (2004), for work that parallels some of our approach.

3. Gunnar Myrdal (1973) first made this distinction. Though largely ignored by traditional economists, a small body of work has continued to emphasize the difference between growth and development, including Boulding (1993), Brinkman (1995), Street (1987), Daly (1996), Norgaard (1994), and Goodwin (1997). For a review of how various schools of economic thought have treated the distinction between growth and development, see Greenwood and Holt (2009).

4. An additional confusion of terms comes from the fact that land development or construction of new buildings is sometimes called "economic development," regardless of its effect on economic growth.

5. This is often called the "Easterlin paradox" (after Richard Easterlin, 1974, 1995, 2003). While this analysis has received some criticism (Hagerty and Veenhoven 2003; Stevenson and Wolfers 2008), it remains clear that income is not the only important factor in determining happiness (Akst 2008) and that relative income matters as much or more than absolute income level. We discuss this more in Chapter 5.

6. Higher standards of living have many different dimensions that go beyond simple economic growth measurements. See Deller, Lledo, and Marcouiller's call for more work to be done to develop "specific indicators of development rather than simplistic and myopic measures of economic growth. Issues that address distributional implications, transitions in economic structure, and regional zero-sum tradeoffs represent a clearer focus on regional development indicators" (2008, 17).

7. Some question the concept of a local economy, since it is impossible to define the boundaries of any particular "economy" inside a nation with one financial currency. Although state or city boundaries are political lines rather than economic boundaries, we believe there is a place for the idea of a local economy. While there are no official boundaries on a "local economy," most people live, go to school, do daily shopping, and work primarily within a particular geographic area. In addition, as we discuss in Chapter 3, quality of life depends heavily on local elements. Therefore, throughout this book we refer to local, state, and regional "economies" with the caveats mentioned above.

8. For a discussion of the important role of amenities and quality of life in rural development, see Deller et al. 2008, Green et al. 2005, and Marcouiller 2005.

9. In defining each of these capitals we note that the products of a capital stock are not necessarily "good," as the products of any kind of capital can sometimes be unhealthy or dangerous.

10. Portions of this discussion are taken from Greenwood and Holt (2009).

11. Recent work of Shaffer, Deller, and Marcouiller (2006) on community development also calls for attention to public capital, technology, society, and institutions along with the traditional factors of production.

12. The origins of this idea can be traced to the work of Robert Frank (1989, 1999, 2007).

13. By fiscal sustainability, we mean relatively constant revenues per person as population increases, land use patterns change, or the community becomes more affluent. This allows services for new residents to be paid for under existing tax levels and structures without a decline in services for existing residents. Higher taxes pay for increased levels of service or costs driven by external forces such as higher worldwide energy prices, rather than coming because of local population growth.

14. The term *conventional wisdom* comes from John Kenneth Galbraith (1969), while Thomas M. Power (1996a) coined the phrase *folk economics*. Both describe widespread beliefs about society or the economy and how it works. Some aspects of each come from what has been called traditional or mainstream economics (Colander, Holt, and Rosser 2004). However, there are also a fair number of "urban legends" nowhere to be found in scholarly economics that make their way into the conventional wisdom or folk economics. Throughout the book we try to identify where ideas are aligned with traditional economic thinking and where they derive primarily from urban legend.

Chapter 2

1. In later chapters, we focus on quality of life, sustainability, and opportunity.

2. Landowners at the fringe of the city, builders, newspaper and television stations, and other local businesses are generally important constituencies that are satisfied.

3. Urban economists and regional scientists are well aware of the defects in export-base models, but many economic development practitioners see them as making intuitive sense and too few explore other alternatives. We thank P. Kozlowski for this observation and for his concise explanation of why the export-base model does not measure economic growth. In technical terms, it is a static model that measures economic impacts, rather than a dynamic model that shows growth. However, in the lore of "folk economics" these impacts turn into growth.

4. Kolko and Neumark (2009) find that some types of local ownership insulate regions from economic shocks. The clearest benefits come from corporate headquarters and, to a lesser extent, from small, locally owned chains.

5. Many urban and regional economists recommend input–output models (such as IMPLAN, REMI, or RIMS) for analyzing local and regional growth, rather than the economic base model (Rickman and Schwer 1995). An even more sophisticated computerized general equilibrium model can differentiate effects on different sectors (Cutler and Davies 2006).

6. In addition to tuition paid by students, direct and indirect state and federal money helps to pay faculty and staff salaries. Students as well as visiting parents spend part of their consumption dollars in the community. In the long term, the university is much less likely than a business to relocate and much more likely to contribute new ideas and vitality to the local economy. Graduates who like the area may stay to work, raise families, and become involved members of the community. One reason for economic vitality in many university towns is the new business start-ups by recent graduates.

7. As we discuss in Chapter 8, there will be different effects on the tax base of the community.

8. The pure fiscal effect on local government is almost always negative, according to Bartik, unless a community has so much overcapacity in infrastructure that it does not have to worry about expansion costs. New taxpayers created by growth then provide a net benefit to local government by increasing the tax base. Otherwise, there is a vicious circle created where more infrastructure is needed for growth, increasing

cost to existing taxpayers. This in turn leads to arguments for more growth to pay for the infrastructure!

9. We note that the match of skills between new jobs and current population in any particular community can cause this to be slightly higher or lower.

10. We say "perceived" because Leroy (2007) documents how many site consultants play both sides of the fence in creating an impression that there are other likely candidates for locations when there may not actually be.

11. We recognize the importance of local educational systems to some businesses, but argue for nonideological indicators of a good business climate that focus on competency measures of local graduates or access to various types of education (vocational, college track, higher education) rather than getting involved in the debate over methods for achieving competency.

12. The BHI index is a "hopeless mishmash of causal and performance variables that render it useless as an overall predictor of anything" writes Fisher (2005, 72), who explores which factors go into a variety of different ratings and the design flaws that plague many of them.

13. Wayslenko and McGuire (1985) found that low taxes helped in some areas, but other areas did very well economically with high taxes if they provided high levels of education and infrastructure. This research was an early indication of the diversity of factors that can attract various types of businesses.

14. After all, if high levels of exports were the way to create wealth, the U.S. economy would have been in the doldrums in the 1950s and 1960s (one of our periods of greatest economic prosperity!) when exports constituted a much lower share of national output. If wealth were based on natural resources, many poor countries in the world like Nigeria or Sierra Leone would be wealthy and countries like Holland and Denmark would be poor.

15. Luria and Rogers (2008) advocate moving toward more "self-supply" for a more people-centered economic development and higher quality of life, as does Shuman (1998). Both emphasize the role of globalization in increased energy usage, lost jobs or lower wages (at least for some), and more dependence. Communities can regain some control over their economy by producing locally when economically feasible for the community rather than only when it meets the profitability target of a distant corporate headquarters, according to Shuman. However, there are pitfalls in going too far with a self-sufficient approach to the economy, as any economist will stress. It may increase costs for consumers and local businesses by limiting outside competition. Local governments can require their own purchases or contracts to give preference to local suppliers, but this may not be an efficient use of taxpayer dollars when other providers offer lower prices. The "going local" strategy requires a carefully thought-through plan as to where it makes sense and where it does not. We discuss examples in Chapters 3 and 4.

16. The South Shore Bank of Chicago, Community Capital Bank of Brooklyn, Union Savings Bank of Albuquerque, and Self-Help Credit Union of Durham, North Carolina, were cited in a list that includes banks, credit unions, thrifts, or lending circles (Sherman 1998). While this contrasts with recent trends in banking and financial services, in the post–subprime mortgage meltdown world there may be more interest in this. There is considerable discussion in favor of smaller banks that are not "too big to fail" and of the relative health of community banks compared to the behemoths.

17. Viking Range Corporation and Brueck Construction, two prominent examples of local companies that have succeeded, both recently received the Main Street Leadership Award for their positive effects on a struggling community.

18. The term *economic gardening* has been attributed to Phil Burgess of the Center for the New West in Denver, Colorado, which was working with the City of Littleton

in the late 1980s. Littleton's economic gardening program won the National League of Cities innovation award in 1998.

19. In contrast, those who ascend the corporate ladder to head a large organization such as a corporation (or a government bureau) have very different temperaments and are likely to be resistant to change. In Myers-Briggs terminology, the NTJ or "Intuitive-Thinking-Judging" types were most successful in INC 500 start-ups, while SJ "Guardians" types dominated the leadership of large corporations. (Center for Application of Psychological Type, Tallahassee, Florida, as cited by Chris Gibbons.)

20. Quote used by permission of Chris Gibbons, July 17, 2009.

21. Beinhocker brings this argument to life with many historical and contemporary examples. Both a recent review (Adkisson 2009b and a discussion in the "Notes and Communications" section (Wunder 2009) comment on Beinhocker's integration of complexity, path dependency, and other post-Keynesian and institutionalist ideas into a very readable, real-world analysis.

22. Communities with a culture of self-employment suffer less when there are lay-offs from large business because workers turn to other, sometimes home-based, earning activities.

23. Hometown businesses are more likely to support local charities, to be involved in civic efforts, and to create the social capital we discuss further in the following chapter. The commercial districts they inhabit are often the ones with the local color that longtime residents and visitors want to frequent as an alternative to the sameness of malls and big-box stores, supporting the quality of place we discuss in Chapter 3.

24. For a recent study sponsored by the Small Business Advocacy office, see Acs, Parsons, and Tracy (2008).

25. Sales-tax revenues, the major source of funding to Littleton's city government, also tripled during the same period from $6.8 million to $19.6 million, despite two major recessions.

26. Discussion of economic gardening has become a formal part of state economic development conferences in California, where Berkeley, Oakland, and San Bernardino are actively pursuing economic gardening. Other communities, including Santa Fe (New Mexico), Lancaster County (Pennsylvania), and Steamboat Springs (Colorado) have experimented with the approach. The South Dakota Rural Enterprise network (www.sdrei.org) lists many other communities around the United States interested in economic gardening. Conferences attract participants from Australia and New Zealand. For more information on economic gardening, including how to join a list serve, see www.littletongov.org/bia/economicgardening.

27. "The heart of the program is mining information from high-powered databases, GIS, and other information tools to increase the competitiveness and success of Littleton businesses. Another pillar of the program is paying attention to infrastructure—creating a city where entrepreneurs want to live and people want to do business. The city has invested heavily in its roads, trails, and cultural amenities, and has provided support to the historic downtown business area. A third emphasis is building connections among the businesses in the city by facilitating industry clusters and cross-marketing opportunities, and strengthening connections between industry and the higher education sector" (Christine Pennell, City of Littleton Business Development Office, *Newsletter* 7, no. 6 [November/December 2004]).

Chapter 3

1. Shapiro (2006) attributes part of the growth in employment of the college-educated in successful urban areas to higher quality of life. There is also a substantial literature

in regional economics on firm location and individual migration and how they relate to amenities of quality of life (Bartik 1991, 2007; Benedetti 2008; Greenwood and Hunt 1989). These include climate and geography, which individual communities have almost no ability to influence. In this book, we focus on the many elements of quality of life that can be influenced by state or local policies.

2. Personal income, the measure most often used at the state and local level, is derived from GDP (gross domestic product) and thus has many of the same strengths and weaknesses. In Appendix 3.1 to this chapter we review briefly the development of GDP as a measure of national economic activity. In Appendix 3.2 we also look at the misuse of GDP as a measure of well-being and discuss an alternative national measure called the genuine progress index (GPI).

3. Income is actually less precise than it first appears. "Census money income" is different from the "adjusted gross income" stipulated by the Internal Revenue Service for tax calculation purposes. Questions about how to best measure income for other purposes are still hotly debated. Should unrealized capital gains be included? Should housing vouchers or food stamps be counted as income? Should the unpaid services of household members providing care or labor to the family be included? Income is a more familiar measure than quality of life but not necessarily an objective or precise one.

4. This is Duesenberry's relative income hypothesis reborn but with some additions by Frank, who points out the real pressures in the workplace and society to meet the higher consumption standards.

5. An example of a somewhat different use of the term *quality of life* comes from the medical field where it deals with individual patient outcomes from treatments for various diseases or injuries.

6. For more on economic uses of happiness data, see Kahneman and Krueger (2006), Di Tella and MacCulloch (2006), and Clark, Fritjers, and Shields (2008).

7. A *Washington Post* article calls the increase in childhood obesity since 1990 an "epidemic" and cites evidence that it is likely to result in a two- to five-year drop in life expectancy for current youth, along with billions of dollars more spent in health care and effects on worker productivity (Levine and Stein 2008). See also Miringoff and Opdycke (2008, 71–74).

8. For example, infant mortality is lower in Cuba and twenty other countries. Patients see a doctor more often in Great Britain and have better health outcomes at every income level, despite far lower spending on health care.

9. Many experts in the medical field suggest that reallocating the way dollars are spent within medicine—more on prevention and less on critical care could produce a higher quality result. For a discussion of varying results from different protocols within the field of medicine see Leonhardt (2009). This is an example of effects on quality from the way income or growth is allocated among different priorities.

10. We thank Bob Powell of Continuous Improvement Associates for early discussions around economic development in which he emphasized the importance of the "attractiveness principle." Equilibrium is reached as the standard of living in the high quality area falls enough that no area has a total package of characteristics that is better than any other area.

11. This is somewhat similar to the contrast between "high and low" roads to economic development. Global market forces can operate to gradually lower the pay and benefits of American workers, or investments in higher productivity can be made in these workers to keep them competitive at higher pay levels.

12. Measures of quality of life should be oriented toward current outcomes and specific community values. Sustainability refers to the preservation of capital stocks used to

produce quality of life in the future. To assess changes in the current standard of living, indicators of quality of life are appropriate. To assess expected changes in the future levels of capital stocks and the inherent linkages between them, sustainability indicators are appropriate. But most indicator projects contain both kinds of measures regardless of their name (see Greenwood 2004 for examples).

13. For example, a recent study of the "Tiebout effect" (voting with your feet) finds that people will pay more to live in an area with high environmental quality (Banzhaf and Walsh 2008; Gabriel, Mattey and Wascher 2004).

14. This deterioration stems primarily from increased traffic congestion due to spending on infrastructure that did not keep up with population growth and also due to air pollution.

15. Other indicators, such as housing affordability and demand for parks or open space, probably reflect both costs of growth and higher demand for amenities.

16. Adkisson (2009a) raises the important question, "Which are the 'right' institutions?" for sustainability

17. However, social capital does not necessarily lead to positive results. Established informal arrangements can support racism or other forms of exclusion, and may be used to block technological or social innovations. Private business capital can also have positive or negative effects. It can help human labor produce much more cheaply and efficiently, but it can also create "bads" of pollution or serious injury. We do not see the fact that bad results can come from "clannishness" to be a valid criticism of the idea of social capital. Instead, it shows that any capital stock can be put to good or bad uses.

18. The question of whether people follow jobs or jobs follow people has been explored by Greenwood (1989), Power (1996a), and Partridge and Rickman (2003, 2006).

19. The "super-creative core" of the workforce is the 12 percent of workers who create new ideas, technology, and creative content in science and engineering, architecture and design, education, arts, music, and entertainment. A broader group of "creative professionals" in finance, law, and health care "engage in complex problem solving that involves a great deal of independent judgment and requires high levels of education or human capital" (Florida 2002, 7–9).

20. Large U.S. cities (San Francisco, Austin, San Diego, Boston, Seattle, Chapel Hill, Houston, Washington, New York, Dallas, and Minneapolis) in Richard Florida's 2002 ranking were those attracting and retaining a super-creative core of workers. Five were also in the top ten just three years earlier—Washington, Austin, San Francisco, Seattle, and Houston. New York moved up from the next ten where it had been in 1999. Between 1999 and 2002, Raleigh-Durham, Boston, Minneapolis, Hartford (Connecticut), and Denver dropped off the top ten. We observe that in an economy with volatile sectors, such as the dot-com and financial sectors, this kind of ranking appears unstable as a short-term indicator, although it provides information about the depth of labor force quality in an area (Florida 2002).

21. A special issue of the *Economic Development Quarterly: The Journal of American Economic Revitalization* includes papers dealing with the Florida approach. See Sands and Reese (2008), Markusen et al. (2008), and Donegan and Lowe (2008).

22. John Kenneth Galbraith wrote the first edition of his classic *The Affluent Society* in 1958, and it has since been continuously in print. In Greenwood and Holt (2007) and other works, we explore his early identification of many of today's problems.

23. The community development literature on rural economies has taken the lead on this (see Shaffer, Deller, and Marcoullier 2006).

24. The index of sustainable economic welfare (ISEW) dates to 1989, according to

Daly (1996, 151). Along with John and Clifford Cobb (1989), Daly developed the index in response to debates over the appropriateness of GDP as a measure.

Chapter 4

1. California's stricter standards have since been proposed for national adoption, demonstrating that sometimes states can act alone and influence national policy (it helps to be big).

2. Preserving habitat for wildlife is a value that many hold as well as having potential tourism and other long-term benefits as well as contributing to quality of life for many people. Many argue that nature has innate value apart from how well it serves the needs of human beings, but we do not believe that debate must be resolved before recognizing the need to deal with preserving natural capital in a new way.

3. While contingent valuation methods can be used to estimate marketlike values, there is substantial criticism of this method.

4. Some environmentalists assert that there is no such thing as sustainable development, although it is more likely that they recognize current growth and consumption patterns as unsustainable. Growth in income (and certainly in well-being) can happen without producing more waste products or depleting natural resources. As a larger share of income is earned through services (child care, massage therapy, landscaping) and the arts and recreation, traditional goods production with its associated environmental costs is greatly reduced. On the other hand, our definition is stricter than some neoclassical economists would agree with. For more on the assumptions behind different definitions of sustainable development, see note 5.

5. The issue of how extensively manufactured capital or new techniques (human capital) can substitute for capital is debated by economists. A "weak" sustainability criterion assumes more substitution possibilities to compensate for lost natural capital, whereas a "strong" criterion assumes less. As a result, neoclassical economists and ecological economists disagree on the definition of sustainable development. Neoclassical economists such as Solow (1992) define sustainability as ensuring that losses of a nonrenewable or renewable resource (natural capital) can be substituted for by additions to human-made capital of equal value (the "weak" definition). Advocates of "strong" criteria define sustainability as preserving existing natural capital stocks due to their unique qualities (Holt 2005, 176).

6. Systems analysis was first used in more limited situations to understand the complex interrelationships within an industrial facility. However, it also applies to the much larger scale of complex interrelationships between economy, environment, and society. Alfeld (1995) provides an excellent summary of applying systems thinking to local economic development. We thank Bob Powell of Continuous Improvement Systems for directing us to this source.

7. According to the U.S. Environmental Protection Agency, "With certain legal exclusions and additions, the term *brownfield site* means real property, the expansion, redevelopment, or reuse of which may be complicated by the presence or potential presence of a hazardous substance, pollutant, or contaminant. Environmental Protection Agency, Brownfields and Land Revitalization (no date), http://epa.gov/brownfields/glossary.htm (accessed June 12, 2009).

8. From ICMA newsletter copyrighted by American City Business Journals, Inc., June 16, 2008.

9. The Clean Water Act (1972) successfully reduced many direct sources of water pollution from industry but left non-point sources to the states. Environmental Protection Agency, Clean Water Act (no date), www.epa.gov/oecaagct/lcwa.html (accessed June 12, 2009).

10. For example, agriculture uses ten times more water than households and thirty-two times as much as industry in eleven western states, as cited by Power (1996b, 193). Some production would be more truly "economic" in other regions or by other methods without the distorting effect on production incentives of subsidized water from federal water projects.

11. Loss of farmland to development and destruction of wildlife habitat (sometimes, unfortunately, from farming practices) has put one-third of the best-known groups of plants and animals native to the United States (including 30 percent of North American bird species) at risk of extinction (2004 report of the National Audubon Society and the Nature Conservancy, cited in Duerksen and Snyder 2005, 2).

12. Suburban and exurban growth compete with feed lots and water-intensive farming in the United States just as they do in many parts of the world (*Economist,* August 21, 2008).

13. For example, water levels in Borrego Valley (San Diego County) have declined two feet per year over the past twenty years through use for intensive agriculture as well as recreation (Ponce 2006).

14. Water disputes have always been a problem in the arid and semiarid lands of the western United States, where agriculture requires irrigation and the water supply of many cities depends on diversion from rivers. They now occur throughout the United States (*Economist,* December 6, 2007).

15. Federally subsidized water began to open western lands to settlement, and New Deal projects provided another major boost. Since the 1970s efforts by President Jimmy Carter, every president has attempted to scale back the most economically inefficient projects, with mixed success. However, the trend is definitely toward much less federal subsidy.

16. Desalination plants date to the Central Arizona Project's plant for treating over-used Colorado River water to meet quality levels, agreed to by treaty, before it entered Mexico. New plants are currently under construction in San Diego and Orange counties (www.carlsbad-desal.com and www.hbfreshwater.com) and similar facilities are being discussed in the Monterrey-Carmel area. Near San Francisco, "Four Bay Area water agencies have teamed up to possibly build as many as three desalination plants, two on the bay, one along the ocean. . . . The East Bay Municipal Utility District (EBMUD), Hetch Hetchy, Contra Costa Water District and Santa Clara Valley Water District are so worried about future water supplies that they are talking about sharing the cost of building the plants." According to the water agencies, "Building an array of desalination plants might mean not having to build new dams and reservoirs." (KPIX-TV report, October 17, 2009, from ICMA newsletter).

17. Pumping water uphill also dates to the Central Arizona Project. However, the water it produced was priced too high to be attractive to crop farms without a federal subsidy. (This demand problem was predicted by water economists, but ignored by water planners.) Colorado Springs city leaders continue to support an ambitious project, the Southern Delivery system, to pump water uphill from the Arkansas River in southeast Colorado to accommodate future population growth and more homes. As a result of the project, average water rates are projected to more than double between 2005 and 2015.

18. Water usage is likely to be significantly less for at least the first five years where trees and lawns are already established than with new landscaping.

19. Environmental Protection Agency, Sustainable Infrastructure for Water & Wastewater (no date), www.epa.gov/waterinfrastructure/ (accessed June 12, 2009). American Public Works Association, Infrastructure Facts, Facts about America's Public Infrastructure (2008), www.apwa.net/Advocacy/Infrastructure/ (accessed June 12, 2009). U.S. General Accounting Office, Water Infrastructure; Comprehensive Asset Management

Has Potential to Help Utilities Better Identify Needs and Plan Future Investments (2004), www.gao.gov/new.items/d04461.pdf (accessed June 12, 2009).

20. This term is borrowed from James and Lahti (2004) and Paul Hawken's *The Ecology of Commerce.*

21. Building an average single-family home creates two to five tons of solid waste, as cited by James and Lahti (2004, 60). See also the U.S. Environmental Protection Agency's Green Building Program for more information on the impact of different materials.

22. "A 2005 report by the Lawrence Berkeley National Laboratory found that U.S. industry could profitably recycle enough waste energy—including steam, furnace gases, heat and pressure—to reduce the country's fossil-fuel use (and greenhouse-gas emissions) by nearly a fifth. A 2007 study by the McKinsey Global Institute sounded largely the same note. It concluded that domestic industry could use 19 percent less energy than it does today—and make more money as a result " (Margonelli 2008, 26).

23. Bureau of Labor Statistics, May 12, 2009, "Table 2. Reason for layoff: Extended mass layoff events, separations, and initial claimants for unemployment insurance, private non-farm sector, selected quarters, 2008 and 2009," www.bls.gov/news.release/mslo.t02. htm (accessed June 12, 2009).

24. Consumer demand for leather shoes tanned the traditional way, with spruce bark rather than chromium, has kept a family-owned business in northern Sweden alive, despite higher costs for the shoe leather (James and Lahti 2004, 88–90).

25. Lawrence Berkeley National Laboratory (2005) and McKinsey Global Institute (2007) as cited in Margonelli (2008, 26).

26. "Computing Sustainability," *Economist,* June 21, 2008, 78.

27. For example, Decker, Nielsen, and Sindt (2005) show that residential housing values are significantly affected by release of pollutants after controlling for the influence of socioeconomic variables. Nelson (1999), finds economic and population growth correlated with environmental amenities.

28. "In the last 15 years, the number of people with diagnosed diabetes in the United States has more than doubled, reaching 17.9 million in 2007. If current trends continue, one-third of all children born in 2000 will develop type 2 diabetes during their lifetime" (Centers for Disease Control 2009).

29. We note that not all defensive expenditures are wasteful, as some problems may be inevitable in the best of circumstances. Moreover, while there are widespread calls for substantial improvement in both the legal and health care administration systems, (areas cited as having high percentages of waste) both include necessary and productive expenditures as well. In addition, one person's waste is another's necessity—a libertarian might answer that people use "unnecessary" health care or abuse drugs and alcohol because they receive value from that use. Nevertheless, there is clearly a substantial percentage of GDP that could be eliminated without harming the standard of living. The question is whether those dollars could be spent more productively on long-term sustainability.

30. See, for example, Power's comparison of the affluence of Silicon Valley in California to its old identity as agricultural Santa Clara County (1996b, ch. 8, especially p. 176).

31. These same problems beset small towns all over the world. In Sweden, a rural village (Overtornea) turned to sustainability as its solution after a major recession brought 20 percent unemployment and substantial out-migration in this region. Its success spawned the eco-municipality and "Natural Step" movements. See James and Lahti (2004) for more examples.

32. For urban and suburban residents, sustainable agriculture is first and foremost about producing food that is healthful and appealing, and second, about ensuring that

food production does not harm other valued aspects of nature. The industrialization of agriculture has lowered prices to consumers but also turned food production into a commodity business. Both price and quality are lower as a result. Taking account of the effects of food production on human health, sustainability of natural systems, and aesthetic quality of life changes the definition of the most "efficient" method of production. If the market price does not take into account all of these negatives, then lowest price is not a good measure of efficiency or consumer satisfaction. The same principles hold for mining and for forestry.

33. Almost fifty cities across the United States were using electric buses in 1996 according to James and Lahti (2004, 58).

34. Austin, the home of the University of Texas; Madison, University of Wisconsin; Eugene, the University of Oregon; and Fort Collins, Colorado State University.

35. See Thaler and Sunstein (2008) for examples of "framing" the context in which decisions are made and of following the herd in public choice behavior, and new examples from the field of behavioral economics.

36. This is difficult to do in large organizations that assign responsibility for roads to one department and health to another without considering the many relationships between roads and health (vehicle accidents, air pollution, opportunities for exercise, etc). That is why a set of broad sustainability or quality-of-life goals that apply to all is necessary.

37. Of course, quality differentials should be factored in for an accurate comparison.

38. Even Smith (1937 [1776]), the champion of the market system, anticipated the need for some kinds of public intervention to help the invisible hand of market success. Since his time, many changes in technology, population growth, and rising expectations have created more areas where the "visible hand" of public policy must be a necessary part of a market-based system.

39. Leasing the services of a computer monitor, phone, or washing machine frees the consumer from needing to evaluate complex scientific information and changes the incentives. If the manufacturer or distributor is responsible for disposal costs at the end of the product life, it will profit by producing longer-lived products made with more materials that are recyclable. Leasing is increasingly common with business equipment and testing technologies (www.livingston.com) and with automobiles. A greater use could lead away from planned obsolescence and cheap materials to a real change in durability and repairability of products (Hawken, Lovins, and Lovins, 1999).

Chapter 5

1. Poverty measures from the U.S. Bureau of the Census, are adjusted annually to reflect household size and changes in the cost of living but they do not reflect local variations in the cost of living. For example, a family of four can afford more on $20,000 in a lower cost part of the U.S. than in high cost areas, unless public goods and services fully compensate for the cost of living difference. Since poverty measures are not adjusted annually for improvements in the standard of living that result from economic growth, the poverty line standard of living falls over time relative to the average American.

2. An American black born into the lowest tenth of the income distribution has a 42 percent chance of staying there, while for American whites the likelihood is 17 percent (Hertz 2005). According to Campbell and colleagues (2005), as income gaps increase the high school dropout rate is three times greater among black children than among white children.

3. We focus primarily on income inequality (see Levy and Murnane 1992 and Madden 2000 for further detail). For trends in wage inequality see Steelman and Weinberg (2005). Wealth differs from income because it is a stock while income and wages are flows. For more on changes in wealth inequality see Wolff (1995, 2002). For changes in broader and more inclusive measures of well-being that include public goods, see Wolff and Zacharias (2007). For a historical perspective on U.S. wealth inequality, see Williamson and Lindert (1980); for a history of wages and incomes in the post World War II period see Levy (1998).

4. It is important not to confuse the terms *poverty* and *inequality*. Often greater inequality does result in more poverty. However, a society in which everyone was guaranteed a minimum income could have substantial inequality, but no poverty. On the other hand, a society in which most people's living conditions were similar could have little inequality but be quite poor.

5. See, for example, Card, Lemieux, and Riddell 2003; Sachs and Shatz 1996; Snower 1999; Wheeler 2005 as well as the references in notes 3 and 6. Readable summaries are Ed Wolff's *Top Heavy* (2002) and Frank Levy's *The New Dollars and Dreams: American Incomes and Economic Change* (1998).

6. The 21.8 percent national income share of the top 10 percent of the population in 2005 was the highest seen in the United States since 1928. Most income growth was concentrated at the very top of this group, where 300,000 people in the top tenth of 1 percent had average increases in income of over $900,000 a year. At the bottom of the distribution, the share of income received by the second lowest 20 percent and lowest 20 percent of the population fell from 10.2 percent and 4.2 percent to 8.7 percent and 3.5 percent, respectively, between 1981 and 2001 (Center on Budget and Policy Priorities 2007; Piketty and Saez 2003, 2006).

7. In contrast, Federal Reserve Board economists Quintin and Saving (2008) summarize a body of research concluding that inequality is as likely to have negative effects on growth as positive effects; see also Panizza (2002). Voitchovsky (2005) finds that the composition of inequality matters—a certain amount at the top is helpful to growth while too much inequality at the bottom is harmful to growth.

8. For more research on declining mobility between income groups, see Bradbury and Katz (2002), Duncan et al. (1997), and Sawhill and Morton (2007).

9. There is growing research on the relationship between child poverty and educational achievement. For example, see Dahl and Lockner 2009; Smith et al. 1997.

10. Virtually all gains in U.S. life expectancy since 1980 been among highly educated groups (Meara 2005). For the relationship between disease and relative income status, see Marmot, Banks, and Oldfield (2006).

11. Indicators of access to basic necessities and to opportunities in most comprehensive local indicators demonstrate concern over too much inequality and not enough opportunity in the United States today as we show in Chapter 8.

12. Economist Robert Frank discusses this in more depth in *Falling Behind: How Rising Inequality Harms the Middle Class* (2007). We build on his insights to explain the rising expectations for what constitutes a "middle-class home" during a period when growth of the U.S. economy has been slower than during the 1950s and 1960s and inequality has increased.

13. Owning any home became a luxury in markets with extreme upward pressure on all housing prices. Gyourko, Mayer, and Sinai (2007) classified only San Francisco and Los Angeles in this category for the 1960–1980 period, but found that twenty additional metropolitan areas, including New York and Boston, were added by 2000. Prices rose far in excess of what could be accounted for by the additional amenities in these homes.

14. Median family income and median home prices are taken from the U.S. Bureau of the Census.

15. There is a much more extensive literature on opportunity-based policies, primarily at the federal level. See, for example, Sawhill and Morton (2007) and Duncan et al. (1997).

16. For a contrary view, see Levy and Murnane (1992) and Steelman and Weinberg (2005).

17. For the highest income families, state spending made no difference in children's success (Mayer and Lopoo 2007). We note that higher-income families are more aware of and participate more actively in the political process than do low-income families, which may explain a lack of focus on these areas.

18. Heckman (2006) and Carneiro and Heckman (2003) find that not every kind of preschool experience has this effect. It is important to invest in the right kind of preschool.

19. Approximately half of the students who begin college complete at least a four-year degree.

20. As Chapter 2 reveals, a small percentage of start-ups succeed and expand into real economic generators. Acs, Parsons, and Tracy (2008) found significant growth between 1998 and 2002 in high-impact "gazelles." The firms were not only in high tech, but ranged across many industries. They accounted for almost all recent private sector employment and revenue growth in the United States. On average, the firms are twenty-five years old (less than the average of low impact firms), have fewer than twenty employees, and had little job loss even during recessions.

21. Junior-high students in 1988 who did very well on a standardized test but came from low-income families were less likely to get through college than students who tested poorly but had well-off parents (National Center for Education Statistics, cited by Paul Krugman, *New York Times,* February 18, 2008).

22. Gottlieb and Fogarty (2003) found some evidence of increased inequality in the metropolitan areas that had less educational investment along with a significant relationship between the number of bachelor degrees granted in one year and local per capita income and employment growth in the next seventeen years.

23. Smith (1937 [1776], ch. 1) cites the need for publicly funded education to offset the dulling effects of repetitive factory work on the citizenry.

24. This effect holds when controlling for income differences associated with education.

25. For example, of workers making less than $15,000 per year, three in four had a high school diploma and 40 percent had some education beyond high school (Carnevale and Rose 2001).

26. Some states restrict coverage to only those seeking a full-time job, although part-time work is increasingly common in this era of two- and three-worker families. The cost of unemployment insurance varies between states, but most of the difference is a result of frequency of unemployment spells in the state. Unemployment benefit levels and duration explained another 3–6 percent, while the voluntary quit exemption explains 6–12 percent of the variation (Blaustein and Kozlowski 1978). Benefits are a small percentage of income for all but the lowest wage workers because most states cap taxes at only a small fraction of what most full-time workers earn. Vroman (2009) recommends increasing this base from an average of $7,000 per worker to $20,000 per worker.

27. Universally available health insurance could relieve employers of the costs of work-related medical treatment and reduce their costs for workers' compensation insurance accordingly.

28. Federal enforcement has been ineffective in certain periods (such as the first decade of the twenty-first century) and federal statutes carry penalties too low to discourage violators, leaving a vacuum to be filled by state enforcement of federal laws. California's Private Attorney General Act allows current and former employees to receive 25 percent of the civil penalties normally paid to the state when they initiate successful actions, and private organizations to devote resources to enforcing state labor laws and increase revenues for the state when lawsuits are successful. Other states could do likewise.

29. Indexing the minimum wage of $1.00 per hour in 1962 to inflation would have raised it gradually to almost $7.00 in 2008. Since changes are made only by amending state or federal statutes increases in the minimum wage lagged behind rising prices in most states during the 1980s and 1990s. Recent increases have corrected that in some areas. As we noted, low minimum wages discourage businesses from adopting methods to increase productivity.

30. The fact that teenagers (many of whom still live with parents) are a large segment of the minimum wage workforce is often cited as a reason not to raise the level. However, adult women are also a major part of the minimum wage population and many play a major support role in their household.

31. The term *small business* is sometimes used for any business with revenues less than $1–2 million. We are talking about true small businesses with fewer than twenty employees.

32. Stricter laws on possession of small amounts of controlled substances are the primary reason for a tripling in the ratio of prisoners to the overall population between 1975 and 2005. One in 100 Americans is in prison now, the highest percentage in history. Since most leave prison within ten years, ever higher numbers of potential workers have felony records (see Bushway, Stoll, and Weiman 2007; Holzer, Raphael, and Stoll 2006).

33. For example, see Silverstein et al. (2003) on underserved inner city retail markets and our discussion of "food deserts" in Chapter 6.

34. Some researchers conclude that any restriction on land use raises prices (Fischel 1990; Levine 1999; Quigley and Raphael 2004).

35. Downs (2002) concludes that (1) a growth boundary is likely to raise the price of land inside it, but does not restrict the number of new units that can be built, and (2) the 1992 decision by Portland's metropolitan government not to increase the size of the boundary may have also played a role in the price spurt.

36. However, Kahn (2001) notes that the net effect on opportunity from the benefits he found associated with buying homes more cheaply in the suburbs must be balanced against the costs of contributing to central city decline.

37. Households spent an average of nearly $3,600 on new and used motor vehicles in 2001, up 47 percent from about $2,500 in 1991. Spending on other vehicle expenses, including insurance, financing charges, maintenance, and repairs, also increased by 14 percent from about $1,720 to nearly $2,400. Meanwhile, gasoline and oil expenditures rose 3 percent to nearly $1,100 in 2001. On average households spent almost $400 on public transportation in 2001, an increase of 6 percent between 1991 and 2001 (Bureau of Labor Statistics 2003).

38. The Urban Institute (2008) calculated that at $4 a gallon for gasoline poverty-level workers (65 percent commuted alone in an automobile to their jobs) were spending an average 8.6 percent of their income on gasoline relative to 2.1 percent of income for workers above poverty, assuming all drove cars with average gas consumption per mile.

39. States with a universally applied sales or property tax rate have less variation than those that depend more on local taxes or those that have many special districts (see Table 7.1).

40. Income is less a factor if selling in a region of high prices and moving to one with

lower prices, because some largely untaxed capital gains are spent in the new area. The 2008–2009 foreclosure crises will cause a new version of that problem. Moving from an area with a housing bubble where prices collapsed will be more difficult than moving from an area where price increases were not as volatile.

Chapter 6

1. A public good is defined by economists as one with two primary characteristics: 1) once it is offered, no one can be excused from its benefit (the good is nonexclusive), and 2) the consumption of the good by one person cannot preclude another's benefiting from the good (this makes it non-rivalrous). Governments usually provide public goods because private businesses have no economic incentives to produce them. We follow the more popular usage of the term to include other goods and services (such as education) that have spillover benefits to the rest of society, and are paid for through tax dollars and are provided by the private sector.

2. As we discuss in Chapter 7, these costs may be higher than the revenues generated, affecting the fiscal sustainability of state or local governments. Taking an active role in setting parameters to accommodate growth rather than letting them be primarily dictated by the private sector can minimize this problem.

3. One of the earliest uses of the word *sprawl* in terms of land use was by Earle Draper, planning director for the Tennessee Valley Authority in a 1937 speech: "Perhaps diffusion is too kind a word. . . . In bursting its bounds, the city actually sprawled and made the countryside ugly . . . , uneconomic [in terms] of services and [of] doubtful social value."

4. To put that in perspective, between 1960 and 1990 the amount of developed land more than doubled while urban population in the United States increased by 50 percent (Benefield et al. 1991, as cited by McGuire and Sjoquist 2003).

5. U.S.D.A., http://ers.usda.gov/publications/aer803/aer803b.pdf.

6. Sprawl is much less common in Canada, which has even more wide-open spaces and less population than the United States (Porter 2008).

7. Dreier, Mollenkopf, and Swanstrom (2004) make a detailed argument that sprawl has been subsidized and encouraged by federal policies dating as far back as the New Deal as well as by many local policies. In addition to paying 90 percent of the cost of local interstate exchanges in the early years, the federal government provided floodplain and other disaster insurance. All of these encouraged commercial and residential development outside central towns and cities.

8. Clark and Herrin (2000) find school quality to be more important to home buyers than crime or environmental quality.

9. For opposing views on this see Madden (2000) and Boustan (2007).

10. For every dollar saved on a home purchase, buyers spent on average 77 cents more on gasoline, and that was before the fuel cost increases of 2007 and 2008 (Lipman 2006).

11. A recent poll conducted for the Congress for the New Urbanism (2001, 8) shows that 30 percent of home buyers want more mixed-use and walkable developments today (Porter 2008, 202).

12. J.E. Frank (1989) finds that public capital (infrastructure) costs associated with a new home can be as high as $120,000 (our conversion into 2008 dollars).

13. The *American Journal of Health Promotion* also had a special issue on "Health Promoting Community Design."

14. "Both fatality and injury rates are much higher for cyclists in the USA compared to Germany, Denmark, and the Netherlands. Averaged over the years 2002 to 2005, the

number of American bicyclist fatalities per 100 million km cycled was 5.8, compared to 1.7 in Germany, 1.5 in Denmark, and 1.1 in the Netherlands. Thus, cycling is over five times as safe in the Netherlands as in the USA, which probably explains why the Dutch do not perceive cycling as a dangerous way to get around. Cycling in Germany and Denmark is not quite as safe as in the Netherlands, but still 3–4 times safer than in the USA" (Pucher and Buehler 2008, 9).

15. However, Brueckner and Largey (2008) analyze data from the Social Capital Benchmark Study and find that density alone is not a determinant of social interaction. Income levels, perceived safety, and the type of development are also important.

16. Jargowsky (2005) subsequently found a dramatic decline in economic segregation over the 1990s relative to his earlier findings. He attributed this to the revitalization of many central cities and increased housing opportunities in the suburbs that occurred during the housing boom. As we acknowledge in Chapter 5, there were temporary increases in opportunity facilitated by easy credit. However, many of these are likely to be reversed as part of the housing bust.

17. This shows the very important role that banks and other mortgage lenders have in shaping land use development.

18. Data from the U.S. Dept of Education's *Digest of Educational Statistics* (2006); the U.S. Department of Transportation's *Nationwide Personal Transportation Study* (1969) and the *National Household Transportation Survey* (2008).

19. Much of the following discussion borrows from ICMA (2008).

20. Adding parking charges to car capital and operating costs could result in a 60 percent or more increase in driving costs according to Robert Dunphy, Senior Fellow at the Urban Land Institute (Porter 2008, 162).

21. A Guide to Metropolitan Transportation Planning Under ISTEA—How the Pieces Fit Together—USDOT, http://ntl.bts.gov/DOCS/424MTP.html.

22. In this paragraph we follow a discussion by DeGrove (2005).

23. For more on the development of zoning laws and past Supreme Court interpretations see Babcock (1966) and Siemon (1985).

24. Yarolavsky (2008).

25. Conclusions of a national conference, University of North Carolina, proceedings cited in ICMA (2008).

26. For example, new priorities might include an increased focus on the health and education of youth for sustainability as well as transportation for the elderly to improve quality of life.

27. See Porter (2008, 20–21) for further discussion of the property rights issue.

Chapter 7

1. We wrote about the effects of tax structure on individual well-being in Chapter 5, focusing on the regressive nature of sales taxes, in particular, and how they affect lower-income residents.

2. Particularly when labor markets are tight, local and state operating budgets are hit with the need to be competitive with private sector salary increases (Baumol 1967, 2001).

3. Brueckner (1997, 2007) finds that this result holds when the growth rate of the population is also less than the interest rate. Of course, dampening growth where marginal costs are rising is exactly what an impact fee or land exaction should do to increase the efficiency of overall land use.

4. Economists refer to the incremental cost of new infrastructure or services as the marginal cost. Over time, a rising marginal cost raises average cost. However, if

only average cost is being measured, it will take much longer to identify rising costs than if costs were measured on an incremental basis. One way to estimate the marginal costs is to divide a city or county into regions (for data collection purposes) that are representative of changing land use patterns. Comparisons can then be made in both operating and capital costs over time between different regions.

5. Either population growth or per capita income growth can increase total personal income on the horizontal axis of Figures 7.2 through 7.6. The new population we refer to is net in-migration (more new residents coming in annually than leaving). Most of the immediate cost effects of population growth come from this in-migration. With smaller families and later age of first birth for most population groups in the United States, births over deaths provides a very slow rate of natural population growth. In addition, when there is growth due to high birthrates, public costs are not affected until children enter school. After that, they will not drive new cars on the road for another ten years and will not move into independent housing units for several more years after that.

6. The Mt. Laurel decisions (http://njlegalib.rutgers.edu/mtlaurel/aboutmtlaurel.php) prohibited "exclusionary zoning." However, its close cousin "fiscal zoning" has a long history, since it is difficult to prove the intent of deliberate discrimination in most zoning patterns.

7. As we have observed earlier, changes in the age composition of the population may temporarily require more services per capita. The costs of education are concentrated in the ages of five to eighteen, and costs of crime control are heavily influenced by the share of population that is between the ages of fifteen and twenty-five. In addition, increased affluence raises the demand for all normal goods, including public goods. Education, parks, and public safety may be superior goods with income elasticities of greater than one. Rising incomes then generate demand for more and better public services. While being a service business can drive costs up more rapidly than the CPI in some periods, better alignment between the tax structure and the cost structure could modify this problem.

8. The original argument comes from a small section of an article by Charles Tiebout (1956) but has been widely cited and developed by others.

9. Brueckner (2004) explores the situations under which benefits of decentralization outweigh the costs of tax competition under varying conditions. However, he does not consider all of the aspects of quality of life and sustainability that we have discussed throughout this book.

10. A progressive rate structure is one for which the marginal rate increases as income increases. In contrast, a proportional tax collects the same percentage of income from all income levels. Sales taxes collect a flat percentage per purchase regardless of income level, but purchases of taxable goods represent a far smaller percentage of income for higher income individuals. Therefore, the sales tax is regressive because it taxes a higher percentage of income at lower incomes. State reliance on sales taxes has increased, making this problem worse (Davis et al. 2009).

11. Perceptions of neighborhood school quality translate directly into the value of homes in the area, making the property tax a user or benefits tax in terms of contributing directly to changes in the wealth of homeowners (Clark and Herrin 2000; Fischel 2001).

12. Tax incidence (how the tax is shifted from the initial payer to the party who actually bears the final burden) is a subject of continued debate among public finance economists, particularly in the case of the property tax.

13. The property tax has a long and tumultuous history in the United States. Although it was one of the first taxes used by the late 1830s Alabama, Georgia, Maryland,

Massachusetts, New York, North Carolina, Pennsylvania, and Rhode Island had completely eliminated it and substituted other business, banking, and transportation taxes, in an early property tax revolt, (Wallis 2001). But lack of other revenue sources led to its restoration and the ensuing property tax revolts later in the nineteenth century.

14. Proposition 13 limits local and state taxing powers in four ways. First, no real property can be taxed at more than 1 percent of its 1975–76 assessed value. Second, assessed value can increase no more than 2 percent per year unless the property changes ownership (at which time it is reassessed at current market value). Third, a local government cannot increase an existing tax or impose a new tax without the approval of two-thirds of the qualified electors. Fourth, state government cannot impose a new tax without approval from two-thirds of the membership in each house of the state legislature (Danziger 1980). For a more extensive discussion of property tax limits in general see O'Sullivan (2001).

15. Spending limits for government will stay even with growth in population and inflation while the benefits of economic growth are refunded to taxpayers. While voters can authorize refunds to be diverted to schools or other government entities this requires special elections, a time lag, and other restrictions. The same would be true for an increase in taxes. In addition, either requires that voters understand the process and the economics of the situation. This understanding is less likely in areas with significant in-migration and many new voters.

Chapter 8

1. Locally developed indicators reflect some of what the genuine progress index (GPI) adds to GDP (the value of public open space and the arts, basic infrastructure maintenance). They also focus on many of the subtractions from GDP (costs of crime, environmental damage, income inequality, or child poverty, and time spent in commuting). Appendix 3.1 reviews the history of current measures such as GDP (gross domestic product) and proposed alternative measures such as the GPI and the Index of Social Health.

2. Individual surveys measure rates of victimization, but the overall crime rate is a better indicator of perceived safety. As crime rates increase, individuals are less willing to walk alone after dark or answer the door for an unknown caller. They spend more on security systems and other methods of private crime prevention in relation to the threat of crime, as well as whether they have been victims of crime.

3. Local school boards are still a major force in budgets, curriculum, and discipline policies in public schools throughout most of the United States, along with state superintendents or boards of education.

4. See Zodrow and Miezkowski (1986), Stiglitz (1983), and Wallace (2008) for alternative perspectives on the efficiency of "Tiebout effects."

5. For example, although quality of life and economic development are impacted by credit availability, unemployment rates, immigration policy, demographic trends, business investment, and housing starts, national and international policies are more important in each of these areas than state or local policies.

6. While the United States has the largest number of projects, there are many in Australia, Canada, Great Britain, and Italy. The rapidly changing list of active indicator projects, combined with the difficulty of keeping Web sites updated, makes it difficult to compile an up-to-date list of these projects. Web sites appear and disappear, and the links on them are even more unstable. Portney (2003) focuses on medium to large cities having a sustainability initiative in January 2000. He lists Scottsdale and Tucson (Arizona), Santa Barbara, San Francisco, San Jose, and Santa Monica (California), Boulder

(Colorado), Tampa (Florida), Brookline and Cambridge (Massachusetts), Cleveland (Ohio), Portland (Oregon), Chattanooga (Tennessee), and Olympia (Washington), in addition to cities already mentioned in this chapter, as having an indicator project that has been active in the past five years. Minneapolis (Minnesota) and Cincinnati (Ohio) are among others that have produced indicators.

7. The city of Seattle's Office of Sustainability and Environment also developed community indicators in the early 1990s, suggesting a widespread interest after the state of Washington's passage of growth management legislation in 1991.

8. Former county executive Ron Sims, as quoted on King County AIMS High Web site (accessed June 5, 2009).

9. The original report included Travis, Hays, and Williamson counties. Bastrop and Caldwell counties are now also included.

10. See www.tbf.org/IndicatorsProject/Transportation/Innovations.aspx#Zipcar (accessed June 4, 2009).

11. For example, if the median income is not increasing at least as fast as local prices, then growth is hurting affordability for many members of the community rather than helping them have more purchasing power.

12. For example, Table 8.4 shows that racism has been measured through survey responses and through measures of activity in juvenile courts. Racism could also potentially be measured using housing data or charges of discrimination, but the small sample size for any single year could make the latter less reliable. Note that no measures of racism or discrimination are available from federally collected data.

13. Other reviews of indicators such as Miringoff and Miringoff (1999) and Connor, Tanjasiri, and Easterling (1999) provide detail on the processes used in the past, but overcoming these issues may require new methods. Hart (1999) provides a Web-based resource for communities starting indicator projects.

14. Rather than releasing a new document once a year, it may be more effective to release changes in the civic indicators in one month and changes in the environmental indicators in another month and so on. Obviously, cooperation of major media outlets is extremely helpful in this regard. As use of the Internet increases and Web sites become more interactive, user friendly, and widespread, more sites can practice continuous updating as information becomes available.

Bibliography

Ackerman, F. 2008. *Poisoned for Pennies: The Economics of Toxics and Precaution.* Washington, DC: Island Press.

Acs, Z.; W. Parsons; and S. Tracy. 2008. "High-Impact Firms: Gazelles Revisited." Office of Advocacy, U.S. Small Business Administration, June. Available at www.sba.gov/advo/research/rs328tot.pdf (accessed December 1, 2008).

Adkisson, R. 2009a. "The Economy as an Open System: An Institutionalist Framework for Sustainable Policy." In *Institutional Analysis and Praxis: The Social Fabric Matrix Approach,* ed. T. Natarajan, E. Wolfram, and S.T. Fullwiler, 25–38. New York: Springer.

———. 2009b. Book Review of the "Origin of Wealth: Evolution, Complexity and the Radical Remaking of Economics." *Eastern Economic Journal* 35, no. 1: 133–35.

Aghion, P.; E. Caroli; and C. Garcia-Penalosa. 1999. "Inequality and Economic Growth: The Perspective of the New Growth Theories." *Journal of Economic Literature* 37, no. 4: 1615–60.

Akerlof, G.A., and R.J. Shiller. 2009. *Animal Spirits: How Human Psychology Drives the Economy, and Why It Matters for Global Capitalism.* Princeton and Oxford: Princeton University Press.

Akst, D. 2008. "A Talk with Betsy Stevenson and Justin Wolfers." *Boston Globe,* November, 23, 2008.

Alfeld, L.E. 1995. "Urban Dynamics: The First Fifty Years." *System Dynamics Review* 11, no. 3: 199–217.

American Journal of Health Promotion. 2003. Special Issue on Community Design. 19, no. 1.

American Journal of Public Health. 2003. Special Issue on Community Design. 93, no. 9.

American Society of Civil Engineers. 2009. Report Card for America's Infrastructure. Available at www.infrastructurereportcard.org (accessed June 12, 2009).

Anderson, M.D., and J.T. Cook. 2003. "Does Food Security Require Local Food Systems?" In *Rethinking Sustainability,* ed. J.M. Harris, 224–48. Ann Arbor: University of Michigan Press.

Annie E. Casey Foundation. 2008. Closing the Achievement Gap: Community and Family Connections. Available at www.aecf.org (accessed January 12, 2009).

Associated Press. 2009. "$350 million in subsidies for Carlsbad desalination plant," November 11.

Ayres, C.E. 1962 [1944]. *The Theory of Economic Progress: A Study of the Fundamentals of Economic Development and Cultural Change,* 2d ed. New York: Schocken Books.

Babbitt, B. 2005. *Cities in the Wilderness: A New Vision of Land Use in America.* Washington, DC: Island Press.

Babcock, R.F. 1966. *The Zoning Game: Municipal Practices and Policies.* Cambridge, MA: Lincoln Institute of Land Policy.
Babcock, R.F., and C.L. Siemon. 1985. *The Zoning Game Revisited.* Cambridge, MA: Lincoln Institute of Land Policy.
Banzhaf, S.H., and R.P. Walsh. 2008. "Do People Vote with Their Feet? An Empirical Test of Tiebout's Mechanism." *American Economic Review* 98, no. 3: 843–63.
Barrett, K., and R. Greene. 2008. "Growth and Taxes: Why Outdated Systems Undercut Economic Vitality and What States Can Do About It." *Governing* (January). Available at www.governing.com/article/growth-taxes (accessed June 2, 2009).
Bartik, T.J. 1991. "Who Benefits from State and Local Economic Development?" Kalamazoo, MI: Upjohn Institute for Employment Research.
———. 1993. "Who Benefits from Local Job Growth: Migrants or the Original Residents?" *Regional Studies* 27, no. 4: 297–311.
———. 2005a. "Incentive Solutions." *Growth and Change* 36, no. 2: 139–66.
———. 2005b. *Taking Preschool Education Seriously as an Economic Development Program: Effects on Jobs and Earnings of State Residents Compared to Traditional Economic Development Programs.* Kalamazoo, MI: Upjohn Institute for Employment Research.
———. 2007. "Solving the Problem of Economic Development Incentives." In *Reining in the Competition for Capital,* ed. Ann Markusen, 103–40. Kalamazoo, MI: Upjohn Institute for Employment Research.
Bartik, T.J., and G.A. Erickcek. 2008. "'Eds & Meds' and Metropolitan Economic Development." In *Urban and Regional Policy and Its Effects,* Vol. 1. ed. M. Turner, H. Wial, and H. Wolman, 21–59. Washington, DC: Brookings Institution.
Baumol, W.J. 2001. "An Interview with William Baumol." *Journal of Economic Perspectives* 15, no. 3: 211–31.
Beacon Hill Institute (BHI). Annually since 2001. *State Competitiveness Report.* Available at www.beaconhill.org/MasterDocumentSCI_A1.pdf (accessed December 24, 2008).
Becker, R.A.; L. Denby; R. McGill; and A.R. Wilks. 1987. "Analysis of Data from the Places Rated Almanac." *American Statistician* 41, no. 3: 169–86.
Beinhocker, E. 2006. *The Origins of Wealth: Evolution, Complexity and the Radical Remaking of Economics.* Boston, MA: Harvard Business School Press.
Benedetti, M. 2008. "Midwest States among Leaders in Redevelopment." *Crain's Detroit Business* 24, no. 18: 18–19.
Benefield, F.K.; D.R. Matthew; and D.T. Chen.1999. *Once There Were Greenfields.* New York: Natural Resources Defense Council.
Bennett, M., and R.P. Giloth. 2007. *Economic Development in American Cities: The Pursuit of an Equity Agenda.* Albany: State University of New York Press.
Berger, M.; G. Blomquist; and W. Waldner. 1987. "A Revealed Preference Ranking of Quality of Life for Metropolitan Areas." *Social Science Quarterly* 68, no. 4: 761–78.
Bernasek, A. 2006. "Income Inequality, and Its Cost." *New York Times,* June 25.
Birch, D.C. 1981. "Who Creates Jobs?" *Public Interest* 65: 3–14.

Blank, R.M. 2009. "Economic change and the structure of opportunity for less-skilled workers." *Focus* 26, no. 2: 14–20. Insititute for Research on Poverty, University of Wisconsin.

Blaustein, S.J., and P.J. Kozlowski. 1978. *Interstate Differences in Unemployment Insurance Benefit Costs: A Cross Section Study.* Kalamazoo, MI: Upjohn Institute for Employment Research.

Blomquist, G.; M. Berger; and J. Hoehn. 1988. "New Estimates of Quality of Life in Urban Areas." *American Economic Review* 78, no. 1: 89–107.

Boulding, K.E. 1964. *The Meaning of the Twentieth Century.* New York: Harper and Row.

———. 1993. "Spaceship Earth Revisited." In *Valuing the Earth, Economics, Ecology and Ethics,* ed., H.E. Daly and K.N. Townsend, 311–13. Cambridge: MIT Press.

Boustan, L.P. 2007. "Was Postwar Suburbanization 'White Flight'? Evidence from the Black Migration." NBER Working Paper, no. 13543.

Bowles, S., and H. Gintis. 2002. "Social Capital and Community Governance." *Economic Journal* 112, no. 483: 419–36.

Bradbury, K., and J. Katz. 2002. "Are Lifetime Incomes Growing More Unequal? Looking at New Evidence on Family Income Mobility." *Federal Reserve Bank of Boston Regional Review.* Available at www.bos.frb.org (accessed April 10, 2009).

Brinkman, R. 1995. "Economic Growth vs. Economic Development: Toward a Conceptual Clarification." *Journal of Economic Issues* 29, no. 4: 1171–88.

Brueckner, J.K. 1997. "Infrastructure Financing and Urban Development: The Economics of Impact Fees." *Journal of Public Economics* 66, no. 3: 383–407.

———. 2001. "Property Taxation and Urban Sprawl." In *Property Taxation and Local Government Finance,* ed. Wallace E. Oates, 153–72. Cambridge, MA: Lincoln Institute of Land Policy.

———. 2004. "Fiscal Decentralization with Distortionary Taxation: Tiebout vs. Tax Competition." *International Tax and Public Finance* 11, no. 2: 133–53.

———. 2007. "Urban Growth Boundaries: An Effective Second-Best Remedy for Unpriced Traffic Congestion." *Journal of Housing Economics* 16, nos. 3–4: 263–73.

Brueckner, J.K., and Hyun-A Kim. 2003. "Urban Sprawl and the Property Tax." *International Tax and Public Finance* 10, no. 1: 5–23.

Brueckner, J.K., and A.G. Largey. 2008. "Social Interaction and Urban Sprawl." *Journal of Urban Economics* 64, no. 1: 18–34.

Brueckner, J.K., and A.S. Luz. 2001. "Do Local Governments Engage in Strategic Property-Tax Competition?" *National Tax Journal* 54, no. 3: 203–29.

Brugmann, J. 1997. "Is There a Method in Our Measurement? The Use of Indicators in Local Sustainable Development Planning." *Local Environment* 2, no. 1: 59–81.

Bruntland, G.H. 1987. *Our Common Future: Report of the World Commission on Environment and Development.* Oxford: Oxford University Press.

Bullard, R.D.; G.S. Johnson; and A.O. Torres, eds. 2000. *Sprawl City: Race, Politics and Planning in Atlanta.* Washington, DC: Island Press.

Burchell, R.W. 2004. *Development Impact Analysis: Feasibility, Design, Traffic, Fiscal, Environment.* Edison, NJ: Transaction.

Burchell, R.W.; D. Listokin; and C.C. Galley. 2000. "Smart Growth: More Than a

Ghost of Urban Policy Past, Less than a Bold New Horizon." *Housing Policy Debate* 11, no. 4: 821–79.

Burchell, R.W.; N. Shad; D. Listokin et al. 1998. *The Costs of Sprawl—Revisited.* Washington, DC: National Academy Press.

Burchell, R.W.; A. Downs; B. McCann; and S. Mukherji. 2005. *Sprawl Costs: Economic Impacts of Unchecked Development.* Washington, DC: Island Press.

Bureau of Economic Analysis. Annual. *State Annual Personal Income.* Available at www.bea.gov/bea/regional/spi/ (accessed December 24, 2008).

Burtless, G. 2007. "Income Supports for Workers and Their Families: Earnings Supplements and Health Insurance." In *Reshaping the American Workforce in a Changing Economy,* ed. H.J. Holzer and D.S. Nightingale, 239–72. Washington, DC: Urban Institute Press.

Bushway, S.D.; M.A. Stoll; and D. Weiman. 2007. *Carriers to Reentry? The Labor Market for Released Prisoners in Post-Industrial America.* New York: Russell Sage Foundation.

Buss, T.F. 2001. "The Effect of State Tax Incentives on Economic Growth and Firm Location Decisions: An Overview of the Literature." *Economic Development Quarterly* 15, no. 1: 90–105.

Campbell, M.; R. Haveman; G. Sandefur; and B. Wolfe. 2005. "Economic Inequality and Educational Attainment Across a Generation." *Focus* 23, no. 3: 11–15.

Card, D.; T. Lemieux; and W.C. Riddell. 2004. "Unions and Wage Inequality." *Journal of Labor Research* 25, no. 4: 519–62.

Carneiro, P., and J. Heckman. 2004. "Inequality in America: What Role for Human Capital Policies?" In *Human Capital Policy,* ed. J. Heckman, A. Krueger, and B. Friedman, 77–240. Cambridge: MIT Press.

Carnevale, A., and S.J. Rose. 2001. "Low Earners: Who Are They? Do They Have a Way Out?" In *Low-Wage Workers in the New Economy,* ed. R. Kazis and M.S. Miller, 45–66. Washington DC: Urban Institute Press.

Carr, D. 2009. "Even Forbes Is Pinching Pennies." *New York Times,* June 19.

Carruthers, J.I., and G.F. Ulfarsson. 2002. "Fragmentation and Sprawl: Evidence from Interregional Analysis." *Growth and Change* 33, no. 3: 312–40.

Centers for Disease Control. 2009. "Healthy Communities: Preventing Chronic Disease by Activating Grassroots Change." Available at www.cdc.gov/nccdphp/ publications/AAG/healthy_communities.htm (accessed May 12, 2009).

Central Texas Sustainability Indicators Project. Annual. *Annual Report 2000.* Available at www.centex-indicators.org (accessed June 29, 2008).

Chernick, H., and A. Reschovsky. 1982. "The Distributional Impact of Proposition 13: A Microsimulation Approach." *National Tax Journal* 35, no. 2: 149–70.

———. 2001. "Lost in the Balance: How State Policies Affect the Fiscal Health of Cities." Discussion Paper. Center on Urban and Metropolitan Policy. Washington DC: Brookings Institution.

Citrin, J. 1979. "Do People Want Something for Nothing? Public Opinion on Taxes and Government Spending." *National Tax Journal* 32, no. 2: 113–29.

Clark, A.E.; P. Fritjers; and M.A. Shields. 2008. "Relative Income, Happiness, and Utility: An Explanation for the Easterlin Paradox and Other Puzzles." *Journal of Economic Literature* 46, no. 1: 95–144.

Clark, D.E., and W.M. Herrin. 2000. "The Impact of Public School Attributes on Home Sale Prices in California." *Growth and Change* 31, no. 3: 385–407.

Clymer, C.; B. Roberts; and J. Strawn. 2001. "Stepping Up: State Policies and Programs Promoting Low-Wage Workers' Steady Employment and Advancement." In *Low-Wage Workers in the New Economy,* ed. R. Kazis and M.S. Miller, 165–202. Washington, DC: Urban Institute Press.

Colander, D.; R.P.F. Holt; and J.B. Rosser Jr. 2004. *The Changing Face of Economics: Conversations with Cutting Edge Economists.* Ann Arbor: University of Michigan Press.

Coleman, J.S. 1988. "Social Capital in the Creation of Human Capital." *American Journal of Sociology* 94: S95–S120.

Coleman, J.S., and T. Hoffer. 1987. *Public and Private High School: The Impact of Communities.* New York: Basic Books.

Collia, D.V.; J. Sharp; and L. Giesbrecht. 2003. "The 2001 National Household Travel Survey: A Look into the Travel Patterns of Older Americans." *Journal of Safety Research* 34, no. 4: 461–70.

Congress for the New Urbanism. 2001. *The Coming Demand.* Available at http://www.cnu.org/node/359 (accessed December 1, 2009).

Connor, R.F.; S.P. Tanjasiri; and D. Easterling. 1999. *Communities Tracking Their Quality of Life: An Overview of the Community Indicators Project of the Colorado Healthy Communities Initiative.* Denver, CO: Colorado Trust. Available at www.coloradotrust.org (accessed August 12, 2008).

Cortright, J., and H. Mayer. 2004. "Increasingly Rank: The Use and Misuse of Rankings in Economic Development." *Economic Development Quarterly* 18, no. 1: 34–39.

Costanza, R. 1991. *Ecological Economics: The Science and Management of Sustainability.* New York: Columbia University Press.

Courant, P.N.; E.M. Gramlich; and D.L. Rubinfeld. 1980. "Why Voters Support Tax Limitation Amendments: The Michigan Case." *National Tax Journal* 33, no. 1: 1.

Cullen, J.B., and S.D. Levitt. 1999. "Crime, Urban Flight, and the Consequences for Cities." *Review of Economics and Statistics* 81, no. 2: 159–69.

Cunningham, W.L. 2001. *Real-Time Ground-Water Data for the Nation.* U.S. Geological Survey. Available at http://pubs.usgs.gov/fs/fs-090–01/ (accessed June 12, 2009).

Currie, J. 2009. "Healthy, Wealthy, and Wise: Socioeconomic Status, Poor Health in Childhood, and Human Capital Development." *Journal of Economic Literature* 47, 1: 87–122.

Cutler, H., and S. Davies. 2007. "The Economic Consequences of Population-and Employment-Led Growth." Working Paper. Colorado State University.

Dahl, G., and L. Lockner, 2009. "The Impact of Family Income on Child Achievement." Discussion Paper no. 1305–05. Madison, WI: Institute for Research on Poverty.

Daily, G. et al. 1998. "Food Production, Population Growth, and the Environment." *Science* 281, no. 5381: 1291.

Daly, H.E. 1996. *Beyond Growth: The Economics of Sustainable Development.* Boston: Beacon Press.

Daly, H.E., and J.B. Cobb. 1989. *For the Common Good: Redirecting the Economy Toward Community, the Environment, and a Sustainable Future.* Boston: Beacon Press.

Daly, H.E., and J. Farley. 2004. *Ecological Economics, Principles and Applications*. Washington, DC: Island Press.

Danziger, J.N. 1980. "California's Proposition 13 and the Fiscal Limitations Movement in the United States." *Political Studies* 28, no. 4: 599–612.

Davis, C., et al. 2009. "A Distributional Analysis of the Tax Systems in All 50 States," 3d ed. Washington, DC : Institute on Taxation and Economic Policy.

Deaton, A. 2008. "Income, Health, and Well-Being Around the World: Evidence from the Gallup World Poll." *Journal of Economic Perspectives* 22, no. 2: 53–72.

Decker, C.S.; D.A. Nielsen; and R.P. Sindt. 2005. "Residential Property Values and Community Right-to-Know Laws: Has the Toxics Release Inventory Had an Impact?" *Growth and Change* 36, no. 1:113–33.

DeGrove, J.M. 2005. *Planning Policy and Politics: Smart Growth and the States*. Cambridge, MA: Lincoln Institute of Land Policy.

Deller, S.C.; V. Lledo; and D.W. Marcouiller. 2008. "Modeling Regional Economic Growth with a Focus on Amenities." *Review of Urban & Regional Development Studies* 20, no. 1: 1–21.

Deller, S.C.; T. Tsai,; D.W. Marcouiller; and D.B.K. English. 2001. "The Role of Amenities and Quality of Life in Rural Economic Growth." *American Journal of Agricultural Economics* 83, no. 2: 352–65.

Denton, N.A. 2001. "Housing as a Means of Asset Accumulation: A Good Strategy for the Poor?" In *Assets for the Poor: The Benefits of Spreading Asset Ownership*, ed. Thomas M. Shapiro and Edward N. Wolff, 232–66. New York: Russell Sage Foundation.

De Souza-Briggs, X. 2005. "More Pluribus, Less Unum? The Changing Geography of Race and Opportunity." In *The Geography of Opportunity: Race and Housing Choice in Metropolitan America*, ed. De Souza-Briggs, 17–44. Washington, DC: Brookings Institution.

De Tocqueville, A. 2000 [1830]. *Democracy in America*, Part II. ed. H.C. Mansfield and D. Winthrop. Chicago: University of Chicago Press.

Diener, E., and Lucas, R.E. 1999. "Personality and Subjective Well-Being." In *Well-Being: The Foundations of a Hedonic Psychology*, ed. D. Kahneman, E. Diener, and N. Schwarz, 213–29. New York: Russell Sage Foundation.

Diener, E., and M.E.P. Seligman. 2004. "Beyond Money." *Psychological Science in the Public Interest* 5, no. 1: 1–31.

Diener, E., and E. Suh. 1999. "National Differences in Subjective Well-Being." In *Well-Being: The Foundations of a Hedonic Psychology*, ed. D. Kahneman, E. Diener, and N. Schwarz, 434–450. New York: Russell Sage Foundation.

Di Tella, R., and R. MacCulloch. 2006. "Some Uses of Happiness Data in Economics." *Journal of Economic Perspectives* 20, no. 1: 25–46.

Donegan M., and N. Lowe. 2008. "Inequality in the Creative City: Is There Still a Place for Old-Fashioned Institutions?" *Economic Development Quarterly* 22, no. 1: 46–62.

Downs, A. 2002. "Have Housing Prices Risen Faster in Portland Than Elsewhere?" *Housing Policy Debate* 13, no. 1: 7–31.

———, ed. 2004. *Growth Management and Affordable Housing: Do They Conflict?* Washington, DC: Brookings Institution.

Draper, E. 1937. Speech Presented at the Tennessee Valley Authority to a National Conference of Planners. In Draper, E.S. Sr. Papers, #2745. Division of Rare and Manuscript Collections, Cornell University Library. Available at http://rmc.library.cornell.edu/EAD/htmldocs/RMM02745.html (accessed April 20, 2009).

Dreier, P.; J. Mollenkopf; and T. Swanstrom. 2004. *Place Matters: Metropolitics for the 21st Century.* 2d ed. Lawrence: University Press of Kansas.

Duerksen, C., and C. Snyder. 2005. *Nature-Friendly Communities: Habitat Protection and Land Use Planning.* Washington, DC: Island Press.

Duncan, G. et al. 1997. "No Pain, No Gain? Inequality and Economic Mobility in the United States, Canada and Europe." In *Poverty and Economic Inequality in Industrialized Western Societies,* ed. N. Keilman, J. Lyngstad, H. Bojer, and I. Thomsen, 257–75. Oslo, Norway: Scandinavian University Press.

Duncan, James and Associates. 1989. *The Search for Efficient Growth Patterns: A Study of the Fiscal Impacts of Development in Florida.* Governor's Task Force on Urban Growth Patterns. Tallahassee: Florida Department of Community Affairs.

Easterlin, R.A. 1974. "Does Economic Growth Improve the Human Lot?" In *Nations and Households in Economic Growth: Essays in Honor of Moses Abramovitz,* ed. P.A. David and M.W. Reder, 89–125. New York: Academic Press.

———. 1995. "Will Raising the Incomes of All Increase the Happiness of All?" *Journal of Economic Behavior and Organization* 27, no. 1: 35–48.

———. 2001. "Income and Happiness: Towards a Unified Theory," *Economic Journal* 111, no. 473: 465–84.

———. 2003. "Explaining Happiness." *Proceedings of the National Academy of Sciences* 100, no. 19: 11176–83.

Easterly, W. 2001. "The Middle Class Consensus and Economic Development." *Journal of Economic Growth* 6, no. 4: 317–35.

Elliott, D.L. 2008. *A Better Way to Zone—Ten Principles to Create More Livable Cities.* Washington, DC: Island Press.

Farrell, A., and M. Hart. 1998. "What Does Sustainability Really Mean? The Search for Useful Indicators," *Environment* 40, no. 9: 4–16.

Ferguson, M.; K. Ali; M.R. Olfert; M.D. Partridge. 2007. "Voting with Their Feet: Jobs Versus Amenities." *Growth and Change* 38, no. 1: 77–110.

Filardo, M. et al. 2006. *Growth and Disparity: A Decade of U.S. Public School Construction.* Washington, DC: The 21st Century School Fund. Available at www.edfacilities.org/pubs/GrowthandDisparity.pdf (accessed April 20, 2009).

Fine, B. 2001. *Social Capital versus Social Theory.* London: Routledge.

Fischel, W.A. 1990. *Do Growth Controls Matter: A Review of Empirical Evidence on the Effectiveness and Efficiency of Local Government Land Use Regulation.* Cambridge, MA: Institute Lincoln for Land Policy.

———. 2001. "Municipal Corporations, Homeowners, and the Benefit View of the Property Tax." In *Property Taxation and Local Government Finance: Essays in Honor of C. Lowell Harriss,* ed. W.E. Oates, 33–77. Cambridge, MA: Lincoln Institute for Land Policy.

Fisher, P. 2005. *Grading Places—What Do the Business Climate Rankings Really Tell Us?* Washington, DC: Economic Policy Institute.

———. 2007. "The Fiscal Consequences of Competition for Capital." In *Reining in the Competition for Capital,* ed. Ann Markusen, 57–85. Kalamazoo, MI: Upjohn Institute for Employment Research.

Fisher, P., and A.H. Peters. 2002. *State Enterprise Zone Programs: Have They Worked?* Kalamazoo, MI: Upjohn Institute for Employment Research.

Fitzgerald, J. 2006. *Moving Up in the New Economy: Career Ladders for U.S. Workers.* Ithaca, NY: Cornell University Press.

Florida, R. 2002. *The Rise of the Creative Class.* New York: Basic Books.

————. 2003. "The New American Dream." *Washington Monthly* 35, no. 2: 26–33.

————. 2009. "How the Crash Will Reshape America." *Atlantic* 303, no. 2: 44–56.

Forbes, K.J. 2000. "A Reassessment of the Relationship Between Inequality and Growth." *American Economic Review* 90, no. 4: 869–87.

Foster-Bey, J.A. 2001. "Metropolitan Growth and Economic Opportunity for the Poor: If You're Poor Does Place Matter?" Manuscript prepared for the Annie E. Casey Foundation.

Frank, J.E. 1989. *The Cost of Alternative Development Patterns: A Review of the Literature.* Washington, DC: Urban Land Institute.

Frank, R.F. 1989. "Frames of Reference and the Quality of Life." *American Economic Review* 79, no. 2: 80–85.

————. 1999. *Luxury Fever: Money and Happiness in an Age of Excess.* Princeton, NJ: Princeton University Press.

_____. 2001. "Traffic and Tax Cuts." *New York Times,* May 11.

————. 2007. *Falling Behind: How Rising Inequality Harms the Middle Class.* Berkeley: University of California Press.

Frank, R.F., and A. Levine. 2006. "Expenditure Cascades," Cornell University mimeograph.

Friedman, B.M. 2005. *The Moral Consequences of Economic Growth.* New York: Knopf.

Fulton, W.; R. Pendall; M. Nguyen; and A. Harrison. 2001. "Who Sprawls Most? How Growth Patterns Differ Across the United States." Brookings Institution, Center on Urban and Metropolitan Policy Program. July.

Gabriel, S.A., and S.S. Rosenthal. 2004. "Quality of the Business Environment Versus Quality of Life: Do Firms and Households Like the Same Cities?" *Review of Economics and Statistics* 86, no. 1: 438–44.

Gabriel, S.A.; J.P. Mattey; and W.L. Wascher. 2003. "Compensating Differentials and Evolution in the Quality-of-Life among U.S. States." *Regional Science and Urban Economics* 33, no. 5: 619–49.

Galbraith J.K., and T. Hale. 2004. "Income Distribution and the Information Technology Bubble." University of Texas Inequality Project. Working Paper 27.

Galbraith, J.K. 1969. *The Affluent Society.* 2d ed. Boston: Houghton Mifflin.

————. 1997. *The Good Society: The Humane Agenda.* Boston: Houghton Mifflin.

Gallagher, K. 2004. *Free Trade and the Environment: Mexico, NAFTA, and Beyond.* Palo Alto, CA: Stanford University Press.

Gardner, G., and P. Sampat. 1998. "Mind over Matter: Recasting the Role of Materials in Our Lives." World Watch Paper 144 (December). Washington, DC: World Watch Institute.

Garoogian, R.; A. Garoogian; and P.W. Weingart. 1998. *America's Top-Rated Cities.* 6th ed. Boca Raton, FL: Universal Reference Publications.

Gittell, R., and T. Edinaldo. 2007. "Did a Strong Economy in the 1990s Affect Poverty in U.S. Metro Areas?" *Economic Development Quarterly* 21, no. 4: 354–68.

Glaeser, E., and J. Gyourko. 2002. "Zoning's Steep Price." *Regulation* 25, no. 3: 24–31.

Glaeser, E.; D. Laibson; and B. Sacerdote. 2002. "The Economic Approach to Social Capital." *Economic Journal* 112, no. 481: 437–58.

Glaeser, E.; J. Scheinkman; and A. Shleifer. 2003. "The Injustice of Inequality." *Journal of Monetary Economics* 50, no. 1: 199–222.

Glennon, R. 2002. *Water Follies: Groundwater Pumping and the Fate of America's Fresh Waters.* Washington, DC: Island Press.

Goodwin, M. 1999. "Space, Scale and State Strategy: Rethinking Urban and Regional Governance." *Progress in Human Geography* 23, no. 4: 503–27.

Goodwin, N.R. 1997. "Overview Essay: Interdisciplinary Perspectives on Well-being." In *Human Well-Being and Economic Goals,* ed. F. Ackerman, D. Kiron, N.R. Goodwin, J.M. Harris, and K. Gallagher, 1–14. Washington, DC: Island Press.

Gottlieb, P.D, and M. Fogarty. 2003. "Educational Attainment and Metropolitan Growth." *Economic Development Quarterly* 17, no. 4: 325–36.

Graves, P.E. 1979. "A Life-Cycle Empirical Analysis of Migration and Climate, by Race." *Journal of Urban Economics* 6, no. 2: 135–47.

Green, G.P. 2001. "Amenities and Community Economic Development: Strategies for Sustainability." *Journal of Regional Analysis and Policy* 31, no. 2: 61–76.

Green, G.P.; S.C. Deller; and D.W. Marcouiller, eds. 2005. *Amenities and Rural Development: Theory, Methods, and Public Policy.* Cheltenham, UK: Edward Elgar.

Greenwood, D.T. 1997. "New Developments in the Intergenerational Impact of Education." *International Journal of Educational Research* 27, no. 6: 503–11.

———. 2004. "Measuring Quality of Life with Local Indicators." In *What Has Happened to the Quality of Life In the Advanced Industrialized Nations?* ed. E.N. Wolff, 334–74. Cheltenham, UK: Edward Elgar Press.

Greenwood, D.T., and R.P.F. Holt. 2007. "Quality of Life and Conventional Wisdom: John Kenneth Galbraith and Economic Development." Working Paper.

———. 2010a. "Growth, Development, and Quality of Life: A Pluralist Approach." In *Economic Pluralism,* ed. R. Garnett, E. Olsen, and M. Starr, 169–75. London: Routledge.

———. 2010b. "Growth, Inequality and Negative Trickle-Down." *Journal of Economic Issues,* forthcoming.

Greenwood, D.T., and M. Skillington. 2008. "What's in a Ranking? Business Climate and Quality of Life." Working Paper. Colorado Center for Policy Studies.

Greenwood, M.J., and G.L. Hunt. 1989. "Jobs versus Amenities in the Analysis of Metropolitan Migration." *Journal of Urban Economics* 25, no. 1: 1–16.

Ground Water Protection Council. 2007. *Ground Water Report to the Nation: A Call to Action. Section 2 Groundwater Use and Availability.* Available at www.gwpc.org/CallToAction/finalpdfs/GWR_FrontMatter.pdf (accessed June 12, 2009).

Gyourko, J., and P. Linneman. 1993. "The Affordability of the American Dream: An Examination of the Last Thirty Years." *Journal of Housing Research* 4, no. 1: 39–71.

Gyourko, J., and J. Tracy. 1991. "The Structure of Local Public Finance and the Quality of Life." *Journal of Political Economy* 99, no. 4: 774–806.

———. 1999. "A Look at Real Housing Prices and Incomes: Some Implications for Housing Affordability and Quality." *Economic Policy Review* (September): 63–77. New York: Federal Reserve Bank of New York.

Gyourko, J.; C. Mayer; and T. Sinai. 2006. "Superstar Cities." NBER Working Paper No. 12355.

Hagerty, M.R., and R. Veenhoven. 2003. "Wealth and Happiness Revisited: Growing National Income *Does* Go with Greater Happiness." *Social Indicators Research* 64, no. 1: 1–27.

Harding, D.; C. Jencks; L. Lopoo; and S. Mayer. 2005. "The Changing Effect of Family Background on the Incomes of American Adults." In *Unequal Chances: Family Background and Economic Success,* ed. S. Bowles, H. Gintis, and M. Osborne Groves, 100–144. Princeton, NJ: Princeton University Press.

Hart, M. 1999. *Guide to Sustainable Community Indicators.* 2d ed. Hart Environmental Data. Available at http:// www.sustainablemeasures.com (accessed May 12, 2009).

Hawken, P. 1994. *The Ecology of Commerce.* New York: HarperCollins.

Hawken, P.; A. Lovins; and L.H. Lovins. 1999. *Natural Capitalism: Creating the Next Industrial Revolution.* Boston: Little, Brown.

Heckman, J. 2006. "Skill Formation and the Economics of Investing in Disadvantaged Children." *Science* 312, no. 5782: 1900–902.

Hertz, T. 2005. "Rags, Riches and Race: The Intergenerational Mobility of Black and White Families in the United States." In *Unequal Chances: Family Background and Economic Success,* ed. S. Bowles, H. Gintis, and M. Osborne Groves, 165–91. New York: Russell Sage Foundation.

Hilber, C., and C. Mayer. 2009. "Why Do Households Without Children Support Local Public Schools? Linking House Price Capitalization to School Spending." *Journal of Urban Economics* 65, no.1: 74–90.

Holdren, J.P. 2007. "Energy and Sustainability." *Science* 315, no. 5813: 737.

Holt, R.P.F. 2005. "Post-Keynesian Economics and Sustainable Development." *International Journal of Environment, Workplace and Employment* 1, no. 2: 174–86.

Holzer, H.; S. Raphael; and M.A. Stoll. 2006. "Perceived Criminality, Criminal Background Checks, and the Racial Hiring Practices of Employers." *Journal of Law and Economics* 49, no. 2: 451–80.

Ingraham, G.K., and Y. Hong, eds. 2008. *Fiscal Decentralization and Land Policies.* Cambridge, MA: Lincoln Institute of Land Policy.

International City Managers Association (ICMA). 2008. "Local Government and Schools: A Community-Oriented Approach." *ICMA IQ Report* 40. Available at www.icma.org (accessed May 27, 2008).

Jacksonville Community Council. 2007. "Quality of life in Jacksonville: Indicators for Progress." Available at www.jcci.org/statistics/qualityoflife.aspx (accessed April 17, 2008).

Jacobs, J. 1992 [1961]. *The Death and Life of Great American Cities.* New York: Random House.

Jaffe, A.B.; S.R. Peterson; P.R. Portney; and R.N. Stavins. 1995. "Environmental Regulations and the Competitiveness of U.S. Manufacturing." *Journal of Economic Literature* 33, no. 1: 132–63 (as cited in Ackerman 2008).

James, S., and T. Lahti. 2004. *The Natural Step for Communities: How Cities and Towns Can Change to Sustainable Practices.* Gabriola Island, BC: New Society Press.

Jargowsky, P.A. 2002. "Sprawl, Concentration of Poverty, and Urban Inequality." In *Urban Sprawl: Causes, Consequences and Policy Responses,* ed. G. Squires, 39–72, Washington, DC: Urban Institute Press.

———. 2005. "Stunning Progress, Hidden Problems: The Dramatic Decline of Concentrated Poverty in the 1990s." In *Redefining Urban and Suburban America: Evidence from Census 2000.* Vol. 2, ed. A. Berube, B. Katz, and R. Lang, 131–71. Washington, DC: Brookings Institution.

Johnson, S. "The Quiet Coup." *Atlantic.* May 2009. Available at www.theatlantic. com/doc/200905/imf-advice/ (accessed April 22, 2009).

Journard, R. 1999. *Methods of Estimation of Atmospheric Emissions from Transport: European Scientist Network and Scientific State-of-the Art Action COST 319 Final Report.* French National Institute for Transport and Safety Research/ Transports and Environment Laboratory. Available at www.inrets.fr/index.e.html (accessed April 22, 2009).

Kahn, M.E. 2001. "Does Sprawl Reduce the Black/White Housing Consumption Gap?" *Housing Policy Debate* 12, no. 1: 77–86.

Kahneman, D., and A.B. Krueger. 2006. "Developments in the Measurement of Subjective Well-Being." *Journal of Economic Perspectives* 20, no. 1: 3–24.

Kane, T.J.; D.O. Staiger; and G. Samms. 2003. "School Accountability Ratings and Housing Values." *Brookings-Wharton Papers on Urban Affairs,* 82–137.

Kasarda, J. 1995. "Industrial Re-structuring and the Changing Location of Jobs." In *State of the Union: America in the 1990s,* ed. R. Farley. 215–68. New York: Russell Sage Foundation.

Katz, P., and V. Scully. 1993. *The New Urbanism: Toward an Architecture of Community.* New York: McGraw-Hill.

Kirst, M. 1980. "The New Political Conflict in State Education Finance." *Taxing and Spending* 3: 46–53.

Knapp, G.J., ed. 2001. *Land Market Monitoring for Smart Urban Growth.* Cambridge, MA: Lincoln Institute of Land Policy.

Krantzberg, G. 2009. "Renegotiating the Great Lakes Water Quality Agreement: The Process for a Sustainable Outcome." *Sustainability* 1, no. 2: 254–67.

Krueger, R., and L. Savage. 2007. "City-Regions and Social Reproduction: A 'Place' for Sustainable Development?" *International Journal of Urban and Regional Research* 31, no. 1: 215–23.

Lang, R.E., and M.Z. Gough. 2006. "Growth Counties: Home to America's New Suburban Metropolis." In *Redefining Urban and Suburban America.* Vol. 3, ed. A. Berube, B. Katz, and R.E. Lang, 61–82. Washington, DC: Brookings Institution.

Lee, D.S. 1999. "Wage Inequality in the United States During the 1980s: Rising Dispersion or Falling Minimum Wage?" *Quarterly Journal of Economics* 114, no. 2: 977–1023.

Leonhardt, D. 2009. "Dr. James Will Make It Better." *New York Times,* November 8. Available at http://query.nytimes.com/gst/fullpage.html?res=9401E0DE1339 F93BA35752C1A96F9C8B63 (accessed November 10, 2009).

Lerman, R.I. 2008. "Are Skills the Problem? Reforming the Education and Training Systems in the United States." In *A Future of Good Jobs? America's Challenge in the Global Economy,* ed. T. Bartik and S.N. Houseman, 17–80. Kalamazoo, MI: Upjohn Institute for Employment Research.

Leroy, G. 2007. "Nine Concrete Ways to Curtail the Economic War among the States." In *Reining in the Competition for Capital,* ed. A. Markusen, 183–98. Kalamazoo, MI: Upjohn Institute for Employment Research.

Levine, N. 1999. "The Effects of Local Growth Controls on Regional Housing Production and Population Redistribution in California." *Urban Studies* 36, no. 12: 2047–68.

Levine, S., and R. Stein. 2008. "Obesity Threatens a Generation. 'Catastrophe' of Shorter Spans, Higher Health Costs." *Washington Post,* May 17.

Levy, F. 1998 [1989]. *The New Dollars and Dreams: American Incomes and Economic Change.* New York: Russell Sage Foundation.

Levy, F., and R.J. Murnane. 1992. "U.S. Earnings Levels and Earnings Inequality: A Review of Recent Trends and Proposed Explanations." *Journal of Economic Literature* 30, no. 3: 1333–81.

Lipman, B.J. 2006. *A Heavy Load: The Combined Housing and Transportation Burdens of Working Families.* Washington, DC: Center for Housing Policy.

Logan, J., and H. Molotch. 1987. *Urban Fortunes: The Political Economy of Place.* Berkeley: University of California Press.

Low, S.; J. Henderson; and S. Weiler. 2005. "Gauging a Region's Entrepreneurial Potential." *Economic Review.* 3d Quarter. Federal Reserve Bank of Kansas City. Available at www.frbkc.org/index.cfm/ (accessed May 27, 2009).

Luger, M., and S. Bae. 2005. 'The Effectiveness of State Business Tax Incentive Programs: The Case of North Carolina." *Economic Development Quarterly* 19, no. 4: 327–45.

Luria, D., and J. Rogers, 2008. "Manufacturing, Regional Prosperity, and Public Policy." In *Retooling for Growth: Building a 21st Century Economy in America's Older Industrial Areas,* ed. R.M. McGahey and J.S. Vey, 249–74. Washington, DC: Brookings Institution.

Lynch, R.G. 2004. *Rethinking Growth Strategies: How State and Local Taxes and Services Affect Economic Development.* Washington, DC: Economic Policy Institute.

———. 2007. *Enriching Children, Enriching the Nation, Public Investment in High-Quality Prekindergarten.* Washington, DC: Economic Policy Institute.

Madden, J.F. 2000. *Changes In Income Inequality Within U.S. Metropolitan Areas.* Kalamazoo, MI: Upjohn Institute for Employment Research.

———. 2003. "The Changing Spatial Concentration of Income and Poverty among Suburbs of Large U.S. Metropolitan Areas." *Urban Studies* 40, no. 3: 481–503.

Magnuson, K.; M.K. Meyers; C.J. Ruhm; and J. Waldfogel. 2004. "Inequality in Preschool Education and School Readiness." *American Educational Research Journal* 41, no. 1: 115–57.

Marcouiller, D.W., and G. Clendenning. 2005. "The Supply of Natural Amenities: Moving from Empirical Anecdotes to a Theoretical Basis." In *Amenities and Rural Development: Theory, Methods and Public Policy,* ed. G.P. Green, S.C. Deller, D.W. Marcouiller, 6–32. Northampton, MA: Edward Elgar.

Margo, R. 1992. "Explaining the Postwar Suburbanization of the Population in the United States: The Role of Income." *Journal of Urban Economics* 31: 301–10.

Margonelli, L. 2008. "Waste Not." *Atlantic Monthly* 30, no. 4: 26–29.

Markusen, A.R. 2007. *Reining in the Competition for Capital.* Kalamazoo, MI: Upjohn Institute for Employment Research.

Markusen, A.R., and K. Nesse, 2007. "Institutional and Political Determinants of Incentive Competition." In *Reining in the Competition for Capital,* ed. A.R. Markusen, 1–41. Kalamazoo, MI: Upjohn Institute for Employment Research.

Markusen, A.; G.H. Wassall; D. DeNatale; and R. Cohen. 2008. "Defining the Creative Economy: Industry and Occupational Approaches." *Economic Development Quarterly* 22, no. 1: 24–45.

Marmot, M.; J. Banks; and Z. Oldfield. 2006. "Disease and Disadvantage in the United States and in England." *Journal of the American Medical Association* 295, no. 17: 2037–45.

Martin, A. 2008. "Reclaiming Contaminated Sites. *New York Times,* March 30. Available at http://www.nytimes.com/2009/11/01/realestate/01njzo.html (accessed December 2, 2009).

Massey, D.S., and M.J. Fischer. 2003. "The Geography of Inequality in the United States, 1950–2000." *Brooking-Wharton Papers on Urban Affairs* 4: 1–40.

Matlack, J.L., and J.L. Vigdor. 2008. "Do Rising Tides Lift All Prices? Income Inequality and Housing Affordability?" *Journal of Housing Economics* 7, no. 3: 212–24.

Mayer, C.J., and K. Pence. 2008. "Subprime Mortgages: What, Where, and to Whom?" Working Paper no. 14083. NBER.

Mayer, S. 2001. "How Growth in Income Inequality Increased Economic Segregation." Working Paper mo. 30. Joint Center for Poverty Research.

Mayer, S.E., and L.M. Lopoo. 2005. "Has the Intergenerational Transmission of Economic Status Changed?" *Journal of Human Resources* 40, no. 1: 169–85.

———. 2008. "Government Spending and Intergenerational Mobility." *Journal of Public Economics* 92, nos. 1–2: 139–58.

McCann, B., and C. Beaumont, 2003. "Build 'Smart.'" *American School Board Journal* 190, no. 10: 24–27.

McGuire, T.J., and D.L. Sjoquist. 2007. "Urban Sprawl and the Finances of State and Local Governments." In *State and Local Finances under Pressure,* ed. David L. Sjoquist, 299–326. London: Edward Elgar.

McMichael, A.J. 2002. "Population, Environment, Disease, and Survival: Past Patterns, Uncertain Futures." *Lancet* 359, no. 9312: 1145.

Meara, E.R.; S. Richards; and D.M. Cutler. 2008. "The Gap Gets Bigger: Changes in Mortality and Life Expectancy, by Education, 1981–2000." *Health Affairs* 27, no. 2: 350–60.

Mills, E.S., and J.F. McDonald, eds. 1992. *Sources of Metropolitan Growth.* New Brunswick, NJ: Center for Urban Policy Research, Rutgers University.

Miringoff, M.L., and M. Miringoff. 1999. *The Social Health of the Nation: How America Is Really Doing.* Oxford: Oxford University Press.

Miringoff, M., and S. Opdycke. 2008. *America's Social Health. Putting Social Issues Back on the Public Agenda.* Armonk, NY: M.E. Sharpe.

Morris, D., and L. Tweeten. 1971. "The Cost of Controlling Crime: A Study in the Economies of City Life." *Annals of Regional Science* 5, no. 1: 33–49.

Mullins, D.R. 2003. "Popular Processes and the Transformation of State and Local Government Finance." In *State and Local Finances under Pressure,* ed. T.J. McGuire and D.L. Sjoquist, 299–326. London: Edward Elgar.

Muro, M., and R. Puentes. 2003. *The Economic Benefits of Smart Growth: A Review of the Fiscal and Competitive Advantages of More Compact, Balanced Development Patterns.* Washington, DC: Brookings Institution.

Myrdal, G. 1973. "'Growth' and 'Development.'" In *Against the Stream: Critical Essays in Economics*, ed. G. Myrdal, 182–96. New York: Pantheon Books.

National Center for Education Statistics, Digest of Education Statistics. 2005. *Expenditures of Educational Institutions Related to the Gross Domestic Product, by Level of Institution.* Table 25. Available at http://nces,ed,gov/programs/digest/d05/lt1.asp/ (accessed August 12, 2008).

National Resources Defense Council. 1998. *Another Cost of Sprawl: the Effects of Land Use on Wastewater Utility Costs.* Washington, DC.

Nechyba, T.J. 1997. "Local Property and State Income Taxes: The Role of Inter-jurisdictional Competition and Collusion." *Journal of Political Economy* 105, no. 2: 351–84.

———. 1998. "Replacing Capital Taxes with Land Taxes." In *Land Value Taxation: Can and Will It Work Today?* ed. Dick Netzer, 183–209. Cambridge, MA: Lincoln Institute of Land Policy.

Nechyba, T.J., and R.P. Walsh. 2004. "Urban Sprawl." *Journal of Economic Perspectives* 18, no. 4: 177–200.

Nelson, P.B. 1999. "Quality of Life, Nontraditional Income, and Economic Growth." *Rural Development Perspectives* 14, no. 2: 32–37.

Nelson, P.B.; J.P. Nicholson; and S.E. Hope. 2004. "The Baby Boom and Non-metropolitan Population Change, 1975–1990." *Growth and Change* 35, no. 4: 525–44.

Neumayer, E. 2001. *Greening Trade and Investment.* Sterling, VA: Earthscan.

New Jersey Law Library. "History of the Mt. Laurel Decision." Available at http://njlegalib.rutgers.edu/mtlaurel/aboutmtlaurel.php (accessed December 8, 2009).

Newman, P., and I. Jennings. 2008. *Cities as Sustainable Ecosystems: Principles and Practices.* Washington, DC: Island Press.

Norgaard, R.B. 1994. *Development Betrayed: The End of Progress and a Coevolutionary Revisioning of the Future.* London: Routledge.

Oates, W.E., and R.M. Schwab. 1997. "The Impact of Urban Land Taxation: The Pittsburgh Experience." *National Tax Journal* 50, no. 1: 1–21.

O'Donoghue, T., and M. Rabin. 2001. "Choice and Procrastination." *Quarterly Journal of Economics* 116, no. 1: 121–60.

Organic Trade Association. 2009. *Organic Food Facts.* Available at www.ota.com/organic/mt/food.html (accessed June 12, 2009).

Organization for Economic Cooperation and Development (OECD). 2009. "Growing Unequal: Poverty and Incomes over 20 Years." *Directorate for Employment, Labour and Social Affairs Newsletter,* no. 7 (October.) Available at www.oecd.org/dataoecd/45/42/41527936.pdf (accessed July 10, 2008).

Pager, D. 2003. "The Mark of a Criminal Record." *American Journal of Sociology* 108, no. 5: 937–75.

Panizza, U. 2002. "Income Inequality and Economic Growth: Evidence from American Data." *Journal of Economic Growth* 7, no. 1: 25–41.

Partridge, M.D. 1997. "Is Inequality Harmful for Growth? Comment." *American Economic Review* 87, no. 5: 1019–32.

Partridge, M.D., and D.S. Rickman. 2003. "The Waxing and Waning of Regional Economies: The Chicken-Egg Question of Jobs versus People." *Journal of Urban Economics* 53, no. 1: 76–97.

———. 2006. *The Geography of American Poverty: Is There a Need for Place-Based Policies?* Kalamazoo, MI: Upjohn Institute for Employment Research.

Patacchini, E., and Y. Zenou. 2007. "Intergenerational Education Transmission: Neighborhood Quality and/or Parent's Involvement?" *IZA Discussion Paper,* no. 2608 (February). Available at http.Ssrn.com/abstract=969370 (accessed May 30, 2009).

Pawasarat, J., and L.M. Quinn. 2001. "Exposing Urban Legends: The Real Purchasing Power of Central City Neighborhoods." Brookings Institution Center on Urban Metropolitan Policy. Working Paper, June.

Pendall, R. et al. 2005. "Connecting Smart Growth, Housing Affordability, and Racial Equity." In *The Geography of Opportunity,* ed. B.X. De Souza Briggs, 219–46. Washington, DC: Brookings Institution.

Piketty, T., and E. Saez. 2003. "Income Inequality in the United States 1913–1998." *Quarterly Journal of Economics* 158, no. 1: 1–39.

———. 2006. "The Evolution of Top Incomes: A Historical and International Perspective." *American Economic Review* 96, no. 2: 200–205.

Pimentel, D. et al. 1992. "Environmental and Economic Costs of Pesticide Use." *Bioscience* 15, no. 10: 750–60.

Pinfield, G. 1997. "The Use of Indicators in Local Sustainable Development Planning: A Response to Jeb Bergmann." *Local Environment: The International Journal of Justice and Sustainability* 2, no. 2: 185–87.

Polzin, P.E. 2001. "Why Some States Grow Faster than Others: New Growth Models for State Economic Policy." *Growth and Change* 32, no. 3: 413–25.

Ponce, V.M. 2006. *Groundwater Utilization and Sustainability.* San Diego State University. Available at http://ponce.sdsu.edu/groundwater_utilization_and_sustainability.html (accessed June 12, 2009).

Porter, D.R. 2008. *Managing Growth in America's Communities.* 2d ed. Washington, DC: Island Press.

Porter, M.C., and C. van der Linde. 1995. "Toward a New Conception of the Environment-Competitiveness Relationship." *Journal of Economic Perspectives* 9, no. 4: 97–118.

Portney, K.E. 2003. *Taking Sustainable Cities Seriously: Economic Development, the Environment, and Quality of Life in American Cities.* Cambridge, MA and London: MIT Press.

Pothukuchi, K. 2005. "Attracting Supermarkets to Inner-City Neighborhoods: Economic Development Outside the Box," *Economic Development Quarterly* 19, no. 3: 232–44.

Power, T.M. 1996a [1988]. *Environmental Protection and Economic Well-Being: The Economic Pursuit of Quality.* 2d ed. Armonk, NY: M.E. Sharpe.

———. 1996b. *Lost Landscapes and Failed Economies: The Search for a Value of Place.* Washington, DC: Island Press.

———. 2005. "The Supply and Demand for Natural Amenities: An Overview of Theory and Concepts." In *Amenities and Rural Development: Theory, Methods and Public Policy,* ed. G.P. Green, S.C. Deller, and D.W. Marcouiller, 63–77. Northampton, MA: Edward Elgar.

Pucher, J., and R. Buehler. 2008. "Cycling for Everyone: Lessons from Europe." *Transportation Research Record: Journal of the Transportation Research Board,* no. 2074 (November): 58–65.

Putnam, R. 1993. "The Prosperous Community: Social Capital and Public Life." *American Prospect* 4, no. 13: 35–42.

———. 2000. *Bowling Alone: the Collapse and Revival of American Community.* New York: Simon and Schuster.

Quigley, J.M., and S. Raphael. 2004. "Is Housing Unaffordable? Why Isn't It More Affordable?" *Journal of Economic Perspectives* 18, no. 1: 191–214.

Quintin, E., and J.L. Saving. 2008. "Inequality and Growth: Challenges to the Old Orthodoxy." *Economic Letter—Insights from the Federal Reserve Bank of Dallas* 3, no. 1. Available at www.dallasfed.org/research/eclett/2008/e10801.html (accessed October 28, 2008).

Rahman, T. 2007. "Measuring the Well-Being Across Countries." *Applied Economics Letters* 14, no. 11: 779–83.

Raphael, S. 2008. "Boosting the Earnings and Employment of Low-Skilled Workers in the United States: Making Work Pay and Removing Barriers to Employment and Social Mobility." In *A Future of Good Jobs? America's Challenge in the Global Economy,* ed. T. Bartik and S.N. Houseman, 245–304. Kalamazoo, MI: Upjohn Institute for Employment Research.

Rappaport, J.M. 2007. "Moving to Nice Weather." *Regional Science and Urban Economics* 37, no. 3: 375–98.

Real Estate Research Corporation. 1974. *The Costs of Sprawl: Environmental and Economic Costs of Alternative Residential Development Patterns at the Urban Fringe.* Washington, DC: U.S. Government Printing Office.

Redefining Progress. 2006. *Community Indicators Handbook.* 2d ed. Available at www.rprogress.org.

Reese, L.A., and G. Sands. 2008. "Creative Class and Economic Prosperity: Old Nostrums, Better Packaging?" *Economic Development Quarterly* 22, no. 1: 3–7.

Resnick, P. 2008. "The Effect of TEL Structure on State Government Finance." Ph.D. dissertation. University of Colorado.

Rickman, D.S., and R.K. Schwer. 1995. "A Comparison of the Multipliers of IMPLAN, REMI, and RIMS II: Benchmarking Ready-made Models for Comparison." *Annals of Regional Science* 29, no. 4: 363–74.

Roback, J. 1982. "Wages, Rents, and the Quality of Life." *Journal of Political Economy* 90, no. 6: 1257–78.

Robison, L.J.; A.A. Schmid; and M.E. Siles. 2002. "Is Social Capital Really Capital?" *Review of Social Economy* 60, no. 1: 1–21.

Rodriguez, C.B. 2000. "An Empirical Test of the Institutionalist View on Income Inequality: Economic Growth within the United States." *American Journal of Economics and Sociology* 59, no. 2: 303–13.

Rogerson, R.J. 1999. "Quality of Life and City Competitiveness." *Urban Studies* 36, nos. 5–6: 969–85.

Roodman, D.M. 1998. *Getting the Signals Right: Tax Reform to Protect the Environment and the Economy.* Washington, DC: World Watch Institute.

Sachs, J.D. 2006. "The Challenge of Sustainable Water." *Scientific American,* December: 48.

Sachs, J.D., and H.J. Shatz. 1996. "U.S. Trade with Developing Countries and Wage Inequality." *American Economic Review* 86, no. 2: 234–39.

Sands, G., and L.A. Reese. 2008. "Cultivating the Creative Class: And What About Nanaimo?" *Economic Development Quarterly* 22, no. 1: 8–23.

Savage, H. A. 2009. *Who Could Afford to Buy a Home in 2004?* U.S. Census Bureau: Current Housing Reports. H121/09-1.

Sawhill, I., and J.E. Morton. 2007. "Economic Mobility: Is the American Dream Alive and Well?" Washington, DC: Pew Charitable Trusts Economic Mobility Project.

Schmid, A. 2000. "Affinity as Social Capital: Its Role in Development." *Journal of Socio-Economics* 29, no. 2: 159–71.

———. 2002. "Using Motive to Distinguish Social Capital from Its Outputs," *Journal of Economic Issues* 36, no. 3: 747–68.

Schrank, D., and T. Lomax. 2007. The 2007 Urban Mobility Report. Texas Transportation Institute, September. Available at http://mobility.tamu.edu (accessed April 20, 2009).

Schweke, B. 1990. *The Third Wave in Economic Development.* Washington, DC: Corporation for Enterprise Development.

———. 2006. *A Progressive Economic Development Agenda for Shared Prosperity: Taking the High Road and Closing the Low.* Washington, DC: Corporation for Enterprise Development.

Sen, A. 1993. "Capability and Well-Being." In *The Quality of Life,* ed. M. Nussbaum and A. Sen, 30–53. Oxford: Clarendon.

Sexton, T.A.; S.M. Sheffrin; and A. O'Sullivan. 1999. "Proposition 13: Unintended Effects and Feasible Reforms." *National Tax Journal* 52, no. 1: 99–112.

Shaffer, R.; S.C. Deller; and D. Marcouiller, 2004. *Community Economics: Linking Theory to Practice.* Oxford: Blackwell.

———. 2006. "Rethinking Community Economic Development." *Economic Development Quarterly* 20, no. 1: 59–74.

Shapiro, J.M. 2006. "Smart Cities: Quality of Life, Productivity, and the Growth Effects of Human Capital." *The Review of Economics and Statistics* 88, no. 2: 324–35.

Shuman, M. 1998. *Going Local: Creating Self-Reliant Communities in a Global Age.* New York: Free Press.

Silva, F., and J. Sonstelie. 1995. "Did Serrano Cause a Decline in School Spending?" *National Tax Journal* 48, no. 2: 199–215.

Silverstein, J.; S. Weiler; K. Chalmers; E. Lacey; W. Rogers; and B. Widner. 2003. "Understanding the Retail Business Potential of Inner Cities." *Journal of Economic Issues* 37, no. 4: 1075–1105.

Simmons, P. 2005. "Rising Affordability Problems among Homeowners." In *Redefining Urban and Suburban America: Evidence from Census 2000.* Vol. 2, ed. A. Berube, B. Katz, and R. Lang, 267–84. Washington, DC: Brookings Institution.

Slottje, D. 1991. "Measuring the Quality of Life across Countries." *Review of Economics and Statistics* 73, no. 4: 684–93.

Smart Growth Network. 2009. *Getting to Smart Growth: 100 Policies for Implementation.* Vols. 1 and 2. International City/County Management Association. Available at wwww.smartgrowth.org (accessed November 10, 2009).

Smith, A. 1937 [1776]. *An Inquiry into the Nature and Causes of the Wealth of Nations.* New York: Modern Library.

Smith, J.R.; J. Brooks-Gunn; and P.K. Klebanov. 1997. "Consequences of Living in Poverty for Young Children's Cognitive and Verbal Ability and Early School Achievement." In *Consequences of Growing Up Poor,* ed. G.J. Duncan and J. Brooks-Gunn, 132–89. New York: Russell Sage Foundation.

Smolko, R.; C.J. Strange; and J. Venetoulis. 2006. *The Community Indicators Handbook: Measuring Progress Toward Healthy and Sustainable Communities.* 2d ed. San Francisco: Redefining Progress.

Snower, D.J. 1999. "Causes of Changing Earnings Inequality." *IZA Discussion Papers* 29, 69–133. Institute for the Study of Labor.

Solow, R.M. 1994. "Perspectives on Growth Theory." *Journal of Economic Perspective* 8, no. 1: 45–54.

Speir, C., and K. Stephenson. 2002. "Does Sprawl Cost Us All? Isolating the Effects of Housing Patterns on Public Water and Sewer Costs." *American Planning Association Journal* 68, no. 1: 56–70.

Squires, G.D., ed. 2002. *Urban Sprawl: Causes, Consequences and Policy Responses.* Washington, DC: Urban Institute Press.

Steelman, A., and J.A. Weinberg. 2005. "What's Driving Wage Inequality?" *Federal Reserve Bank of Richmond Economic Quarterly* 91, no. 3: 1–17.

Stewart, C., and A. Morris. 2002. "Development in Underserved Retail Markets." International Council of Shopping Centers and Business for Social Responsibility. Available at http://www.bsr.org (accessed June 15, 2008).

Stern, M.J. 2001. "The Un-Credit Worthy Poor: Historical Perspectives on Policies to Expand Assets and Credit." In *Assets for the Poor: The Benefits of Spreading Asset Ownership,* ed. T.M. Shapiro and E.N. Wolff, 269–301. New York: Russell Sage Foundation.

Stern, N. 2006. *The Economics of Climate Change: The Stern Review.* Cambridge: Cambridge University Press.

Stevenson, B., and J. Wolfers. 2008. "Economic Growth and Subjective Well-Being: Reassessing the Easterlin Paradox." *Brookings Papers on Economic Activity,* 1–102.

Stewart, C., and A. Morris. 2002. "Development in Undeserved Retail Markets." International Council of Shopping Centers and Business for Social Responsibility. Available at http://www.bsr.org (accessed June 15, 2008).

Stiglitz, J.E. 1983. "The Theory of Local Public Goods Twenty Five Years After Tiebout: A Perspective." In *Local Provision of Public Services: The Tiebout Model After Twenty Five Years,* ed. G.R. Zodrow, 17–53. New York and London: Academic Press.

Stolarick, K. 2003. "Inequality and the Creative Economy." *Creative Intelligence* 1, no. 5: 1–6.

Stover, M.E., and C.L. Leven. 1992. "Methodological Issues in the Determination of the Quality of Life in Urban Areas." *Urban Studies* 29, no. 5: 737–54.

Street, J.H. 1987. "The Institutionalist Theory of Economic Development." *Journal of Economic Issues* 21, no. 4: 1861–87.

Sustainable Development Indicators. *Community Indicators.* Available at www.sdi.gov/example.htm (accessed June 29, 2008).

Sustainable Seattle. 1998. *Indicators of Sustainable Community.* Available at www.sustainableseattle.org/Programs/RegionalIndicators/1998IndicatorsRpt.pdf (accessed April 17, 2008).

———. 2006. *Sustainability Report 2006.* Available at http://www.sustainableseattle.org/ (accessed June 29, 2008).

Sustainlane. 2006. *The SustainLane 2008 US City Rankings.* Available at www.sustainlane.com/us-city-rankings/ (accessed June 29, 2008).

Swanstrom, T.; P. Dreier; and J. Mollenkopf. 2002. "Economic Inequality and Public Policy: The Power of Place." *City and Community* 1, no. 4: 349–72.

Swanstrom, T.; P. Dreier, C. Casey, and R. Flack. 2006. "Pulling Apart: Economic Segregation in Suburbs and Central Cities in Major Metropolitan Areas, 1980–2000." In *Redefining Urban and Suburban America: Evidence from Census 2000,* Vol. II. ed. A. Berube, B. Katz, and R. Lang, 143–66. Washington, DC: Brookings Institution.

Sweeney, M. 2004. "The Challenge of Business Incentives for State Policymakers: A Practitioner's Perspective." *Spectrum the Journal of State Government* 77, no. 1: 8–11.

Talberth, J.; C. Cobb; and N. Slattery. 2007. *The Genuine Progress Indicator 2006: Executive Summary.* Redefining Progress, The Nature of Economics. Available at www.rprogress.org/publications/2007/GPI2006_ExecSumm.pdf#search=%221950–2004%22/ (accessed June 29, 2008).

Texas Transportation Institute. 2007. *Urban Mobility Report*. Texas A&M University. Available at http://tti.tamu.edu/publications/ (accessed May 25, 2009).

Thaler, R.H., and C.R. Sunstein. 2008. *Nudge: Improving Decisions about Health, Wealth and Happiness*. New Haven: Yale University Press.

Theobald, D.M. 2001. "Land-Use Dynamics beyond the American Urban Fringe." *Geographical Review* 91, no. 3: 544–64.

Thomas, K.P. 2007. "The Sources and Processes of Tax and Subsidy Competition." In *Reining in the Competition for Capital*, ed. A. Markusen, 43–56. Kalamazoo, MI: Upjohn Institute for Employment Research.

Tiebout, C. 1956. "A Pure Theory of Local Expenditures." *Journal of Political Economy* 64, no. 5: 416–24.

Turner, R. 1999. "Entrepreneurial Neighborhood Initiatives: Political Capital in Community Development." *Economic Development Quarterly* 13, no. 1: 15–22.

Tyler Norris Associates et al. 1997. *The Community Indicators Handbook*. San Francisco: Redefining Progress. Available at http://www.tylernorris.com/pubs/indicats.html (accessed November 2, 2009).

Urban Institute. 2005. "Assessing the New Federalism. Low-Income Working Families: Facts and Figures." Available at www.urban.org/publications/900832.html (accessed April 22, 2009).

U.S. Census Bureau. 2008a. *Historical Income Table—Income Equality*. Available at www.census.gov/hhes/www/income/histinc/ie3.html (accessed December 8, 2008).

———. 2008b. *Income, Poverty, and Health Insurance Coverage in the United States, 2007*. Available at www.census.gov/prod/2008pubs/p60–235.pdf (accessed December 6, 2008).

U.S. Centers for Disease Control and Prevention. 2005. "Barriers to Children Walking to or from School—United States, 2004." *Morbidity and Mortality Weekly Report*, September 30.

U.S. Department of Agriculture. 2009. *Summary and State Data*. February. Available at www.agcensus.usda.gov/Publications/2007/Full_Report/CenV1US1.txt (accessed June 12, 2009).

U.S. Department of Commerce. 2007. *Statistical Abstract of the United States: 2006. The National Data Book*. Economic and Statistics Administration, U.S. Census Bureau.

U.S. Department of Education, 2006. *Digest of Education Statistics*. Available at http://nces.ed.gov/pubSearch/pubsinfo.asp?pubid=2007017 (accessed August 28, 2008).

U.S. Department of Transportation.1969. *Nationwide Personal Transportation Study*. Washington, DC: Government Press.

———. 2008. Federal Highway Administration. 2007. *NHTS Brief National Household Travel Survey*. Washington, DC: Government Press.

U.S. Environmental Protection Agency. 2001. *Our Built and Natural Environments*. Washington, DC: Government Press.

U.S. Geological Survey. 2003. *Ground-Water Depletion Across the Nation; U.S. Geological Survey Fact Sheet 103–03*. Available at http://pubs.usgs.gov/fs/fs-103–03/ (accessed June 12, 2009).

Veblen, T. 1899. *The Theory of the Leisure Class: An Economic Study in the Evolution of Institutions*. New York: Macmillan.

Vey, J.S. 2007. *Restoring Prosperity: The State Role in Revitalizing America's Older Industrial Cities.* Washington, DC: Brookings Institution Metropolitan Policy Program.

Voitchovsky, S. 2005. "Does the Profile of Income Inequality Matter for Economic Growth? Distinguishing Between the Effects of Inequality in Different Parts of the Income Distribution." *Journal of Economic Growth* 10, no. 3: 273–96.

Vroman, W. 2009. "Unemployment Insurance: Current Situation and Potential Reforms." Working Paper. Washington, DC: Urban Policy Institute.

Waldfogel, J. 2007. "Work-Family Policies." In *Reshaping the American Workforce in a Changing Economy.* ed. H.J. Holzer and D.S. Nightingale, 273–92. Washington, DC: Urban Institute Press.

Wallis, J. 2001. "A History of the Property Tax in America." In *Property Taxation and Municipal Government Finance: Essays in Honor of C. Lowell Harris,* ed. W.E. Oates, 123–47. Cambridge, MA: Lincoln Institute of Land Policy.

Warner, K., and H. Molotch. 2000. *Building Rules: How Local Controls Shape Community Environments and Economics.* Boulder, CO: Westview Press.

Wassmer, R.W. 2002. "Fiscalisation of Land Use, Urban Growth Boundaries and Non-Central Retail Sprawl in the Western United States." *Urban Studies* 39, no. 8: 1307–27.

Wasylenko, M., and T. McGuire. 1985. "Jobs and Taxes: the Effect of Business Climate on States' Employment Growth Rates." *National Tax Journal* 38, no. 4: 497–511.

Watson, T. 2006. "Metropolitan Growth, Inequality, and Neighborhood Segregation by Income." *Brookings-Wharton Papers on Urban Affairs,* 1–52.

Weiler, S. 2000. "Information and Market Failure in Local Economic Development: A New Role for Universities?" *Economic Development Quarterly* 14, no. 2: 194–203.

Wheeler, C.W. 2005. "Cities, Skills, and Inequality." *Growth and Change* 36, no. 3: 329–53.

Whisler, R.L.; B.S. Waldorf; G.F. Mulligan; and D.A. Plane. 2008. "Quality of Life and the Migration of the College-Educated: A Life-Course Approach." *Growth and Change* 39, no. 1: 58–94.

Whyte, W.H. 1980. *The Social Life of Small Urban Spaces.* New York: Project for Public Spaces.

Williamson, J., and P.H. Lindert. 1980. *American Inequality: A Macroeconomic History.* New York: Academic Press.

Wolff, E.N. 1998. "Recent Trends in the Size Distribution of Household Wealth." *Journal of Economic Perspectives* 12, no. 3: 131–50.

———. 2002 [1996]. *Top Heavy: The Increasing Inequality of Wealth in America and What Can Be Done About It.* New York: New Press.

———. 2006. *Does Education Really Help? Skill, Work and Inequality.* Oxford: Oxford University Press.

Wolff, E.N., and A. Zacharias. 2007. "The Levy Institute Measure of Economic Well-Being: United States, 1989–2001." *Eastern Economic Journal* 33, no. 4: 443–70.

Wu, J. 2007. "How Does Suburbanization Affect Local Public Finance and Communities?" *Review of Agricultural Economics* 29, no. 3: 564–71.

Wunder, T.A. 2009. "Mainstream Amnesia: Why Evolutionary Ideas in the Mainstream Are Not Being Recognized for What They Are and How Institutional Economics Can Benefit." *Journal of Economic Issues* 42, no. 1: 266–76.

Yaroslavsky, Z. 2008. "Don't Be Dense, The Growth Policies Favored by Some City Officials Threaten L.A.'s Livability." *Los Angeles Times,* April 13.

Yinger, J. 1998. "Who Pays Development Fees?" In *Local Government Tax and Land Use Policies in the United States: Understanding the Links,* ed. Helen F. Ladd, 218–33. Cheltenham, UK and Northampton, MA: Edward Elgar.

You, J., and S. Khagram. 2005. "A Comparative Study of Inequality and Corruption." Paper presented at the annual meeting of the Midwest Political Science Association, Chicago. Referenced in Bernasek, A. 2006. "Income Inequality, and Its Cost." *New York Times,* June 25. Available at www.allacademic.com/meta/p86534_index.html.

Zax, J.S. 1990. "Race and Commutes." *Journal of Urban Economics* 28, no. 3: 336–48.

Zhao, Z., and R. Kaestner. 2009. "Effects of Urban Sprawl on Obesity." NBER Working Paper no. 15436.

Zodrow, G., and P. Miezkowski. 1986. "Pigou, Tiebout, Property Taxation and the Underprovision of Local Public Goods." *Journal of Urban Economics* 19: 356–70.

Index

About the Authors

Daphne T. Greenwood is professor of economics and director of the Colorado Center for Policy Studies at the University of Colorado, Colorado Springs. She has published a number of book chapters and a variety of articles in academic journals as well as work on local economic development, quality of life and tax policy at the Center. She has been a visiting professor at the U.S. Naval Academy and a visiting scholar at the Institute for Research on Poverty at the University of Wisconsin in Madison. She has also worked at the Office of Tax Analysis in the U.S. Department of Treasury, and as an economist for Esmark, Inc., Division of Corporate and Strategic Planning, Chicago. From 1991 to 1994 she was a state representative, District 17, in the Colorado House of Representatives.

Richard P.F. Holt is professor of economics and university seminar at Southern Oregon University. He has authored, coauthored or edited a number of books, including *A New Guide to Post Keynesian Economics* and the prize-winning *The Changing Face of Economics*. His latest books include *European Economics at a Crossroads* and the edited volume *Post Keynesian and Ecological Economics: Confronting Environmental Issues*. He has also published over fifty articles and book reviews in a variety of academic journals. His research areas include environmental and ecological economics, post-Keynesian economics, history of economic thought, complexity economics and game theory. His present research focuses on the ethics of human rights and the environment.